THE FUTURE OF THE INTERNATIONAL
MONETARY SYSTEM

The Future of the International Monetary System
Change, Coordination or Instability?

Edited by
Omar F. Hamouda
Robin Rowley
Bernard M. Wolf

M. E. SHARPE, INC.
Armonk, New York

Copyright © 1989 by Omar F. Hamouda, Robin Rowley, Bernard Wolf

Published in the United States by M. E. Sharpe, Inc.
80 Business Park Drive, Armonk, New York 10504.

Published in Great Britain by Edward Elgar Publishing Limited

Printed in Great Britain

Library of Congress Cataloging-in-Publication Data

The Future of the international monetary system.

    1. International finance.   I. Hamouda, O. F.
II. Rowley, J. R. C.   III. Wolf, Bernard M.
HG3881.F873   1989   332'.042   88-35567
ISBN 0-87332-567-2

Contents

List of contributors   vii
Acknowledgements   ix

1 Disturbance in the world economy *Robin Rowley and Omar Hamouda*   1
2 Banks, governments and international debt: where do we go from here? *Thomas J. Berger*   4
3 International monetary reform: the future is not what it used to be! *Robert Solomon*   10
4 International monetary reform, coordination and indicators *Andrew Crockett*   17
5 The search for exchange stability: before and after Bretton Woods *Edward M. Bernstein*   27
6 The international monetary system and the paper-exchange standard *Robert Triffin*   35
7 Purchasing power parity as a monetary standard *Ronald I. McKinnon and Kenichi Ohno*
  Comment by *Charles Goodhart*   42
8 The international monetary system: an analysis of alternative regimes *Marcus H. Miller and John Williamson*
  Comment by *Michael Jones*   68
9 The future of the international monetary system *Sidney Dell*
  Comment by *Michael Dealtry*   89
10 External impacts of the United States' financial policies *Peter M. Oppenheimer*
  Comment by *L. D. D. Price*
  Comment by *Michael Dealtry*   118
11 Some reflections on the LDC debt crisis *Kari Levitt*   131
12 Macroeconomic adjustment policy issues *Fred Z. Jaspersen*
  Comment by *B. V. Gestrin*   149
13 A return visit to the international debt problem of the LDCs *Lorie Tarshis*
  Comment by *M. H. I. Dore*
  Comment by *Charles Goodhart*   160
14 LDC debt: towards a genuinely cooperative solution *Benjamin J. Cohen*
  Comment by *Rita Tullberg*   174

15 A neglected monetary standard alternative: gold/commodity
   bimetallism *Albert Gailord Hart*
   Comment by *John N. Smithin*
   Comment by *Robert W. Dimand*   197
16 The international monetary system: a look ahead *Bernard
   M. Wolf*   214

Name index   221

Contributors

Thomas J. Berger, Deputy Assistant Secretary for International Monetary Affairs, US Treasury Department

Edward M. Bernstein, Senior Fellow, Brookings Institution

Benjamin Cohen, William L. Clayton Professor of International Economic Relations, Fletcher School of Law and Diplomacy, Tufts University

Andrew Crockett, Deputy Director, Research Department, International Monetary Fund

Michael Dealtry, Manager and Deputy Head, Monetary and Economic Department, Bank for International Settlements

Sidney Dell, Senior Fellow, United Nations Institute for Training and Research

Robert Dimand, Professor of Economics, Brock University

Mohammed Dore, Professor of Economics, Brock University

Berger V. Gestrin, Executive Vice-President and Economic Advisor, Canadian Imperial Bank of Commerce

Charles Goodhart, Professor of Economics, London School of Economics

Omar Hamouda, Professor of Economics, Glendon College, York University

Albert Hart, Professor of Economics, Columbia University

Frederick Z. Jaspersen, Principal Economist, Macroeconomic Adjustment Policies, Country Economics Department, The World Bank

Michael Jones, Professor of Economics, Bowdoin College

Kari Levitt, Professor of Economics, McGill University

Ronald I. McKinnon, Professor of Economics, Stanford University

Marcus Miller, Professor of Economics, University of Warwick

Kenichi Ohno, Economist, International Monetary Fund

Peter M. Oppenheimer, Professor of Economics, Oxford University

Lloyd D. D. Price, Head, International Division, Bank of England

Robin Rowley, Professor of Economics, McGill University

John Smithin, Professor of Economics, York University

Robert Solomon, Senior Fellow, Brookings Institution

Lorie Tarshis, Professor of Economics, Glendon College, York University

Robert Triffin, Professor Emeritus, Yale University and Université de Louvain

Rita Tullberg, Senior Researcher, Stockholm International Peace Research Institute

John Williamson, Senior Fellow, Institute for International Economics

Bernard M. Wolf, Professor of Economics, York University

Acknowledgements

The editors wish to express their thanks to the following persons and organizations, all of whom have given invaluable support and encouragement in various ways, both for the Conference and the preparation of this volume: President Harry Arthurs, York University; Ms Marjorie Latour, C-I-L Inc.; Ms Valerie Vanstone, Communications Department, York University; Ms Noli Swatman, Office of Research Administration, York University; Mr Jacques Aubin-Roi, Executive Office, Glendon College; Ms Eve Woods, Printing Services, Glendon College; Mr Bryne Purchase, Ministry of Treasury and Economics, Government of Ontario; Mr Murray Fitzsimmons, C-I-L Inc.; and Mr John Kirton, Centre for International Studies, University of Toronto.

Financial support for the Conference was provided by the Ministry of Treasury and Economics, Government of Ontario; C-I-L Inc.; The Municipal Programme on the 1988 Toronto Summit; The Ontario Centre for International Business; York University Ad Hoc Research Committee, and Glendon College.

Special mention must be made of the hard work put in by present and former students of Glendon College for the Conference: Franque Grimard, Eric Armour, Andrew Bacque, Lisa Durkin, JoAnn Gore, Nicholas Ignatieff, Elisabeth King, Milos Kostich, Louise Laliberté, James Laver, Diana O'Reily, Colm O'Shea, Jonathan Quaglia, Craig Sangster, Elisabeth Sherman, Tod Smyth and Marc Vezina.

We would also like to thank Professors Lorie Tarshis, Betsey Buchwald and David McQueen for their advice, enthusiasm and encouraging support for the Conference. Judy Rowley supervised the editorial process, prepared the final typescript and generally contributed to the speed and accuracy with which this volume was produced.

Finally, we would like to express our appreciation to our publisher, Mr Edward Elgar, for guiding us in the publication of this volume with his customary thoroughness and professional expediency.

1 Disturbance in the world economy
Robin Rowley and Omar Hamouda

Crises are not rare occurrences in the world economy. We can readily point to major problems of excessive debt, financial fragility, exchange-rate volatility, extraordinary levels of governmental and international deficits, commodity imbalances and inadequate political leadership – all present with marked severity during the last decade. Diligence in searching the historical record may demonstrate that such disturbed conditions were experienced in irregular instances throughout the life of capitalistic pro-duction and exchange. However, the present incidence of debt, lack of hegemonic leadership and fragility of the international monetary system (perhaps, of banking and stock markets too) are special. We have moved into a phase of crisis rather than one of modest disturbances to the world economy. Even the powerful elite of the IMS have recognized some need for corrective actions although considerable doubts persist as to what these should entail – primarily because of the ideological pressures of familiar beliefs and, to some extent, because of plain ignorance or fear. Few economists and politicians presume that the present crisis must lead to an extensive collapse of the world economy but most of them are gradually acknowledging the hazards of the situation in which we find ourselves. Almost no one anticipates that these hazards will be expeditiously resolved either by the individual acts of the principal players on the international scene or by their collaborative efforts. We are, indeed, 'groping' for guided choices of appropriate actions and for the fora or mechanisms by which or through which such choices can be imple-mented without making the IMS or impoverished nations susceptible to future shocks.

To some extent, we are both hindered and helped by the relative com-placency of three decades of economists, who developed their attitudes and methods in a climate of apparently successful performance (with strong confidence in their ability to assess policy needs, their ability to design remedial programmes, and their means of influencing govern-mental and corporate responses). Earlier 'successes' in dealing with instability, energy shocks and the emergence of new locations for economic power reinforced the commitment to existing attitudes and

1

methods ('fashions', as we have called them elsewhere) although modest drifts from the rhetoric of Keynesianism to that of 'private' enterprise and supply-side prophecy are discernible. The attendant complacency restrains our willingness to accept both novel proposals and the revival of older views, previously rejected for adoption in different situations of the world economy, even though such deviations from fashion might provide important ingredients for solutions to our present difficulties. On the other hand, incrementalism and familiarity with the bureaucratic robustness of both international organizations and national governments prevent the frozen immobility of panic and the frenetic search for utopian dreams. We are required from this background to find a middle path between torpidity and excess, to demonstrate sufficient concern (perhaps, indignation) without being preoccupied with the search for 'villains', and to act humanely with due concern for the needs of impoverished countries (while conscious, of course, that much of their discomfort might stem from the adverse influences of particular macroeconomic developments affecting the richer and more powerful countries).

The questions to be addressed now are many and diverse. First we have to identify (1) which attributes of the present situation are especially troublesome for the well-being of the world economy; (2) to what extent the burdens associated with particular problems have reached 'critical' proportions; (3) those primarily affected by these burdens; (4) what new measures of relief, discipline or collaboration are called for and what form they should take; and (5) who should provide leadership to escape from these problems. Beyond this first round of questions, there are significant issues of intensity, speed and magnitude. Should gentle intellectual debate be discarded for a more intense promotion of particular 'solutions' because the problems are so severe, unfair and (potentially) catastrophic for some groups of the world's population, both rich and poor? Should we act now (even if unsure of the consequences) rather than later? Should we do 'much more' rather than continue to use existing facilities with their conventional absence of dramatic shifts in leadership, process or emphasis?

Clearly the present environment is ripe for major steps (1) to ease the incidence and magnitude of international debt; (2) to amend the international monetary and financial systems with new criteria for permissible exchange-rate adjustments or changes in the effective 'rules of the game' that govern conduct of national governments; (3) to facilitate meaningful coordination of national macroeconomic policies in the light of wider objectives; and (4) to provide hope for improvement in economic, social and political relationships. Besides deciding what must be done and assessing an appropiate temporal framework for actions, we must deal with political reality. Thus we must know how to bring about change in the present political environment with its four-fold weaknesses; namely, lack of consensus, biases, mutual distrust among different constituencies, uncertainties and plain ignorance. Utopian dreams, excessive (academic) abstraction and lack of realism are not conducive to rational action. On the other hand, we cannot rely solely on either bureaucrats or politicians for we need innovative ideas and well-structured initiatives with a long-term commitment – not unduly stifled by an oppressive proximity to existing 'institutional thinking' nor preoccupied with transitory whims and expedients.

In setting up the programme for our Conference on the Future of the International Monetary System, we sought the participation of academic economists, bankers, bureaucrats in significant international organizations, governmental officials, journalists, and researchers in major private-sector 'think tanks', with a wide spectrum of the 'old' and the 'new' in terms of our participants' experience. We had extraordinary good fortune both in assembling a stellar cast and in finding the right 'mix' of ingredients to provide a comfortable situation for the exchange of facts, proposals and views. The papers that are reproduced below are a selection of those presented at the Conference. As active editors, we have compressed the drafts of our authors and 'interfered' with them to meet our space limitations, without (we hope) distorting their substance. Our gratitude for the tolerance, timeliness and clarity of our authors is immense as we were able to present the final typescript of this volume to our publisher within about seven weeks of the end of the Conference. Our primary disappointment was an inability to include all of the papers presented – exclusions are always painful, especially when attributable to difficulties of communication, timing and space. The pain is ours as much as that of the potential contributors.

We offer the fourteen papers and their attendant comments as part of a necessary dialogue on the present state of the world economy. One book can achieve little on its own but the effort of producing it was, nevertheless, worthwhile for the contributors. We hope our readers are equally encouraged to think and act on the need for improvement of our present world environment.

2 Banks, governments and international debt: Where do we go from here?

Thomas J. Berger

I welcome this opportunity to review recent developments and current prospects for addressing international debt problems. The debt crisis which emerged six years ago posed potentially serious risks to the debtor-nations and the global economy. Through mutual effort and cooperation, we have reduced these risks and improved the debtors' prospects for a return to steady growth and creditworthiness. In my remarks I would like to summarize the basic principles underlying the current debt strategy; review recent progress; touch on the role of creditor governments and commercial banks; and consider with you the key issues we now have to address.

The international debt strategy
The strategy we embarked upon in the autumn of 1985 has helped move us a considerable distance towards our goals. It also has provided a basis for meeting the changing circumstances of individual countries while maintaining a steady focus on the following four key principles. First is the central importance of *economic growth* in easing the debt burden over time. Second, in order to promote growth, *market-oriented policy reforms* within the debtor-nations are crucial. Third, to support these reforms, *additional capital* is needed in the form of equity, debt and the return of flight capital. Finally, *each case* should be dealt with *on its own merits*, recognizing the inescapable fact that the particular circumstances of each country are different. I firmly believe that this strategic framework remains the only viable long-run approach. The logic is irrefutable. The problems of debt and development can only be solved through the growth of debtor-countries. Growth necessitates capital and continuing access to the credit markets. Growth also requires durable, market-oriented economic reforms. These adjustments will make debtor-nations more attractive for future investment – both domestic and foreign. Together with that investment, the reforms promise stronger growth, higher standards of living, and more productive and flexible economies.

The debt strategy's key principles are constant, but its execution is dynamic. Indeed, one of the greatest strengths of this approach is its adaptability. Early in 1987 we suggested a 'menu' of financing options – which I shall discuss in greater detail later – to make sure that investment opportunities evolve with this long-term problem. The problems of debt and development did not arise overnight. They unfolded over a period of years, and it will take years to solve them. I recognize, of course, that some critics urge another path – the development of large-scale, generalized, mandatory debt-forgiveness schemes. We strongly oppose such 'quick-fix' approaches, including the creation of an international debt facility, for a number of reasons.

First, this approach will preclude debtors from gaining access to credit markets for years to come – including vital trade finance and might well exacerbate existing problems with the flight of local capital. Second, this approach would forgo the benefits of case-by-case actions, taken over time, to secure economic adjustments to make investments more productive. It ignores that a major part of the solution is to improve the productivity of investments, enabling them to pay their own way. The debt burden is one constraint – like those posed by politics, history, culture, sociology and local economic structures – and it should not be our sole preoccupation. Third, these debt forgiveness schemes, which generally rely on a consolidating mechanism, would irreparably politicize the problem, distracting creditors and debtors alike from the difficult but fundamental economic adjustment tasks. Fourth, this method would actually encourage counterproductive debt repudiations to depreciate the value of the debt so as to maximize the so-called 'benefits' of forgiveness. Fifth, in addition to all these costs, this approach does not even score well according to its supposed rationale of delivering significant debt-service savings. An across-the-board 30 per cent forgiveness of all the bank debt of all top 15 debtors would lower annual debt service by about $7 billion. To put that figure in perspective, the drop in LIBOR interest rates since 1981 saves the major debtors almost four times as much. Last, but perhaps most important, proposals to have the public sector purchase private sector debt would necessitate a large, not-to-be-returned infusion of public funds, with the continuing risk of these loans also shifted to the tax-payer. Not only is it inappropriate for governments unilaterally to force private financial institutions to sustain losses, but those governments would then end up paying for debtor wards around the globe.

Progress to date
Admittedly there is fatigue among both debtor-countries and commercial banks, but contrary to those who would argue that wholesale debt relief

is the only solution, I believe the present strategy *is* producing results and moving us towards resolution of this difficult problem. Allow me to draw your attention to the following facts. According to World Bank data, eight of the 15 major debtor countries grew at 4–5 per cent or more in 1987, compared with only three countries in 1985. We should bear in mind that growth for the 15 countries was a negative 3 per cent in 1983. Debt-service ratios for the group have fallen by a quarter and interest-service ratios by one-third in the past few years. This is largely due to the substantial decline in interest rates since 1982. Aggregate current account deficits have been sharply reduced from a peak of $50 billion in 1982 to $15 billion in 1986, and $8 billion in 1987. Export earnings rose by 13 per cent to near-record highs in 1987, while imports in 1988 were expected to be the highest since 1982. The adoption of debt/equity swap mechanisms in some countries, as well as broader policy reforms, has encouraged the return of flight capital, while also helping to reduce debt and debt-service burdens. On a more general basis, the concentration of resources on the debt problem has been impressive. Since October 1985, the World Bank has agreed to provide nearly $14 billion in new loans to support reform efforts in the major debtor-nations, while the IMF has provided $5 billion in temporary balance of payments assistance to these nations. Official creditors have rescheduled some $18 billion in outstanding debt, including interest payments. Commercial banks have committed some $17 billion in new finance. Banks have also rescheduled over $211 billion in outstanding debt, reduced spreads, and provided longer grace periods and maturities.

The role of creditor governments
Let me now touch upon the part being played by creditor governments in the debt strategy. In my view, it is not the role of governments to take the banks out of their LDC exposures, nor to assume for their taxpayers part of the risk on commercial bank LDC loans, nor to put up massive amounts of funds from their budgets through a new international debt facility to purchase existing commercial bank debt at a discount. Furthermore, it is not the role of the international financial institutions to offer credit enhancements more routinely; specifically, World Bank guarantees of commercial bank debt are exceptional and their use should remain limited. Commercial bank numbers in terms of reschedulings may look impressive, but we must remember that commercial banks lent more to begin with and, therefore, have much more debt to reschedule. Commercial banks have been rescheduling principal, while creditor governments, through the Paris Club, have rescheduled interest as well as principal.

Creditor goverments have also been contributing in many other ways. First, the major industrial nations have maintained a sound international economic environment with sustained growth, low inflation and open markets. This is especially true for the United States, which took over 50 per cent of the increase in non-oil LDC exports between 1982 and 1986. Second, the industrial countries have provided leadership in international efforts to address the problems of various debtor-countries, often providing bridge financing at key moments. This has involved helping a number of countries to resume normal relations with financial institutions and re-establish fruitful negotiations with the IMF and World Bank. Third, the US and a number of other industrial nations have helped to remove regulatory obstacles to new loans and innovative financing techniques. Fourth, creditor goverments have provided sustained support for the international financial institutions. In 1983 these governments provided the major share of a quota increase for the International Monetary Fund of $33 billion and recently have agreed to support a $75 billion general capital increase for the World Bank. Finally, the industrial nations have secured the implementation of important innovations to strengthen the debt strategy generally.

For example, at the IMF Interim Committee on 14 April 1988, it was agreed in principle to establish a combined Compensatory and Contingency Financing Facility. This new facility will help cushion the effect on IMF standby programmes of unforeseen external developments such as weaker commodity prices, natural disasters, or sustained higher interest rates that might force a performing country off its economic course. We expect the new facility to expand potential access for the 15 major debtors by more than 25 per cent – potentially more than $12 billion, depending of course upon external developments. Creditor governments have also taken a number of significant measures to assist low-income developing nations. The IMF's new Enhanced Structural Adjustment Facility will provide concessional resources totalling six billion SDRs to low-income countries facing protracted balance of payment problems. In addition, donor governments have pledged $6.4 billion of bilateral financing to be used in cooperation with the World Bank for low-income African countries with severe debt problems that have undertaken adjustment programmes.

The role of commercial banks
What is the role of the commercial banks at this point in the long-term resolution of the debt problem? To facilitate commercial bank financing packages, Treasury Secretary Baker proposed last year the development of a 'menu' of financing options. Such menus can help meet the diverse interests of both debtor-nations and the banking community, and can include both new money and debt conversion options. Some of the menu

items that might be included in future financing packages are: (1) *trade and project loans* to support private sector production and growth; (2) *new money bonds* which have some of the characteristics of senior debt; (3) *bonds or notes* that are *convertible into equity*; (4) *exit bonds* for banks wanting to exit from the future new money obligations; (5) *on-lending rights* permitting loans to be targeted to specific enterprises; (6) *debt/equity swaps* to help reduce debt and debt-service burdens; (7) *debt/charity swaps* to advance health, education and conservation programmes; and (8) traditional *balance of payment loans*.

This 'menu' approach has gained broad acceptance as the basis for new financing packages. The newest 'option' is reflected in the recent Mexican debt-exchange offer. Through this transaction, Mexico was able to exchange $3.7 billion in outstanding commercial bank debt for $2.6 billion in new Mexican bonds collateralized by a special US Treasury 20-year security, for a net $1.1 billion in debt retired and $1.6 billion in interest saved over 20 years. We expect additional debt conversions techniques to be developed in the period ahead. In order to be successful, such efforts must be voluntary, privately financed, and developed within the market to benefit commercial banks and debtor-nations alike. In sum, the 'menu' approach emphasizes a negotiated, market-orientated way of resolving debt problems. Both commercial banks and debtors should actively pursue efforts to develop further the menu approach, while creditor-governments can help assure that regulatory impediments do not stand in their way.

Unfortunately, however, it has generally been the debtor-governments rather than the commercial banks which have taken the lead in developing menus and orchestrating new transactions. This was true in the case of the Mexican debt-exchange offer, the Philippine Investment Notes and the Argentine exit bonds. Commercial banks should not wait for innovative financing options to be offered by debtor-governments; nor should they call on creditor-governments and the international financial institutions to 'enhance' new bank credits through guarantees or other support mechanisms. Rather, banks should challenge the most creative minds among their executive ranks to develop financing options that can advance common interests in dealing with the debt problem. In addition, the banks should discuss with the international financial institutions and debtor-governments those areas where policy reforms can best assist debtors' return to creditworthiness. Banks must also work to improve communication within the banking community and to further streamline the new lending process to help assure that new financing is made available in a more timely fashion. In short, banks must lead rather than react; work cooperatively rather than individually; and support innovation in order to advance the process.

In conclusion, let me summarize the tasks before us. Indebted countries must be steadfast in their pursuit of sound policies. Commercial banks and the international financial institutions must be willing to support these adjustment efforts with increased capital flows. Finally, the industrial countries must sustain their rate of demand growth and improve the access of debtor-nations to their markets. Such a cooperative solution to the debt problem is the only real answer.

3 International monetary reform: the future is not what it used to be!

Robert Solomon

I address you as a reformed international monetary reformer. I recognize that considerable dissatisfaction exists concerning present international monetary arrangements, especially the exchange-rate regime. I am aware that a desire for reform is sitting in the breasts of numerous economists and of the officials of some countries. I am not going to defend the current system by reminding you what Churchill said about democracy. That is not my punchline. It will come along in due course. Let me start with a few words about the relevance of international monetary arrangements to the principal ills troubling the world economy today. What are those ills?

At the top of the list, I would put the plight of the debt-ridden developing countries. According to IMF data, real GDP per capita in the 15 most heavily indebted countries fell 8 per cent between 1980 and 1987, after increasing at an annual rate of 3.3 per cent in the 1970s. Gross capital formation as a fraction of GDP decreased from almost 25 per cent in 1980 to 17 per cent in 1987, while net foreign borrowing declined by no less than 80 per cent. Do international monetary arrangements have anything to do with this sorry, indeed tragic, state of affairs? Very little, I would say. I see two other major problems in the world economy. One is the high rate of unemployment in Europe. It averaged almost 11 per cent in 1987, compared with about 4 per cent in the 1970s. Much has been written about this problem (recently, for example, by my Brookings colleagues, Lawrence and Schultze, in *Barriers to European Growth*, 1987). No one that I know of attributes the high unemployment in Europe to deficiencies in the international monetary system. Whether the exchange-rate mechanism of the European Monetary System is in any way responsible is an intriguing question to which I do not have an answer. The other major problem is, of course, the existence of large current-account imbalances in some of the leading industrial countries. Does the emergence of these imbalances reflect shortcomings in the international monetary system? One cannot in this case give a quick negative reply as I did for the other two problems.

I turn therefore to the international monetary system and its possible need for reform. Machlup, I believe, classified potential problems of the system under the three headings: adjustment, liquidity and confidence. By 'adjustment' is meant the correction of large and persistent deficits and surpluses in the balance-of-payments positions of countries. If the system allows, or fails to reduce such imbalances, it presumably needs reform. By 'liquidity' is meant the international reserves of countries. If the international monetary system creates either an excess or a deficiency of official reserves, it needs improvement. By 'confidence' is meant stability in the holdings of international reserves. This concept was formulated when the US Treasury stood ready to convert dollars into gold for monetary authorities and a 'run on the bank' was considered possible. Although such convertibility into gold no longer exists, shifts of official holdings among reserve currencies may occur. Of course, destabilizing movements of private funds are even more possible.

How can the present system be characterized with respect to these potential problems? Regarding adjustment, large payments imbalances have certainly developed in the 1980s. The fundamental question is whether the large current-account deficits and surpluses can be attributed to the operation of the international monetary system? Does the system therefore need reform? Regarding liquidity, neither generalized shortages nor generalized excesses of reserves have been evident in recent years. Intervention in foreign exchange markets by industrial countries has been the major explanation for their reserve changes. These countries would have little difficulty in replenishing reserves by borrowing in capital markets. The argument has been made, however, that developing countries could use additions to their official reserves. The mechanism for accomplishing this exists in the form of Special Drawing Rights in the International Monetary Fund

Regarding confidence, little, if any, instability in the composition of official reserve holdings has been evident. In 1977–78, when the dollar depreciated, some monetary authorities apparently switched out of dollars into Deutschmarks and other reserve currencies. This experience led to consideration of a substitution account in the Fund, which would have permitted reserves in the form of currencies to be transformed into SDRs. Interest in a substitution account has waned in recent years. Instability of private holdings of foreign assets is certainly possible – much more possible than in the past as the result of the enormous increase in cross-border assets and liabilities. The external liabilities of banks in the industrial countries were 15 times larger at the end of 1987 than at the end of 1972, while money supply in these countries was less than four times larger. International transactions in securities have also increased enormously. This aspect of increased interdependence – the potential for large and sometimes destabilizing shifts of private funds – has evoked a number of proposals that come under the heading of reform and are related to adjustment. Thus the principal international monetary problems have to do with balance-of-payments adjustment and stability.

Until the 1980s, a movement of exchange rates was usually regarded as a means of correcting balance-of-payments surpluses or deficits that had developed for other reasons. In contrast, the large current-account deficit in the US balance of payments in recent years is, to a large extent, a consequence of the appreciation of the dollar. The analysis should begin, therefore, with an explanation for the rise in the foreign-exchange value of the dollar from 1980 to 1985. This rise was of record proportions, the largest movement of a real exchange rate in modern history. Measured by the Federal Reserve's trade-weighted index, the dollar went up about 80 per cent from 1980 to the peak in February 1985

Why did the dollar appreciate so much? The most common explanation – the 'conventional wisdom' – starts with the US budget deficit, which increased markedly as tax rates were lowered and defence spending increased. The combination of the budget deficit and domestic investment exceeded domestic saving. If the US had been a closed economy, the enlarged budget deficit would have driven up US interest rates to the point where they reduced investment or increased saving by enough to offset the budget deficit. In the interdependent world in which we live, somewhat higher interest rates in the US than abroad attracted funds from other currencies into dollars, pushing up the value of the dollar. This was the mechanism by which foreign savings were brought in to supplement US savings. The counterpart of the inflow of foreign savings was a current-account deficit in the US balance of payments. Thus, instead of American investment being crowded out by the budget deficit, American exports and domestic import-competing output were crowded out.

In Germany and Japan, the situation was the mirror-image of that in the US. These countries reduced their structural budget deficits: in fact, they did so by more, relative to their GNP, than the US increased its structural budget deficit. The excess saving in these countries showed up as current-account surpluses. Germany and Japan were able to cut back their budget deficits without creating recessions precisely because their exports were expanding as the result of US policies. Thus the exchange-rate movements of 1980–85 reflected fiscal policies of the major countries and helped to generate the external imbalances appropriate to those fiscal policies.

Suppose an attempt had been made to hold exchange rates at their 1980 levels (for example, through a system of target zones) with the budget policies that were actually in force in the three countries. What would have happened? The higher interest rates in the US would have made dollar assets look attractive to investors relative to assets denominated in Deutschmarks, yen and other currencies. This would have created upward pressure on the dollar's exchange rates. How could the monetary authorities have held exchange rates near their 1980 levels? Presumably, central banks would have intervened in foreign-exchange markets, selling dollars and buying the currencies of other industrial countries. If the intervention had been sterilized, it would probably not have succeeded in holding exchange rates against the pressures that existed in 1981–85. Therefore, central banks might have reverted to unsterilized intervention and the direct use of monetary policy to try to hold exchange rates. In either case, the Federal Reserve would have eased its policy and the central banks of Germany, Japan and other industrial countries would have tightened their policies. If the central banks had been willing to act in this way, the result would have been greater inflation in the US and even more sluggish economies in Europe and Japan. Higher inflation would have had the same effects on American exports and imports as the appreciation of the dollar. The ill-effects of the dollar's rise, including protectionist pressure, would have been felt anyway.

In practice, the Federal Reserve would not have followed such an inflationary policy. More realistically, the target zones for the dollar would have been adjusted upward from time to time, assuming they were not abandoned completely. Thus the dollar would have appreciated in any event. Whether the dollar had to appreciate as much as it actually did is a question to which I shall return. I find it difficult to avoid the judgment that, given the fiscal policies adopted by the larger countries in the first half of the 1980s, the world was better off with an appreciating dollar than it would have been with an attempt to keep exchange rates stable.

Where do these considerations lead us on the question of international monetary reform? It seems clear that the primary cause of the dollar appreciation of 1981–85 was not the nature of the exchange-rate regime but the fiscal policies of the leading countries. The movement of exchange rates reflected fiscal imbalances and helped bring about the accommodating current-account imbalances. In other words, the movement of exchange rates was the messenger. If a messenger brings unwelcome news, one does not try to reform the messenger. One tries to get at what led to the unwelcome news. It follows that one of the first priorities of those who would like to see improved performance of the world economy should be reform of fiscal policy, especially in those industrial countries that have a large impact on the world economy. Reforms to make fiscal policy more sensible and more flexible in the larger industrial countries would lead to better macroeconomic performance of these countries individually and as a group. This alone would probably result in more stable exchange rates over time.

Now I would like to go back and consider what is wrong or what is missing from the story I have been telling. One thing that is wrong is that the higher interest rates in the US in the first half of the 1980s do not provide a convincing explanation for the persistent rise of the dollar. At most, US interest rates exceeded those in Germany and Japan by 5–6 percentage points, often less. Was that spread sufficient to explain the continuing appreciation of the dollar when a 6 per cent dollar depreciation could have wiped out the annual interest gain from investing in dollar rather than Deutschmark or yen securities? To explain the appreciation, one also has to posit that market participants did not expect the dollar to depreciate or that they expected it to continue to appreciate. Thus the dollar was rising in part on expectations, in a self-fulfilling prophecy. This became clearer when, in the latter half of 1984, US interest rates declined and the differential in favour of dollar securities narrowed or disappeared. Yet the dollar kept rising until February 1985. The term 'speculative bubble' seems applicable.

Continuing with my second thoughts, I find myself in agreement with Krugman who argues, in his Robbins Lectures, that the large movements of exchange rates have, in effect, desensitized trade quantities and trade prices to changes in exchange rates. It is precisely because trade has become less responsive to alteration in currency values that those currencies could move so far in the 1980s. The explanation for the sluggish response of trade to exchange rates has several strands. The sunk costs of creating productive capacity for export and of establishing distribution systems abroad lead firms to delay entering new markets when that looks profitable and to delay leaving markets when losses are incurred. However, sunk costs are hardly a new phenomenon. What is new is that exporting firms may expect rates to reverse themselves after a large movement in one direction. Even if reversal is not expected, mere uncertainty about future exchange rates leads firms to delay entering or leaving markets. Thus large exchange-rate movements have led to inertia or sluggishness in the real responses to those movements. The word that economists have adopted to characterize this phenomenon is 'hysteresis'.

Policy implications

If exchange rates are subject to speculative runs that push them too far and if this, in turn, makes trade volumes and prices less responsive to changes in exchange rates, a case exists for more active management of exchange rates so as to moderate the amplitude of their medium-term swings. I hasten to say that a case does *not* exist for fixed rates. I also assert that McKinnon's 'gold standard without gold' (with its PPP-determined fixed rates among the three key currencies and its world money supply) is misconceived and would lead us far astray. Meade and Johnson taught us in the 1950s that the simultaneous achievement of internal and external balance requires expenditure-switching as well as expenditure-reducing, or expenditure-increasing, policies. Some flexibility of exchange rates is imperative in a world where countries have differing economic structures, differing rates of productivity growth, differing rates of inflation, and where the main impact of changes in fiscal or monetary policy is felt at home rather than abroad.

While I am being critical, a brief word is in order regarding some rational-expectations interpretations of exchange-rate movements. How can the gradual appreciation of the dollar over several years and its gradual depreciation in 1985–88 be reconciled with rational expectations? In a world of rational expectations, would not the dollar have jumped to its peak level immediately in the early 1980s when the US budget policy was established? Could the speculative bubble of late 1984–85 occur in a world of rational expectations?

Let me repeat my policy conclusion regarding exchange rates; namely, they need some management so as to give the market a centre of gravity, a point of focus, a norm. Whether this calls for formal target zones or something looser such as we have under the Louvre Accord is a matter for future determination, as far as I am concerned. The dilemma is to combine a sufficient degree of exchange-rate flexibility with some constraint on how far markets are permitted to push rates.

Concerning the other international monetary problem of destabilizing short-term capital flows, I shall be brief. Tobin has proposed a small tax on foreign-exchange transactions – to put 'some sand in the wheels' – without significantly affecting trade. Such a tax would be difficult to enforce in a world of global financial markets. Dornbusch has proposed dual exchange rates, one for commercial and the other for capital transactions. This would require exchange controls to assure that the system was respected. There are no easy answers here. I would not *in principle* reject the notion of some deterrent to speculative capital movements, if it could be done without interfering with either current-account transactions or capital flows to developing countries.

To return to my main theme, while I see the need for more managed exchange rates, the time for that reform is not now. For one thing, every forecast or projection (I know of) shows that, at present exchange rates, the US current-account deficit will not fall below $100 billion. Even if exchange rates were at levels that would eliminate the existing current-account imbalances, domestic policies, at least in the US and Germany, are not yet consistent with correcting those imbalances while meeting the other goals of policy. Another reason why this is not the time to reform the exchange-rate regime is that fiscal policy is immobilized in the US and far from flexible in Germany, where fiscal restraint seems to have become a goal rather than an instrument of policy. If a more managed system of exchange rates requires monetary policy to be directed at times to stabilizing currency values, a flexible fiscal policy will be needed to assure that the domestic goals of policy are met. For all these reasons, I believe that reform of the exchange-rate regime is a goal for the future rather than the present.

What deserves earlier attention, in my view, is the macroeconomic policy coordination process. At the Economic Summit meeting in Tokyo in 1986 the heads of government of the seven leading countries agreed on a procedure for policy coordination aimed not at exchange-rate stabilization *per se* but at improved macroeconomic performance. That procedure will not yield spectacular results in the short run. Numerous obstacles impede it, and it too requires improved fiscal policies. We can hope that the Toronto Summit in 1988 will provide additional momentum to that coordination process. Let me conclude by suggesting that, in the meantime, we direct our reformist zeal to one instrument and two targets of policy. Fiscal policy needs to be reformed in the United States, Germany, and perhaps other countries. As to the objectives of policy, we can hardly say that all is well with the world when unemployment in Europe exceeds 10 per cent. Finally, the debt problem of developing countries cries out for a solution that will permit capital imports and economic growth to be renewed.

4 International monetary reform, coordination and indicators

Andrew Crockett

The subject of international monetary reform has been attracting increasing attention in recent years. This conference provides a good opportunity to take stock of the state of thinking on this important issue. My remarks are in three parts. First, I discuss some of the reasons why there is dissatisfaction with the way in which the international monetary system (IMS) is functioning. This illustrates the basic motivation for seeking reforms to present arrangements. Second, I consider certain alternative proposals to introduce more fixity into exchange-rate relationships. Lastly, I deal with the way in which more systematic policy coordination can be used to improve the efficiency of the IMS within the framework of present arrangements. My conclusion is that the most feasible way of strengthening the working of the IMS is through incremental improvements to present arrangements rather than by attempting to design a new system with different rules.

Weaknesses in current arrangements

Perhaps the most obvious shortcoming of the way in which the IMS has worked in the floating-rate period has been the extreme exchange-rate instability that has occurred. This instability is manifested both in greater day-to-day volatility of rates (which probably do not have very serious medium-term effects) and in longer-lasting exchange-rate swings. The resulting exchange-rate misalignments can have much more substantial implications for economic performance. To take only the most prominent example, the US dollar appreciated by roughly 70 per cent in real effective terms in the first five years of the current decade, only to fall by an even larger amount in the subsequent three years. This development, it seems clear, cannot be conducive to an optimal allocation of real economic resources either across countries or over time. Fundamental factors cannot change over a few years by amounts that would justify movements in relative prices of such a magnitude.

A second unsatisfactory development under current international monetary arrangements has been the emergence of payment imbalances that appear to be unsustainably large. These imbalances are of course intimately linked to the exchange-rate trends just mentioned. The current-account deficit of the US reached about $160 billion in 1987, equivalent to some $3\frac{1}{2}$ per cent of GNP. At the same time, the surpluses of Japan and Germany, in relative terms, have grown to a broadly comparable size. Looking beyond the three largest countries, a situation has arisen in which the industrial world as a whole is absorbing real resources from the developing countries – hardly an optimal situation in a dynamic world economy. This 'reverse transfer' was more the result of the debt crisis than the IMS, *per se*. Nevertheless, it is a troublesome feature of the international economic landscape.

A third source of dissatisfaction with the functioning of the IMS is the lack of discipline that it seems to permit in domestic policies. The absence of an exchange-rate constraint means that domestic fiscal and monetary policies are freed from some discipline that operates under fixed exchange rates. Perhaps the most obvious example of undisciplined policies in recent years is the US fiscal deficit, which continued to increase even as the US external deficit was growing. More generally, current arrangements do not have any mechanism to restrain inflation. This was particularly obvious in the 1970s and early 1980s, when price increases ratcheted upwards in the industrial world, accommodated by expansionary monetary and fiscal policies.

This development reflects a fourth shortcoming in the present system, namely the absence of a 'nominal anchor' as a stabilizing focus for prices and price expectations. Under the gold standard, the nominal anchor was the price of gold. Under a dollar standard, a similar function was performed by the Federal Reserve, which, if it can ensure the stability of the US dollar in terms of goods, can provide an anchor for countries that wish to peg their currency to the dollar. With flexible exchange rates and no agreed system of currency management, the price level in each country depends on the policies the country itself follows. This may not be troublesome when policies are disciplined and credible; in other circumstances, the absence of a nominal anchor may be more costly.

These various shortcomings in current international monetary arrangements have potentially significant welfare cost. Exchange-rate volatility and misalignment, for example, lead to inefficient resource allocation in several ways. In the first place, the volatility creates uncertainties that (presumably) encourage producers to move into markets where they will be less exposed to international competition. There is, therefore, a bias towards sheltered markets and non-traded goods which contributes to a misallocation of resources in static terms. Secondly, there are costs of shifting resources when exchange rates change by large amounts. Exchange-rate movements cause shifts in profitability so resources have to be moved from one use to another. The movement of factors of production back and forth from traded to non-traded goods industries cannot be achieved without frictional costs. Moreover, it usually involves transitional unemployment. Thus one consequence of exchange-rate misalignments is likely to be a lower level of output and investment than might have been achieved had exchange rates been more stable.

The fact that there is no credible and established anchor for the domestic price level reduces the pressure on governments to follow stable domestic policies. Even where responsible policies are pursued, their credibility may be harder to establish in the minds of decision-makers in the private sector. Market participants will be aware that inflation may, at some future stage, be seen as a viable option and they will require additional incentives to enter into longer-term contracts. Lastly, but by no means least, the period of exchange-rate volatility has been associated with a revival of protectionism – fostered, at least in part, by attempts on the part of producers in internationally exposed sectors to insulate themselves (as they see it) from some of the adverse effects of currency volatility.

The conclusion to be drawn is that, if an international monetary regime could be devised that led to a greater degree of exchange-rate stability, this new regime would contribute to better domestic economic policies and stronger economic performance. However, the relationship between exchange-rate stability and economic performance is not simple. The fact that exchange-rate volatility is associated with certain more or less identifiable economic costs does not mean that simply fixing exchange rates would unequivocally improve welfare. In matters of economic policy, one must be very careful to distinguish symptoms from causes. The large exchange-rate swings of the last decade are, at root, *symptoms* of inconsistent and, in some cases, ill-conceived domestic policies. To improve economic performance, any new international monetary arrangements must deal not just with the symptoms of bad policies but also with the root causes. Thus incentives must be created to promote mutually compatible and internally consistent domestic policies. Only in such circumstances will it be possible for the IMS to facilitate the efficient allocation of real and financial resources across national frontiers.

There are two basic approaches to achieving compatible domestic policies and exchange-rate stability. One starts with an obligation to defend a set of exchange-rate parities or ranges. This obligation can create a framework within which the domestic policies of individual countries, being geared to a similar external objective, are mutually consistent. The approach can thus be thought of as a 'top-down' framework for consistency. The other approach focuses on the development of rules or guidelines for the formation of domestic policies. If these guidelines are well conceived and reasonably faithfully adhered to, then market mechanisms should produce exchange-rate stability – a 'bottom-up' approach. It is with these two broad approaches that I wish to deal in the remainder of this chapter.

Target zones and fixed exchange rates
One possible approach to reforming the IMS is to explicitly introduce more fixity into exchange-rate relationships through some kind of arrangement that establishes levels or ranges for variation among currencies. There are a variety of proposals of this type, covering the spectrum from fairly rigidly fixed rates to rather loose arrangements for target zones. What they have in common is the use of the exchange rate as a focal point for disciplining domestic policies and achieving international consistency. I do not propose to spend much time discussing the polar case of rigidly fixed exchange rates. Despite the attractiveness of fixed rates as an analytical construct, I believe they cannot be considered feasible at the present time. Bernstein's interesting and provocative paper (see Chapter 5 below) offers several reasons for doubting the practicability of fixed rates in current circumstances. I would add that a tight fixing of exchange rates (to be effective and credible) requires a greater willingness to subject domestic policies to international discipline than is likely to prevail outside countries that have already achieved, or are close to, a political union. The three large currency blocs of Japan, the US and the European Monetary System (EMS) are some distance from reaching such a stage.

What is more feasible and is certainly very much more in the forefront of debate – at least in academic circles – is the question of target zones. Is it possible and desirable to develop a system in which bands of exchange-rate fluctuation would be established and defended by means of agreements reached among the major countries? Target-zone schemes also come in a variety of specific forms. They have become increasingly sophisticated over the years as their proponents adapted earlier schemes to deal with objections or difficulties that were identified. Target-zone proposals, however, all involve the selection of an appropiate pattern for exchange-rate relationships among currencies; the establishment of bands of fluctuation around those relationships; and the obligation to intervene in foreign-exchange markets and to adapt domestic policies so as to help prevent rates moving outside the established bands.

The advantages of target zones are several and they are well understood.

In the first place, they stabilize exchange rates directly and, therefore, avoid some of the costs associated with the wide swings that have been experienced over the past decade. Secondly, a regime in which there are specific international objectives promotes a focus on the international spillovers of policy. It therefore encourages policy-makers to take into account the international implications of domestic developments and policies, more so than might be the case under a floating exchange-rate regime. Exchange-rate obligations exert a discipline on domestic policies that, it can be argued, induce policy-makers to avoid policy extremes and respond (rapidly and firmly) to destabilizing disturbances. At the same time, the fact that a range of fluctuation is accepted around the centre of a target band provides a safety valve permitting speculative pressures to be absorbed without breaking the system. Lastly, most formulations of the target-zone proposal allow for judgmental movements of the target range to accommodate fundamental changes in international competitiveness.

To set against these potential benefits of a target-zone system, there are a number of less positive features. Some of them can be dealt with by modifying specific features of the target-zone proposal; others pose more fundamental difficulties. A first problem is that any target-zone proposal requires the authorities to be confident that they can select a more suitable and sustainable rate than would emerge from the interplay of market forces. As someone whose professional responsibilities embrace the need to make regular economic forecasts, I would like to believe that economists can do better than the market. In fact, I believe there are occasions when we can, but the experience of the past few years should teach us a humility in this regard! It is also salutary to recall that researchers approaching this problem from different methodological standpoints have occasionally come up with quite different results. While McKinnon and Ohno (1989) suggest the dollar would have to appreciate by at least 30 per cent to reach its purchasing-power parity equilibrium rate, Dornbusch (1987) and others have estimated that the dollar still needs to depreciate substantially further in real terms to achieve a sustainable payments position!

Perhaps more fundamental than the difficulty of selecting an appropriate equilibrium rate, a focus of policy on the exchange rate confuses the symptom with the cause. This may, in certain circumstances, induce an inappropriate policy reaction. Consider the case of the appreciation of the US dollar between 1980 and 1985. It is now widely (though, perhaps, not universally) believed that the growth of the US fiscal deficit was a major motive force behind the appreciation of the US dollar and the widening of the US current account deficit in the early 1980s. Given the stance of fiscal policy, the only instruments available to counteract the appreciation of the dollar were intervention in the foreign-exchange market and monetary policy. (Further, since sterilized intervention is generally thought to have only limited results, the only truly independent instrument was, in effect, monetary policy.) If, in order to counteract the appreciation of the US dollar, the instrument of monetary policy had been applied, a more expansionary monetary stance would have been required. This would have added to the already expansionary effects of fiscal policy and would have worsened the domestic imbalance. Economic activity would have expanded even more rapidly in the US, thus contributing to possible overheating; meanwhile, in the rest of the industrial world, sluggish domestic demand would not have been offset by growing exports and the problem of unemployment would have been exacerbated.

A further drawback of target zones is that they reintroduce the need for politically sensitive adjustments of rates. If circumstances arise in which differential inflation (or some other development affecting competitiveness) cause the need for an adjustment of the real effective exchange rate, it will be necessary to make an adjustment in the bands of the target zone. The more there is a public focus on the exchange rate, the more politically sensitive it is likely to become. Hence, needed adjustments may take place with delays.

Lastly, target zones in themselves do not solve the 'N-1' problem; nor do they provide a nominal anchor for the system. There will always be one more currency in the system than there are exchange rates so understandings will be needed concerning which currency should be regarded as the *numéraire* whose value cannot be changed unilaterally. If there is a *numéraire* currency, there is no guarantee that the relevant issuing authority will manage its currency in such a way as to deliver the appropriate and acceptable degree of price stability.

These various objections have not gone unanswered by the proponents of target zones. Take, for example, the charge that a target zone can prompt an inappropriate policy response when official action is directed at the symptom of misalignment rather than the cause. The response elaborates on the guidance provided by the target-zone system so that not only are countries obliged to act in order to remain within the target zones, but also the nature of the action to be taken is specified. For example, if the original problem is a divergence in fiscal policies, then the solution will be sought through a convergent fiscal policy adjustment rather than by offsetting monetary policy.

It is also possible to add mechanisms providing solutions to both the N-1 problem and the nominal anchor problem. The former can be overcome either by designating one country as the hegemonic leader of the system or by developing a process of coordination, in which all countries relinquish part of the responsibility for their own currency in order to obtain a voice in setting the multilateral pattern of rates. The nominal anchor issue can be dealt with by agreeing to a collective monetary-growth rule (for example, as suggested by McKinnon, 1988) or by developing some kind of commodity-price rule, whereby one or more monetary authorities pursue a monetary policy to stabilize the value of their currency in terms of a basket of commodities (as proposed by Hart).

These modifications to the target-zone proposal do not, to my mind, get around the fundamental difficulty that there is an excess of targets over instruments. There are at least four major targets that governments are interested in pursuing and maybe 1½ instruments they have any latitude in using. The four targets would be output, inflation, exchange-rate stability and the balance of payments. The only instrument that is available on a continuous basis to regulate the economy or achieve exchange-market stability is monetary policy. Fiscal policy can perhaps be considered half of an instrument but not more. In some countries, most notably the US, fiscal policy is not available as an independent instrument for constitutional reasons, while in others, its use is also limited by essentially economic considerations. Most countries are now pursuing medium-term fiscal objectives. Within the framework of those objectives, there is limited scope to adjust fiscal policy for short-term demand management or exchange-rate purposes. I have not assigned intervention any weight here as an independent policy instrument – non-sterilized intervention is essentially an application of monetary policy while sterilized intervention has rather limited effects on exchange rates beyond the short term. Still, there probably are occasions when sterilized intervention can play a useful signalling and 'credibility enhancing' role and its usefulness should not be entirely discounted.

With an excess of targets over instruments, trade-offs have to be accepted so countries will not be able simultaneously to achieve all their objectives in the fields of growth, inflation, exchange-rate stability and payments adjustment. They will have to accept more of some and less of others. Also the choice of trade-off is likely to change over time and to be affected by the corresponding choices made by trading partners. Thus there may be costs to establishing rules that fix (in advance) the manner in which certain elements of the trade-off are to be decided. For this reason, I believe that a 'top-down' approach, using target exchange-rate relationships to determine domestic policy responses, risks putting the cart before the horse. At best, it is an indirect way of achieving harmonized and appropriate domestic policies.

Strengthening existing arrangements through enhanced coordination
Now I want to focus on ways in which, within the framework of existing international monetary arrangements, incremental improvements can be achieved by strengthening both the process and the substance of policy coordination. There are several steps in the process of effective policy coordination. The first and most fundamental step is to improve the basis for national decision-making through sharing information. Such sharing, together with improved understanding of how economies interact, enables governments to frame their individual policies with a better knowledge of what the global environment is likely to be. For example, if a country's trading partners contemplate the adoption of strongly expansionary policies, the authorities of that country might then choose a more restrained policy stance in order not to add to domestic and international inflationary pressures.

A second step in policy coordination is to make informed and mutually consistent choices about the trade-offs among economic objectives. Given the excess of objectives over instruments, countries cannot simultaneously achieve all their economic goals. Further the pursuit of a particular objective by one country has implications for the objectives of its trading partners. Exchange-rate stability, for example, implies that inflation rates must be similar across countries. It is thus essential for countries to reach a *consensus* on the relative emphasis to be accorded to objectives such as exchange-rate stability, balance-of-payments adjustment, inflation control and the promotion of economic growth. The third step of coordination is to adapt policies in individual countries so as to make them internationally consistent and mutually supportive. What does this mean in practice? How can the present IMS be modified in order to serve better the process of international policy coordination? What is the role of indicators in this process?

Let me focus on three areas in which I think there is scope for solid progress: strengthening the analytical basis for coordination; establishing an adequate objective standard to monitor developments and assess the need for policy changes; and finding an appropriate forum for discussing sensitive issues of international economic management. Concerning the analytical framework, there is a need to develop common understandings about key international economic relationships, expressed in the language of everyday political discourse and not just in the language of econometricians. That need is the motivation for the development of indicators which received attention at the Tokyo and Venice Summits. At one level, indicators seem like the emperor's clothes – not very much there! The initial list of indicators consists of familiar variables such as GNP, inflation, balance of payments, interest rates, fiscal deficits, and so on.

Nobody can object to considering these variables; indeed they have always been the subject of discussion whenever international economic officials meet. What has to be developed (and what I believe is being developed) is a common way of looking at these indicators and of viewing how policy measures (monetary and fiscal policies) affect intermediate variables (interest rates, exchange rates and domestic demand growth) and, thereby, influence performance variables such as GNP, inflation and the balance of payments.

There is now a clear recognition that the key to reducing external imbalances among the major countries is for changes in competitiveness (that have already occurred) to be accompanied by a sustained differential in rates of domestic growth in demand among countries – with faster demand growth in the surplus countries absorbing their surpluses, and lower demand growth in the US releasing resources for balance-of-payments improvement. This is perhaps not a novel discovery for economists but its wider acceptance has clear implications for the setting of monetary and fiscal policies.

There is also increased understanding about the limitations of demand-management policies. The major countries all broadly agree that the main goal of monetary policy has to be price stability and that fiscal policy must be kept on a steady course without fine-tuning if an environment conducive to private-sector activity is to be created. The second requirement is to have some established (and broadly objective) standard for assessing whether policies are on their intended track. This goal is expressed in the Louvre Communiqué, which stated that the major industrial countries will 'regularly examine, using performance indicators, whether current economic developments and trends are consistent with the medium term objectives and projections and consider the need for remedial action.' This perspective suggests an approach in which the major countries establish a desired path for key economic variables and use departures from this path as a signal that corrective actions may need to be considered. Mechanical responses may not be called for but the indicators serve as a sort of early warning system, with the actual policy response being determined in the light of the specific circumstances.

My last point is on the subject of the *forum*. At the present time, the main focus of coordination efforts is the Group of Seven, which has achieved much of value over the past three years or so. A difficult adjustment was begun while the momentum of world economic growth was sustained. However, the G-7 is not a particularly satisfactory forum from the point of view of an international monetary reform because it is a restrictive group that does not include representatives of the remainder of the international community. This reflects an inherent dilemma for the choice of a forum within which coordination is to be conducted has to balance two objectives. First, there needs to be some degree of universality. In other words, there must be a channel or a mechanism by which all members of the international community have a voice in the kind of coordination that takes place. At the same time, direct participation must be limited because it is quite clear, as a practical matter, that sensitive bargains will not be struck in large groupings.

Current arrangements provide for a rough-and-ready balancing of these desiderata. The G-7 is the focus for specific policy coordination decisions among the major countries. The managing director of the IMF participates in these meetings and can represent the interests and views of the remainder of the Fund membership. Moreover, meetings of the G-7 normally take place at the same time as meetings of the IMF's Committee of Governors (The Interim Committee). This permits a wide variety of views to be expressed and considered, even if not all countries are privy to the discussions on specific coordination proposals.

Where does all this leave us? The incremental approach to improving the working of the IMS is certainly not very elegant or tidy but, when the world itself is not tidy, this is not necessarily a disadvantage. There is a strong impulse to cooperation among the major countries, reinforced by the realities of interdependence. I believe the cooperative impetus provides a valuable basis for building both the process and substance of policy coordination. A codification of rules may be possible at some stage but to attempt such a codification prematurely could well be counterproductive.

References

Dornbusch, R. (1988), 'Doubts about the McKinnon standard', *Journal of Economic Perspectives*, **2**, 105–112.
Hart, A.G. (1989), 'A neglected monetary-standard alternative: gold/commodity bimetallism', chapter 15 below.
McKinnon, R.I. (1984), *An International Standard for Monetary Stabilization*, Institute for International Economics, Washington.
McKinnon, R.I. (1988), 'Monetary and exchange rate policies for international financial stability: a proposal', *Journal of Economic Perspectives*, **2**, 83–103.
McKinnon, R.I. and K. Ohno (1989), 'Purchasing power parity as a monetary standard', chapter 7 below.

5 The search for exchange stability: before and after Bretton Woods

Edward M. Bernstein

Until the middle of the nineteenth century, governments gave little attention to stability of foreign exchange rates. As long as the coinage was not debased and bank notes were convertible in gold or silver coin, the monetary system was regarded as in good order. When the convertibility of Bank of England notes was suspended during the war with France, the House of Commons appointed a select committee in 1810 'to enquire into the Cause of the High Price of Gold Bullion, and to take into consideration the State of the Circulating Medium, and of the Exchanges between Great Britain and Foreign Parts'. The exchange rate was given so much attention in the Bullion Report only because it was regarded as one of the tests of the depreciation of a paper currency.

As a practical matter, exchange rates were seldom stable before the 1870s. As Adam Smith noted, when silver coins were legal tender by tale, the pound was below its theoretical par value because the coins contained less silver than the mint standard as a result of abrasion and clipping. When gold coins (guineas) became the only unlimited legal tender, the exchange rates in Amsterdam and Hamburg – which were on the silver standard – varied because of changes in the gold price of silver. Exchange rates in France and the United States, which were on a bimetallic standard, were affected not only by changes in the gold price of silver but also by legislation changing the ratio of gold to silver and the seignorage in standard coins.

Although the state of the foreign exchanges became one of its guides to credit policy in the 1820s, the Bank of England did not regard it as necessary to take measures that were specifically directed to the exchange rates. The customary practice of the bank had been to raise the discount rate in steps of 0.5 per cent when necessary to restrain the demand for credit. In 1860, on the recommendation of Goschen (then a director), the bank adopted the policy of raising the discount rate by 1 per cent when the purpose was to strengthen the exchange rate. The new policy was unpopular with the business community which objected to the larger rise in the discount rate even though, as Bagehot noted, 'the beneficial results of the improved policy were palpable and speedy.'

About this time, a wider interest developed in the international aspects of money. At a conference in Paris in 1867, the delegates of 18 countries recommended that 'all gold coins hereafter struck in any of the countries which are parties to the convention should either be of the value of five francs or multiples of that sum, [and that] a gold coin of the value of 25 francs should be struck by such countries as prefer it, and be admitted as an international coin.' The advantages claimed for this universal coin were that it would be convenient for travellers and facilitate international payments. Another objective was to convert British coinage to the decimal system. Jevons was a strong supporter of the plan; Bagehot opposed it.

Conditions became favourable in the 1870s for the large trading countries to join Britain on the gold standard. The new German Empire, whose constituent states had been on the silver standard, decided to base the mark on gold. The rest of Europe followed Britain and Germany rather than continue on a silver standard. When France resumed convertibility of the franc after the war with Prussia, it was on a gold not a silver standard. The United States, which had suspended specie payments during the Civil War, resumed convertibility of the dollar in gold in 1876. Russia and India adopted a gold exchange standard. By the end of the nineteenth century, all of the large trading countries were on a gold standard.

This lasted only until 1914. Inflation during and after World War I compelled all countries – neutral as well as belligerents – except the United States, to terminate the gold convertibility of their currencies. An international monetary conference in Genoa in 1922 recommended an early return to the gold standard. By 1930, all of the large trading countries were back on the gold standard, some with new parities, others at historic parities. The new pattern of exchange rates overvalued some currencies, notably the pound, and undervalued others, particularly the French franc. This created centres of deflation, with deficits on current and capital account financed by gold settlements and held in check by large-scale unemployment. International payments were further distorted by the very high US tariff rates of 1930. In any event, the reduced production of gold after the war could not support an international monetary system at prices 45 per cent higher in dollars than before the war and the gold value of the dollar and sterling the same as before the war.

The gold standard, restored with so much difficulty in the 1920s, collapsed in the 1930s. As each country let the foreign exchange value of its currency fall, it increased the payments difficulties of countries still supporting the previous parities. The best that could be said for the successive reduction in the foreign exchange value of the major currencies is that competitive depreciation was preferable to competitive deflation. Attempts to secure international cooperation on exchange policy failed until 1936. On that occasion, to give international sanction to the devaluation of the franc, the US, the UK and France issued a Tripartite Declaration that recognized international responsibility for exchange policy – not only on rates but on exchange restrictions as well. Belgium, the Netherlands and Switzerland announced their adherence to the Declaration.

The Bretton Woods system
The Bretton Woods system of fixed but adjustable par values was intended to provide exchange stability without the rigidity of the gold standard. The automatic adjustment of the classical gold standard had come to an end in the 1920s, when the ties between the money supply and gold were loosened and the Central Banks gave greater emphasis to managing the money supply. Moreover, under the classical gold standard, balance-of-payments adjustment was shared by surplus and deficit countries in inverse proportion to the size of their economies. Under the managed gold standard, the burden of adjustment fell much more on the deficit countries as the surplus countries could neutralize the expansionary effect of an increase in their reserves. As a consequence, in the 1920s and 1930s, deficit countries resorted to deflation as an important means of balance-of-payment adjustment.

It was implicit in the Bretton Woods system that the large trading countries would follow policies directed to maintaining exchange stability. The basic requirement of a par value system is that prices should behave in a manner conducive to maintaining an appropriate pattern of international payments. As the only price policy that could be generally acceptable was one of stability, the objective had to be to maintain the trend stability of the price level of export goods. To achieve this, wage rates in each country would have to increase as much as the increase of productivity in its export industries. This rule would have to be modified to take account of trend changes in reciprocal demand. In countries where world demand for their exports grew more (less) than their demand for imports, wages would have to increase more (less) than the increase of productivity in their export industries.

Exchange stability also requires compatibility of the employment and balance-of-payments objectives of the large trading countries. That does not mean that their cyclical fluctuations must be synchronized but rather that the average level of utilization of their productive resources should be much the same over the course of a business cycle – about as high as is consonant with price and wage stability. Further, their balance-of-payments objectives must be compatible with an appropriate pattern of international payments – one in which the high-income countries usually have a surplus on current account, but not of equal proportionate magnitude.

In the discussions prior to Bretton Woods, the US emphasized the central role of price stability. In fact, it expected greater inflationary pressures after the war. That was one reason why it was unwilling to accept without qualification the principle that surplus countries had a responsibility for balance-of-payments adjustment equal to that of deficit countries. Most countries were concerned about the possibility of a recurrence of a great depression after the war and an excessive surplus in the US balance of payments. If this should happen, they wanted the United States to have the primary responsibility for adjustment. The US pointed out that its payments surplus in the 1930s was entirely due to a capital flight from Europe and that its balance on current account had fallen sharply in the depression. More important, the US held that the great depression was the result of the restoration of the gold standard after World War I at inappropriate parities and that this need not happen after World War II. Nevertheless, the US agreed that if a scarcity of the dollar should occur, the International Monetary Fund would have authority to deal with it.

The discussions before the Bretton Woods Conference did not set forth the conditions for maintaining exchange stability in a systematic way. The fullest statement of the US views was in the *Questions and Answers on the International Monetary Fund*, a document issued at the Bretton Woods Conference. One question was on the measures the IMF would recommend to a country whose currency was scarce – that is, to a super-surplus country – which led to the following statement:

> In general, there is little reason to expect that it will be necessary to recommend measures designed to encourage domestic expansion in the country whose currency is scarce. Nevertheless, if such recommendations are needed, they should be made . . . It is quite possible that the rise in productivity has been greater than the rise in wage rates, efficiency rates of remuneration have fallen, and that an upward adjustment should be encouraged.

The answer also stated that deficit countries could be partly at fault for the huge surpluses of other countries and that 'in such cases the responsibility for the correction of the maladjustment is not a unilateral one.'

It is much more difficult for countries to follow policies that are compatible with exchange stability than had been assumed at Bretton Woods. The basic difficulty is that countries differ in the emphasis they place on maintaining high levels of employment and on maintaining stability of prices. This difficulty is enormously greater when it becomes necessary to change a customary wage policy. Countries in which the growth of productivity has slowed may be unable to slow the rise of wages correspondingly, and those countries in which the growth of productivity has accelerated may be unwilling to increase the rise of wages to the same extent. Furthermore, to offset changes in reciprocal demand, unit labour costs would have to rise in countries whose position in world markets has strengthened and fall in those whose position has weakened. As experience shows, the countries whose relative international economic position has deteriorated are unable to restrain the rise of wages as much as necessary and those whose position has improved are unwilling to allow a greater rise of wages.

Is a modified Bretton Woods system feasible?

It may seem excessively pessimistic to conclude that a system of fixed but adjustable par values is no longer possible because countries are unable or unwilling to follow the policies required by such a system. After all, the gold standard, which was more rigid than the Bretton Woods system, lasted nearly 100 years in the UK and about 40 years as a universal standard. The Bretton Woods system lasted 25 years before it broke down and had to be abandoned. In the past nine years, the European Monetary System has operated as a regional exchange system, with wider margins around central rates that are adjusted frequently.

The gold standard lasted so long because it was believed by the public, and by most economists, that there could be no other satisfactory basis for a monetary system. Its long reign was marked by prolonged recessions, conditions which became intolerable by 1930 and led to its abandonment. The Bretton Woods system was able to last 25 years because it started with the US in an exceptionally strong payments position and huge gold reserves. The system collapsed because the US did not follow policies that would have offset the gradual deterioration in its relative international economic position and prevented the sharp depletion of its reserves. The EMS has been successful in maintaining orderly exchange markets, although exchange rates for its principal currencies have been far from stable. At present, the value of the Deutschmark in French francs is 47 per cent higher than at the end of March 1979, while it is less than 10 per cent higher in terms of the highly volatile dollar. The real achievement of the EMS was to facilitate the necessary adjustment of central rates in small steps to offset changes in the price-competitive position of its members.

It will not be possible to restore a general system of par values even after the US balance of payments has been adjusted. That is mainly because of the differences in the policy objectives of the US, Germany and Japan on the level of employment, stability of prices and the appropriate balance of payments on current account. For the US there is the further difficulty of maintaining convertibility of the dollar under a system of fixed parities, even with wide margins and frequent adjustment of central rates. The very limited reserves of the US, apart from its gold holdings, are not enough to finance the ordinary cyclical swings in the balance on current account. Beyond that, with the huge amount of dollar assets of private foreigners in this country, there is the possibility of a disruptive capital outflow even with a satisfactory balance on current account. If the dollar is to be convertible, it will have to be through the exchange market with the occasional use of reserves through intervention.

Although it is not possible to restore a modified Bretton Woods system, it should be possible to avoid large fluctuations in exchange rates after the foreign-exchange value of the dollar becomes appropriate to the relative international economic position of the US. If the system of floating rates was working properly, changes in the dollar rates for the major currencies would mainly reflect differences in their rates of inflation. If export prices in the US, for example, rise by 2 per cent a year more than in Germany and Japan, the dollar would have to tend downward by 2 per cent a year against the Deutschmark and the yen in order to maintain the price-competitive position of the US in world markets. The trend decline in the foreign exchange value of the dollar would have to be somewhat greater if there were also an adverse change in the reciprocal demand for exports and imports in the US and a favourable change in Germany or Japan.

The trend changes in the foreign-exchange value of the dollar that would be necessary to maintain an appropriate balance on current account would be small and gradual. There would be cyclical pressure on the payments position because of differences in the stage of the business cycle. If the cyclical expansion in the US came earlier or was larger than in other industrial countries, the US balance on current account would fall, and if the cyclical contraction in the US came earlier or was larger, its balance on current account would rise. The foreign-exchange value of the dollar would tend to fall in a cyclical expansion and rise in a cyclical contraction. However, intervention by the monetary authorities of the US and other countries could limit cyclical fluctuations in exchange rates if that were regarded as desirable.

Apart from exchange rates that reflect the relative international economic position of the large trading countries, it is necessary to have a pattern of interest rates that will result in net capital flows to match their balances on current account. The basic principle is that the difference in interest rates in the principal financial centres should, ordinarily, be the same as the differences in the rate of inflation or more precisely, the expected changes in exchange rates. If the dollar is expected to fall by 2 per cent a year relative to the Deutschmark and the yen, then interest rates in the US would have to be 2 per cent higher than in Germany and Japan. That would make the holding of funds equally attractive in these countries. What German and Japanese investors would gain in higher interest rates in the US would be offset by the fall of the dollar in terms of the Deutschmark and the yen.

This would not prevent the monetary authorities from using monetary policy to deal with their economic problems. If the cyclical expansion were synchronous in the large trading countries, they could all lighten monetary policy without affecting the difference in interest rates. If the US alone tightens monetary policy, US interest rates will rise and the interest differential will widen. This would encourage a capital flow and tend to raise the foreign-exchange value of the dollar, although much less than is generally assumed. If the interest rate differential is widened from 2 to 4 per cent and this is expected to continue for two years, then the dollar should rise promptly by about 4 per cent (the value of the extra 2 per cent for two years) and then decline at a rate of 4 per cent a year over the next two years. After that, when US monetary policy is eased and US interest rates decline to their previous level, the dollar will again fall at the trend rate of 2 per cent a year. Actually, the foreign exchange value of the dollar should rise less, if at all, as the effect of the higher interest rates would be offset to some extent by the cyclical fall in the balance on current account.

The key to greater stability is for the monetary authorities to recognize that the behaviour of the foreign-exchange value of the currency is an integral part of monetary policy. From a domestic point of view, an exchange rate for a currency that is high relative to the trend rate necessary for an appropriate balance on current account is like a tight monetary policy – it helps in holding down prices and costs but also restricts output and employment. An exchange rate that is low relative to the trend rate is like an easy monetary policy – it has an expansionary effect on output and employment but also facilitates a rise in prices and costs. From a broader point of view, overvalued and undervalued currencies cause a distortion of international trade. That is because an undervalued currency acts as a bounty on exports and a tax on imports, while an overvalued currency acts as a tax on exports and a bounty on imports. With large fluctuations in exchange rates, international trade is no longer determined by comparative advantage.

The money authorities cannot abdicate their responsibility for preventing fluctuations in exchange rates from having an adverse effect on the domestic economy and on the balance of payments. Under ordinary circumstances, these authorities would have a reasonable idea of what the trend rate of exchange should be to generate an appropriate balance on current account over the course of a business cycle. The authorities would have no reason for intervening unless the exchange rate departed by about 5 per cent from the trend rate. Even then, the purpose of the intervention should be to slow the rise or fall significantly rather than to prevent any further change in the exchange rate. The market may be saying that it foresees a change in the relative international economic position that requires a change in the trend rate of exchange. After the rate has risen or fallen by about 10 per cent from the trend rate, the monetary authorities should intervene as much as is necessary to stabilize the rate. They can do so on the assumption that underlying economic conditions do not change so much so fast. When there are large changes in exchange rates that call for intervention, they must be due to capital flows. The authorities should therefore consider whether their intervention should be accompanied by a change in monetary policy – higher interest rates if the exchange rate is falling, lower interest rates if the exchange rate is rising.

Such a policy on intervention could have greatly limited the fluctuations in the foreign-exchange value of the dollar in the past eight years. The huge rise of the dollar in 1980–85 was due to the capital inflow. It is frequently said that this was a response to higher real interest rates in the US. Actually, those who place uncovered liquid funds in the US are concerned less with interest rates than with prospective changes in the foreign-exchange value of the dollar. About 40 per cent of the foreign capital inflow in 1980–85, excluding official funds, were claims of foreign banks. They did not place their own funds in the US because of higher interest rates as that would have involved an exchange risk. Instead, they were responding to the demand of speculators who bid up the rate for forward dollars relative to the spot rate. This enabled the banks to engage in covered interest arbitrage, selling dollars forward and covering their position by buying dollars spot. The speculation on the dollar could have been halted by the end of 1980, after the dollar had risen by 11 per cent against the Deutschmark. As it was, the speculation continued until it became apparent that the risks of a fall in the dollar outweighed the prospects of a continued rise.

The large fluctuations in exchange rates in the past eight years have been in the dollar rates for the major currencies. The exchange rates of other currencies in terms of each other have fluctuated very much less than against the dollar. Because of the importance of the dollar in international trade and payments, large fluctuations in its foreign-exchange value are of concern to other countries. For this reason, the policy of the US on intervention in the exchange market should be made after consultation with the IMF and coordinated with intervention by the other large trading countries.

6 The international monetary system and the paper-exchange standard

Robert Triffin

I deplored 30 years ago (in 1957) the restoration of the 'gold-exchange standard' anchored to the use of a few national currencies (primarily the dollar) as major units of account in international contracts, settlements and reserve accumulation by the Central Banks and, as a consequence, by commercial banks and other major international transactors. I warned that such a system was unviable in the long, or even medium, run since it would tend to feed the reserve increases needed to finance the growth of world transactions through a continuous expansion of liabilities for the reserve-centre countries, exceeding the feasible growth of the gold holdings available to preserve the convertibility of their currency. I proposed, therefore, to create a truly international reserve instrument to replace gradually gold as well as reserve currencies: reserve deposits in the International Monetary Fund, enabling it: (1) to meet the requirements of feasible non-inflationary growth of world trade and production through the expansion of its loans and investments portfolio; and (2) to earmark this expansion for the financing of agreed high-priority objectives, including among others the development of the less developed countries of the Third World.

This analysis and prescription were broadly endorsed by the executive directors of the IMF, and by Jeremy Morse's Committee of Twenty, after two decades of debates and negotiations at the highest level between Ministers of Finance, Governors of Central Banks and their technical experts. Yet, they were thrown under the carpet by the Jamaica Agreement and the Second Amendment of the IMF Articles of Agreement. They continue to be ignored at the repeated summit meetings of the major financial powers at the Plaza Hotel in New York, the Louvre Museum in Paris and other palaces in Tokyo, Venice and elsewhere. These meetings persist vainly in focusing attention on the thermometer only, that is, the exchange rate of the dollar and its wild waves of successive undervaluation and overvaluation, rather than their root cause, that is, the acceptance of one or a few national currencies as world so-called 'parallel' currencies.

35

The consequences of this absurd system – denounced first by Emmanuel Kant in 1795, by the Gold Delegation of the League of Nations in the early 1930s, and by multiple other international conferences since then – have been as disastrous for the United States as for other countries. They are the main explanation of the wildest inflation in world history over the years 1970–88, and of unprecedented world trade and payments disequilibria under which the richest and most heavily capitalized country – except for a handful of Persian Gulf oil-exporting countries – experienced in 1987 current account deficits of $160 billion financed – by definition – by equivalent net capital imports from poorer and less adequately capitalized countries (about $660 per habitant, nearly $2 500 per household, or more than the total income per head on which some 3.5 billion people of the Third World must survive or starve). This situation is obviously unacceptable, economically as well as humanely, and in total contradiction with often repeated pious resolutions of the United Nations Assembly urging the richer countries to devote at least 1 per cent of their GNP to capital exports to the poorer and less developed countries.

These huge and unsustainable inflows of net capital are obviously at the root of the October 1987 Wall Street boom and collapse (reminiscent of 1929) and of the wild gyrations of the dollar exchange rates. Private capital inflows practically came to a halt in 1987, while dollar stabilization interventions on an unprecedented scale (nearly $140 billion) by Central Banks and other official institutions succeeded only in slowing down – but not arresting – a substantial fall of the dollar *vis-à-vis* its major rival currencies such as the mark and the yen.[1] I neither wish nor believe that such massive interventions could continue indefinitely, enabling the United States to finance huge and persistent deficits through the accumulation of a $2 000–3 000 billion foreign debt by the end of the 1980s, as happily foreseen and welcomed by the great monetarist and supply-side experts of President Reagan. The fundamental world monetary reforms previously advocated by the IMF and the Committee of Twenty will, sooner or later, be imposed by US and foreign statesmen on shortsighted politicians. The countries best able to take the initiative in this respect are obviously those of the European Economic Community.

The ECU (European Currency Unit), now defined as a basket of the participating countries' currencies, should be redefined as a final reference currency, in terms of which each member country will define the par value of its currency and its occasional – and hopefully less and less frequent, as is already the case – realignments upward or downward. Professor Kindleberger correctly argues that the 'paper standard dollar' has proved more acceptable in fact than Volapuk or Esperanto, but that world interests require its management be entrusted to an enlarged

Table 6.1   The international balance sheet of the United States: 1939–87 ($ billions)

	End of year							Period changes		Annual changes		
	1939	1949	1970	1979	1982	1986	1987 (pr)	1980–82	1983–86	1980–82	1983–86	1987 (pr)
I Exchange market, net:	+1	−2	+12	−15	−69	−564	−724	−54	−495	−18	−124	−159
A. Gross assets	11	18	122	441	739	967	1032	+298	+228	+99	+57	+65
B. Gross liabilities (−)	−10	−20	−110	−456	−809	−1532	−1756	−353	−723	−118	−181	−224
C. Official and banks, net	−3	−5	−33	−120	−15	−242	−334	+105	−227	+35	−57	−92
D. Customers, net	+4	+3	+45	+105	−54	−322	−390	−159	−268	−53	−67	−68
II Gold and foreign aid assets	18	36	44	194	195	192	215	+1	−3	—	−1	+23
III Net total (I+II)	+19	+34	+56	+179	+126	−373	−509	−53	−498	−18	−125	−136
Assets	29	54	166	635	934	1159	1248	+299	+225	+100	+56	+88
Liabilities (−)	−10	−20	−110	−456	−809	−1532	−1756	−353	−723	−118	−181	−224

Source: Survey of Current Business. The 1987 columns are provisional estimates unadjusted (except gold) for exchange-rate and price fluctuations, whose estimates will probably appear in the June 1988 Survey.

open-market committee including representatives of foreign countries. Such a proposal seems to me far more unrealistic than even the most utopian versions of the Triffin plan. While many countries might not only be willing, but determined, to negotiate appropriate controls over the issue of any joint reserve, or parallel, currency, none will ever accept having its own currency controlled by foreigners.

Nine years of functioning of the European Monetary System have amply demonstrated its ability to perform the essential role of an exchange-rate system, which is to preserve or restore with reasonable speed the stability of real exchange rates among member currencies at competitive levels, consonant with desirable and feasible surpluses and deficits in their international accounts. Exchange-rate realignments have proved negotiable whenever necessary to avoid excessive financing of the persistent inflationary price and cost differentials that participating countries were politically unable to avoid. This success, however, was undoubtedly due in part to the strength of the dollar *vis-à-vis* the mark and other strong EC currencies until the end of 1984. The strong dollar eased exchange-rate tensions considerably within the Community. Unfortunately, it weakened Germany's interest in implementing paragraph 4 of the Annex to the Bremen agreement of 6 and 7 July 1978, and thus in consolidating 'not later than two years after the start of the scheme, the existing arrangements . . . in a European Monetary Fund'. This objective has acquired a new urgency in view of the awesome foreign-exchange and bank crises likely to erupt at any time as a consequence of the enormous US deficits and of the decision of various Latin American countries to suspend or limit contractual amortization and even interest payments on their huge bank indebtedness. It is particularly necessary to avoid disruptive realignments of intra-community exchange-rates – those that are not required by significant inflation differentials. The last such realignment (on 12 January 1987) was only a weak foretaste of foreseeable future tempests.

The success and even the feasibility of such progress, however, require that it be planned in such a way as to avoid further aggravation of the dollar crisis. Indeed, the European Monetary Fund should enable the Community to help resolve the severe dollar problem, particularly through the conversion of short-term dollar indebtedness into exchange-guaranteed 'consols' and the extension of *conditional* credit to finance further US deficits that cannot possibly be eliminated overnight. This decentralization of the defunct Bretton Woods system would help rally to it not only many disaffected countries of the Third World but even countries of the Communist bloc. I urge you to read, in this connection, the unprecedented and revolutionary statement of the delegate from the

USSR Institute of World Economics, Dr D.V. Smyslov, at the Round Table East–West Conference on the Future of the International Monetary System, held at Szirak (Hungary) on 28–29 August 1986 (see Szabó-Pelsóczi (ed.), forthcoming). The major obstacle to the adoption of these suggestions lies in the obdurate opposition of Central Banks in general, not just of the Bundesbank.[2]

The completion of the economic and monetary – and therefore political – union of the Community has been repeatedly promised by its heads of state or governments since their first summit meeting at the Hague in December 1969. Progress towards it, however, has been slowed down for years by the opposition of central bankers – not only in Germany, but in most other countries – understandably fearful to see the inflationary proclivities of some member countries automatically transmitted thereby to the Community as a whole. These fears have been quelled to some extent by the relative success of the EMS, but are by no means extinct. What needs to be emphasized, however, is the revolutionary change of political perspectives now in process and of which very few people are aware, not only outside Europe, but even in Europe itself. It is increasingly recognized by its political as well as by its economic leaders that radical steps toward full monetary union are indispensable to the completion of the fully integrated internal market envisaged for 1992 in the Single European Act signed in February 1986 and ratified by all member countries in 1986 and 1987.

The two founding fathers of the EMS and the ECU, Valéry Giscard d'Estaing and Helmut Schmidt, have formed a committee designed to promote sweeping reforms that include the creation of a European reserve currency and of the European Central Bank indispensable to its management. Those who equate wisdom with scepticism will, of course, dismiss such ambitious proposals as utopian. They will point out – rightly – that Ministers of Finance and Governors of Central Banks are prone to advocate, when out of office, the fundamental reforms which they consider as unfeasible when in office! You may be more interested, therefore, in the treaty concluded on 20 January 1988 between the governments now in power in France and Germany, on the 25th anniversary of the Franco-German treaty signed in 1963 by President de Gaulle and Chancellor Adenauer. President Mitterrand and Chancellor Kohl paragraphed solemnly, in company with about twenty of their ministers, two additional protocols, soon to be ratified by their Parliaments and creating a Defence and Security Council and an Economic and Financial Council. An important task of the latter will be to assure a closer coordination of monetary policy between the two countries than that already in effect today, and to enable them to accept and promote the creation of a European Central

Bank. The Presidents of the Bank of France and of the Bundesbank and the French and German Ministers of Finance and Ministers for Economics will make up this Council.

The President of the Bundesbank, Dr Otto Pöhl, expressed the agreement of the Bank's Council, but noted that

> since the Council is to be established in the context of a treaty that is binding under international law and an examination of the legal position was not possible in the brief period of time given to the Central Bank Council to take its decision, the agreement of the Central Bank Council is given with the reservation that the supplementary protocol does not affect the content of Sections 3 and 6(1) and 12, sentence 2, Bundesbank Act. The Bundesbank requests the Federal Government to communicate this decision also to the French partner to the Treaty and to take it into account when ratifying the Treaty.

He explained that this meant 'that the freedom of decision and the independence of the Bundesbank in monetary policy affairs must not be restricted', and answered some critical remarks of Prime Minister Chirac about the Bundesbank's policies.

It is well known of course, that the Bundesbank's authorities have long been radically divided about the creation and development of the European Monetary System, to which its former President, Dr Emminger, was adamantly opposed, as is still today its Vice-President, Dr Schlesinger. Dr Pöhl, recently reappointed as President for a term of eight years, undoubtedly shares the German fears about 'premature' commitments to the EMS, and particularly to full monetary union, until the primary objective of price stability, as well as exchange-rate stability, can be implemented by a better coordination of national monetary and fiscal policies, and guaranteed by the independence of a European Central Bank and its federated national Central Banks from undue political pressures. Yet, he reiterates relentlessly and indefatigably in all his speeches that the ultimate goal of full economic and monetary union, including the merging of all national currencies into a single European currency, under a European Central Bank, must be kept in mind in the formulation of immediately feasible policies. The Basle Central Bank's agreement, ratified by the Nyborg European Council, indicates that his views are now prevailing within the Bundesbank itself, and most commentators agree that it functions in fact even better than initially hoped for by its proponents.

The European Parliament has also expressed repeatedly, under the leadership of Lord Plumb, Otmar Franz and Fernand Herman particularly, its strong support for the measures leading to full economic and monetary union of the Community. Equally encouraging is the totally unexpected success of the Brussels Summit of mid-February 1988 regarding the financing of an increased Community budget, the doubling of subsidies to its poorest members, and the initiation, at least, of overdue radical reforms of the Common Agricultural Policy.

Let me note, in conclusion, that the EMS has modified radically the transitory provisions toward full monetary union initially envisaged in the 1970 Werner Plan. These began with the gradual elimination of exchange margins and exchange-rate fluctuations between the national currencies and ended with their sudden replacement by the ECU at the end of the process only. The EMS, on the contrary, began with the creation and development of the ECU as a parallel currency for external transaction, as described earlier in this paper. Its success would transform into ECUs the equivalent of well over $1 trillion of bank loans (and deposits) and of securities now denominated in so-called Eurocurrencies or Xeno-currencies. The completion of the monetary union would then merely require the gradual extension of the use of the ECU in domestic as well as external transactions throughout the Community. This could be done at a different pace in the various countries and is likely to proceed faster in Luxembourg, Belgium and Italy for instance, and even in Austria, which has recently indicated its desire to join the Community, than in the United Kingdom or Germany. As an inveterate optimist, I hope to live long enough to see the end of this venture!

Notes

1. See the 1986 and 1987 estimates of the US balance of payments in the March 1988 *Survey of Current Business*, and the tables and commentary on international monetary developments and policy in the remarkable *Report of the Deutsche Bundesbank for the Year 1987*, pp. 56–75, from which this $140 billion estimate is derived.
2. See Michel Aglietta (1986), 'L'ECU et la vieille dame: Un levier pour l'Europe', with a Preface by Robert Triffin (*Economica*, Paris); and Robert Triffin (1985), 'Proposals for the strengthening of the European Monetary System: a discussion of Germany's objections', *Info-digest*, Munich, **8**, 6–11.

7 Purchasing power parity as a monetary standard

Ronald I. McKinnon and Kenichi Ohno

From its initial formulation by Gustav-Cassel in the unsettling monetary aftermath of World War I, through the modern experience with fluctuating exchange rates since 1973, economists have been fascinated by the relationship between purchasing power parity (PPP) and exchange rate equilibrium. Indeed, Cassel took it as a virtual truism that 'As long as anything like the free movement of merchandise and a somewhat comprehensive trade between two countries takes place, the actual rate of exchange cannot deviate very much from . . . purchasing power parity' (Cassel, 1918, p. 413).

However, the experience with floating exchange rates in the early 1920s, to be painfully relearned in the 1970s and 1980s, disabused people of the idea that the natural forces of international commodity arbitrage would be sufficient to align national price levels when exchange rates were not fixed. Since 1973, fluctuations in the important yen/dollar and mark/dollar rates have been unexpectedly large, and seemingly as often away from PPP as towards it. This unpredictability of exchange rates, combined with the natural stickiness of the prices of domestically-produced goods invoiced in domestic currencies, inhibits arbitrage in international markets for manufactured goods so that cross-country prices of very similar products can differ greatly (Isard, 1977; Levich, 1986).

To explain this anomaly, the modern theory (Frenkel and Mussa, 1980) has it that 'forward-looking' floating exchange rates are determined in asset markets – and continually move according to new information about, say, how policy in country A might change *vis-à-vis* that in country B. Because international asset markets clear much faster than commodity markets or movements in national price levels, exchange rates almost always appear to be misaligned – at least by the criterion that the purchasing powers of national monies be equated across countries. Indeed, one cannot reject the hypothesis that floating exchange rates move like a random walk (Meese and Rogoff, 1983). Clearly, with the diverse monetary conditions now prevailing among the United States, Japan and

Germany (representing the Western European bloc), PPP must be rejected as a positive theory for explaining or predicting movements in floating nominal exchange rates over the course of months or even years.

Nevertheless, there is a more normative sense in which the theory is valid, and potentially very useful. Because of the high degree of trade and financial integration among the three major blocs, suppose the Federal Reserve System, the Bank of Japan, and the Bundesbank decide to approximate conditions prevailing in a single currency area. Not only would nominal exchange rates be fixed (at least within narrow bands), but each national money supply would adjust to maintain these rates as if a common monetary standard were in operation. The details of how symmetrical monetary coordination could take place are spelled out in McKinnon (1974, 1984, 1988). Here it suffices to note that each Central Bank must gear domestic money growth to exchange rate stabilization: when its exchange rate tends to appreciate *vis-à-vis* the agreed parity rate, the Central Bank must expand domestic money growth above normal – and contract should its currency weaken in the foreign exchanges. Assuming the necessary international monetary coordination indefinitely sustains the new exchange-rate regime, Cassel would be vindicated, for purchasing power parity – with respect to appropriately chosen definitions of national price levels for tradable goods – would prevail.

Our purpose is to show how, for this hypothetical new international monetary order, past information (on exchange rates and national price indices – producer prices, consumer prices, GNP deflators, unit labour costs, wages, and so on) can be used to calculate alternative estimates for the concurrent yen/dollar and mark/dollar exchange rates that best approximate PPP; and to chart how various national price and wage indices might evolve if nominal exchange rates were fixed. While some price indices would move together, others would diverge because of international differences in productivity growth. The statistical problem is essentially one of taking noisy data from the unsettled 1970s and 1980s (when exchange rates floated and national inflation rates often differed) and using them to project what the monetary authorities in the US, Japan and Germany could expect once exchange rates were stabilized through monetary cooperation.

Alternative estimates of PPP exchange rates

Consider first the conceptual issues for calculating PPP exchange rates at any point in time from disequilibrium data. If nominal exchange rates are fixed for a long time and trade is fairly free, international arbitrage should roughly align the average national levels for prices of tradable goods – as measured, say, by each country's producer price index (PPI). Similarly, because the common monetary standard would tend to equalize the cost of capital everywhere, so too the unit labour cost (ULC) of producing a broad basket of manufactured goods should be roughly the same in different countries. Any differences in labour productivity would be offset by wage differentials. In contrast, international or inter-regional arbitrage in goods markets need not align the prices of non-tradables that also enter CPIs or GNP deflators. Thus, national PPIs or ULCs are more appropriate indices for measuring whether price levels are internationally aligned. Major statistical problems, however, prevent the use of *current* observations on PPIs or ULCs to directly estimate (absolute) PPP exchange rates for national price indices are not directly comparable and, given the recent sharp and unexpected fluctuations in relative currency values, one cannot presume the existing values of PPIs or ULCs are in equilibrium.

International comparability
Countries use different quantity or value weights in constructing price indices and their absolute values are not scaled the same way – each index is a price relative to some base year and is not the price of a basket of internationally comparable commodities. Ideally, the cross-country information we would like to have for, say, the PPI would be

$$(1) \qquad\qquad E^{PPP} = P_a/P_a^*,$$

where P_a is the (absolute) yen price and P_a^* is the dollar price of the same broad basket of manufactured goods at the 'factory gate', before any indirect taxes or subsidies are imposed. Instead, national indices for PPIs are price relatives such that

$$(2) \qquad\qquad E^{PPP} \simeq \theta P/P^*,$$

where θ is an unknown scale factor. The price relatives, P and P*, represent domestic currency prices of commodity baskets which are similar in composition but of arbitrary size – say, 100 in 1980. All officially published price indices take this form. The approximate equality ($\simeq$) reflects the fact that the two commodity baskets may have different weights.

Cassel (1922) resolved the reconciliation problem with his 'relative' method of estimating E^{PPP}: choose a base year when one could reasonably presume that PPP held; then use the subsequent (differing) rates of national price inflation to adjust the base period's exchange rate and get a new estimate of PPP at the time t, given by

$$(3) \qquad\qquad E_t^{PPP} = e_0(P_t/P_0)/(P_t^*/P_0^*),$$

where e_0 is the actual and PPP exchange in the base period 0 and the θ

in equation (2) is $e_0 P_0^*/P_0$. This methodology was well suited to Cassel's historical circumstances. The gold standard effectively imposed a common monetary policy on the principal industrial countries from the late 1870s, so 1913 was a natural base year from which to project PPP exchange rates after World War I. Recent evidence (Triffin, 1964; McCloskey and Zecher, 1976) suggests that the price of tradable goods in the late nineteenth century remained about as well aligned internationally as within regions of the same country. Although tradable goods prices moved considerably through time under the gold standard, they tended to rise and fall together on a worldwide basis. In August 1914, the sudden shock of World War I abruptly terminated the common monetary policy. Currencies were no longer freely convertible into one another so all the belligerent countries and many neutral ones began to inflate at different rates. With the limited data for national wholesale prices then available, Cassel (1922) used equation (3) to estimate various PPP exchange rates for 1920. These could, in principle, have been the basis for a new fixed-rate postwar monetary standard but the necessary international monetary cooperation was not forthcoming in the interwar period.

To re-establish a common monetary standard in the late 1980s our problem of comparing price indices across the major industrial economies differs somewhat from that of Cassel. After a long period of fluctuating exchange rates, there is no single – not too distant – base year (like 1913) for which one could confidently assert PPP held among the yen, dollar and mark. Various authors, using Cassel's relative method in the 1970s and 1980s, have made a case for PPP equilibrium holding for this or that base year but a wide dispersion of estimates resulted for current PPP exchange rates. On the other hand, national price relatives (PPI, CPI, GNP deflator, ULC and wages) are now available going fairly far back in time. Could evidence of which price indices tend eventually to realign themselves internationally be used to compute some long-period average 'real' exchange rate, the θ in the equation (2)?

Initially, let us arbitrarily choose a real exchange-rate series based on 1970, the last year of the Bretton Woods system of (weakly) pegged exchange rates. Starting with 1960, define the 'real' exchange rate at any subsequent point in time:

(4) $$\bar{E}_t = E_t/E_t^{PPP}(1970),$$

where E_t is the concurrent yen/dollar or mark/dollar exchange rate and $E_t^{PPP}(1970)$ is the corresponding PPP rate using 1970 as the base. With quarterly data for 1960–86, Figures 7.1 and 7.2 plot the real exchange rate (defined by this equation) for the dollar/yen and dollar/mark, respectively. The alternative US, Japanese, and German price indices used to

Figure 7.1   Yen real exchange rates, 1960–86 (against the dollar)

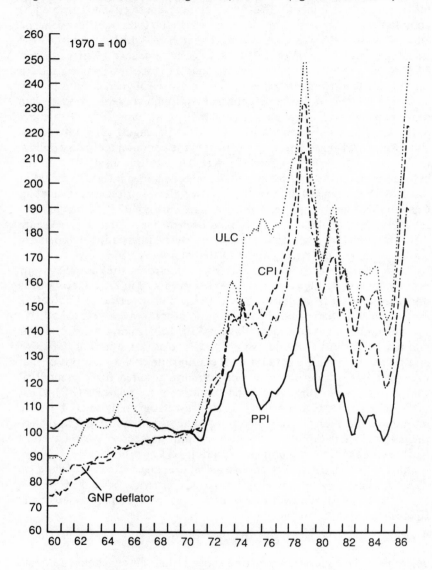

Note: ULC means the dollar/yen exchange rate deflated by the relative unit labour costs of Japan and the United States, CPI by relative consumer prices, PPI by relative producer prices.

Sources: OECD, *Main Economic Indicators* for all price indices (quarterly); IMF, *International Financial Statistics* for exchange rates (quarterly).

Figure 7.2   Mark real exchange rates, 1960–86 (against the dollar)

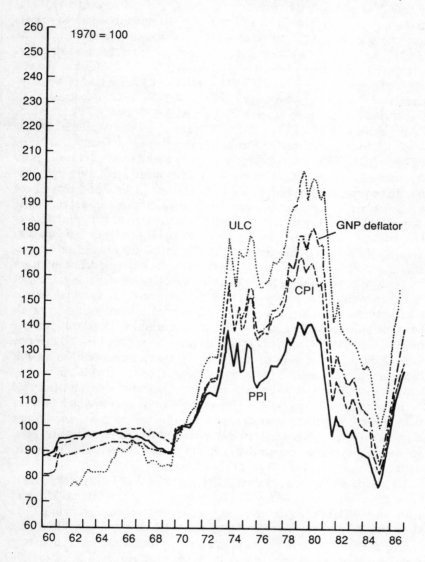

Note: ULC means the dollar/mark exchange rate deflated by the relative unit labour costs of Germany and the United States, CPI by relative consumer prices, PPI by relative producer prices.
Sources: OECD, *Main Economic Indicators* for all price indices (quarterly); IMF, *International Financial Statistics* for exchange rates (quarterly).

calculate E_t^{PPP} (1970) are producer prices, unit labour costs, consumer prices and GNP deflators. Of the four corresponding sets of measures for the real exchange rate, those based on PPI show the strongest tendency to regress to some *normal* level, associated with the period of pegged rates in the 1960s. The Japanese/US data in Figure 7.1 show this effect most strongly. Even the PPI's unprecedented large deviation from PPP (due to the yen appreciation of 1985–87) could well regress over a long period of time. International commodity arbitrage should eventually bring pressure to align tradable-goods prices so as to achieve a rough PPP by the PPI criterion.

In contrast to the PPI, Figures 7.1 and 7.2 show a much weaker tendency for international arbitrage to reassert itself in terms of CPIs or GNP deflators. This is not surprising since each has a substantial non-tradable component which cannot be directly arbitraged, although non-tradables prices could 'line up' if factor-price equalization holds in the tradables sector and production technology is everywhere the same (Komiya, 1967). However, Japan and Germany started with much lower levels of economic productivity in 1960 than the US and they subsequently experienced more rapid technical progress, particularly in industries producing tradable goods. Hence, from the Scandinavian model of inflation (Balassa, 1964; Lindbeck, 1979; Marston, 1986), one expects service prices to rise more (relative to goods prices) in high-growth economies. This is what is observed in Figures 7.1 and 7.2: graphs for real exchange rates, based on either the CPI and GNP deflator, continually rise *vis-à-vis* those based on the PPI, particularly in the Japanese case. The upshot is that one must discard price indices with high service components (CPI and GNP deflators) in calculating PPP exchange rates consistent with commodity market equilibrium. If a common monetary standard were implemented in the late 1980s among the US, Japan and Germany (for which productivity growth is quite dissimilar), participating governments should not expect that their CPIs or GNP deflators to increase at the same rate. However, they should expect their PPIs to remain roughly aligned and to define the common price level in tradable goods.

The remaining apparent anomaly in Figures 7.1 and 7.2 is the behaviour of unit labour costs. Why should the graphs show Japan/US and Germany/US labour costs increasing relative to their corresponding PPIs since 1960? After all, we argued above that ULCs should line up across countries in the long run (and much faster under a common monetary standard). Measurement error could be the problem. In a more rapidly growing economy like that of Japan, the faster introduction of new products imparts a relative upward bias to measures of its ULC. When a new product is introduced, domestic costs of production implicitly fall from some very high number to an internationally competitive level. As ULC indices are constructed to splice in new products without showing any fall in the index, they fail to capture the true improvement in relative productivity. Japan's international cost competitiveness is thus understated relative to that of the US. This (biased) divergent growth in relative ULCs diminished sharply after 1973 (Figures 7.1 and 7.2) because Japanese and German productivity growth slowed down *vis-à-vis* US growth. Nevertheless, this problem of international comparability cautions one against using very long-term unadjusted averages of ULCs, by themselves, for calculating PPP exchange rates in the late 1980s.

The method of long-run averaging
With these caveats about the comparability of price indices in mind, consider Table 7.1. Alternative calculations of PPP are presented for the fourth quarter of 1986, according to the format of equation (2). Of the large number of base periods employed in Table 7.1, most are invalid in the sense of PPP actually holding in these intervals. Nevertheless, suppose international arbitrage tends in the long run to align international price levels, despite the disruption of great exchange-rate fluctuations on a quarterly or annual basis. Then period averages (27 and 14 years in Table 7.1) could replace the choice of any single base year in equation (3) for calculating PPP exchange rates in the last quarter of 1986. That is, our scale factor in equation (2) becomes $\theta = 1/T \sum_{k=0}^{T-1}(e_{t-k}P_{t-k}^*/P_{t-k})$, where T is either 27 or 17 years. How long is the optimal interval over which the data should be averaged? If the data are subject to noise but otherwise unbiased, the period should be as long as possible, perhaps 27 years. On the other hand, if bias in relative price indices accumulates with the passage of time – because of differential productivity growth or measurement errors – then the optimum period average could well be less than 14 years. There is an uncomfortable trade-off. The base period of 1973–86 seems a plausible choice here. First, in comparison to the 1960s, the big differences in productivity growth between Japan, the US and Germany had narrowed by 1973, the end of what the Japanese call their 'era of rapid economic growth'. Second, the last 14 years provide the more recent data.

We have argued that PPIs are the most likely to reflect accurately international arbitrage and that base-period averaging over the most recent 14 years is not implausible. Hence, in Table 7.1, our 'best' point estimates of PPP exchange rates for the fourth quarter of 1986 are 205 yen/dollar and 2.24 marks/dollar while the actual spot-exchange rates are 160 yen/dollar and 2.01 marks/dollar, respectively. Fortunately, in Table 7.1, all the PPP estimates based on 14-year averaging (but using alternative price indices) are quite tightly bunched. Estimates range from 205 to 224 for the yen/dollar rate and from 2.07 to 2.27 for the mark/dollar in the

Table 7.1   Alternative PPP exchange rates for 1986: IV (with different base years and price indices)

Base period	Index	PPI	yen/dollar ULC	CPI	GNP defl.	PPI	mark/dollar ULC	CPI	GNP defl.
1960		231	439	468	373	2.77	—	2.92	3.45
1961		223	431	449	352	2.60	—	2.75	3.19
1962		226	396	425	344	2.57	4.46	2.71	3.13
1963		223	382	400	335	2.55	4.20	2.66	3.07
1964		224	380	392	327	2.52	4.19	2.63	3.02
1965		226	346	373	319	2.53	3.85	2.60	2.99
1966		229	360	367	316	2.57	3.73	2.59	2.99
1967		226	382	362	308	2.60	3.85	2.61	3.02
1968		231	390	357	304	2.69	4.02	2.65	3.10
1969		234	396	355	304	2.69	3.97	2.70	3.08
1970		234	393	348	298	2.47	3.43	2.56	2.80
1971		238	342	332	289	2.33	3.01	2.43	2.60
1972		215	285	285	249	2.18	2.69	2.17	2.36
1973	• 189	252	243	211		1.94	2.18	1.81	1.96
1974		191	228	235	205	1.97	2.06	1.82	1.94
1975		207	214	234	211	1.98	2.04	1.78	1.90
1976		206	216	225	208	2.05	2.14	1.84	1.98
1977		192	200	201	189	1.95	2.02	1.75	1.86
1978		164	170	163	152	1.80	1.79	1.58	1.66
1979		183	195	182	167	1.76	1.72	1.54	1.58
1980		188	223	198	184	1.86	1.77	1.65	1.64
1981		198	223	202	190	2.38	2.23	2.13	2.14
1982		227	255	236	224	2.49	2.50	2.30	2.32
1983		221	239	227	221	2.61	2.65	2.42	2.48
1984		226	247	230	228	2.90	2.94	2.73	2.81
1985		227	251	234	235	2.92	3.10	2.86	2.97
1986		164	171	167	168	2.16	2.22	2.15	2.18
Average of 27 years (1960–86)		230	286	276	253	2.60	2.89	2.49	2.64
Average of 14 years (1973–86)		205	224	217	205	2.24	2.27	2.07	2.13
1986: I		180	193	186	187	2.33	2.43	2.30	2.36
1986: IV (actual)		160	160	160	160	2.01	2.01	2.01	2.01

Note: German ULCs for 1960 and 1961 are unavailable.
Sources: IMF, *International Financial Statistics* (exchange rates); OECD, *Main Economic Indicators* (PPI, ULC, CPI, GNP deflator).

fourth quarter of 1986. By contrast, estimates based on 27-year averaging are considerably higher and they are much more greatly dispersed in the Japanese case.

The price-pressure method
Under the floating exchange-rate system, we can extract further information about bilateral PPPs from the movement in relative prices

themselves. The modern asset-market approach (Frenkel and Mussa, 1980) suggests that exchange-rate fluctuations behave as if they are exogenous or 'forward-looking' with respect to other important macro-economic variables. On the other hand, national prices tend (through international commodity arbitrage) to realign themselves at the PPP level in the long run. Hence, if an exchange rate moves away from PPP, it would seem to 'cause' differential rates of national price inflation. When observed inflation rates in the prices of tradables markedly diverge between two countries, we know PPP is not holding. To take a recent example, the sharp appreciation of the yen against the dollar in 1985–86 induced a considerable deflation in the Japanese PPI relative to the American. While the US inflation rate was only slightly negative due to worldwide deflation, the Japanese PPI fell much faster because of the additional downward price pressure from the high yen.

Over a much longer time-period, we can exploit information about price movements due to exchange misalignments if any movement of the exchange rate away from PPP systematically affects domestic prices; and if there are at least two kinds of goods and services whose prices respond differently to the exchange rate. This latter condition enables us to use the less sensitive price index as the benchmark against which changes in the more sensitive price index are measured. Ohno (1987) presents a price-pressure method for estimating bilateral PPPs for the situation when these conditions hold. Let us define the logarithm of E^{PPP} in terms of PPIs:

$$(5) \qquad p_t = \log(\theta_1 P_t / P_t^*),$$

where θ_1 is the unknown scale factor in equation (2). Here p_t is a measure of the PPP exchange rate (with its anti-log having dimensions of, say, yen/dollars) but it also measures relative price levels. If there was a burst of internal (PPI) inflation in Japan *vis-à-vis* the United States, then p_t would increase.

Alternatively, define the logarithm of E^{PPP} in terms of unit labour costs:

$$(6) \qquad c_t = \log(\theta_2 C_t / C_t^*),$$

where θ_2 is an alternative definition of the unknown scale factor in equation (2) while C_t and C_t^* are price relatives for ULCs. Both p_t and c_t are not directly observable but their unknown scale factors can be estimated if we postulate how relative prices and costs interact:

$$(7) \qquad p_t - c_t = \alpha(e_{t-1} - c_{t-1}) + u_{1t}$$

$$(8) \qquad c_t - c_{t-1} = \gamma + \beta(p_{t-1} - c_{t-1}) + u_{2t},$$

where e is the logarithm of the nominal exchange rate and the u's are error terms. Equation (7) presumes that the price pressure (p − c), the deviation of relative prices from underlying relative costs, directly depends on how much the nominal exchange rate is misaligned from PPP based on relative costs. With a one-quarter lag, international arbitrage in commodity markets moves relative PPIs in the same direction as the nominal exchange rate compared to the more slowly adjusting ULCs. Equation (8) postulates that relative ULCs change because of an exogenous (known) time trend, γ, and the profit squeeze brought about by the price pressure, which tends to dampen nominal wage claims. For example, the current relative (and absolute) fall in the Japanese PPI (from the overvalued yen) has slowed down the rate of growth of nominal wage claims in Japan *vis-à-vis* the US.

In order to estimate θ_1 and θ_2, Ohno first calculates the observable relative prices and costs (unadjusted for these scale factors):

$$(9) \qquad \tilde{p}_t = \log(P_t/P_t^*)$$

$$(10) \qquad \tilde{c}_t = \log(C_t/C_t^*).$$

Then substitution implies the system can be reduced to 2 estimable equations:

$$(11) \quad \tilde{p}_t - \tilde{c}_t = (1 - \alpha)\log\theta_2 - \log\theta_1 + \alpha(e_{t-1} - \tilde{c}_{t-1}) + u_{1t}$$

$$(12) \quad \tilde{c}_t - \tilde{c}_{t-1} = \gamma + \beta(\log\theta_1 - \log\theta_2) + \beta(\tilde{p}_{t-1} - \tilde{c}_{t-1}) + u_{2t}.$$

Using quarterly data for 1975–86, these equations yield estimates for α, β, $\log\theta_1$, and $\log\theta_2$. In effect, this price-pressure method is another way of calculating PPP exchange rates without resorting to the traditional Cassel technique. Since it relies on relative changes in prices and costs from exogenous exchange-rate fluctuations, it can systematically incorporate information from many years of experience with fluctuating relative-currency values.

The upper panel of Table 7.2 summarizes price-pressure estimates of p and c for the fourth quarter of 1986. The estimated PPP exchange rates that would have aligned national PPIs are 202 yen and 2.26 marks per dollar; whereas those that would have aligned national ULCs are 217 yen and 2.27 marks per dollar. These are very close to those estimates obtained by the alternative long-period averaging technique, as shown in Table 7.1. The lower panel of Table 7.2 shows how PPE estimates can be projected forward from subsequent movement in national price levels. As the Japanese and German PPIs are falling relative to that of the US, Table 7.2 shows that PPP exchange rates fell to about 200 yen and slightly less than 2.2 marks per dollar toward the end of 1987.

Table 7.2   Purchasing power parity exchange rates

Method	Best PPP estimates: 1986: IV yen/dollar	mark/dollar
PPI: 14-year average (Table 7.1)	205	2.24
PPI: Price pressure (Ohno)	202	2.26
ULC: Price pressure (Ohno)	217	2.27
Actual nominal rate	160	2.01

	Projections for 1987 Producer price indices (OECD, 1980 = 100)			PPP exchange rates	
	United States	Japan	Germany	yen	mark
1986: IV	111.1	92.1	113.6	205	2.24
1987: I	112.5	91.7	113.9	202	2.22
II	114.1	91.8	113.5	199	2.18
III	114.4	93.0	114.1	201	2.18
IV				200^P	2.17^P
1988: I				199^P	2.16^P
Suggested target ranges for 1988: I for smooth convergence of tradables prices				160–180	1.9–2.1

Note: P = projected. Using the PPI 14-year average for the fourth quarter of 1986 as the base, PPP exchange rates into 1987 and 1988 are projected by

$$\text{yen} \quad E_t^{PPP} = 205 \times \frac{PPI_t^J/92.1}{PPI_t^{US}/111.1}$$

$$\text{mark } E_t^{PPP} = 2.24 \times \frac{PPI_t^G/113.6}{PPI_t^{US}/111.1}$$

Simulating wage and price profiles when exchange rates are fixed

These estimates of current PPP exchange rates are *not* predictions for future values of the yen/dollar and mark/dollar rates. Indeed, the under-valuation (by the PPP criterion) of the US dollar in 1986 and 1987 seems more likely to be eliminated by price inflation within the US (relative to that in Japan and Germany) than by equilibrating adjustments in nominal exchange rates. Without systematic monetary cooperation among the Bundesbank, Federal Reserve System and Bank of Japan, nominal exchange rates move randomly. However, if these Central Banks are to cooperate in establishing a common standard, knowing the prevailing PPP exchange rates is very useful. Fixing existing exchange rates at *con-current* PPPs may only be appropriate if the internal rates of inflation in all three countries are suitably aligned as they were at the beginning of 1986. In 1987, the internal trend of price inflation in the US seems higher than that in Japan due to the current undervaluation of the dollar so the yen/dollar rate could initially be set somewhat less than its concurrent PPP in order to converge more smoothly to a common price level for tradables.

Be that as it may, suppose the countries succeeded, by mutual monetary adjustment, in fixing their nominal exchange rates into the indefinite future and anchor their common price level in tradable goods. McKinnon (1984, 1988) indicates how such a policy could be actually implemented. In a nutshell, G-3 should mutually adjust short-term interest differentials on a daily or weekly basis in order to accommodate international portfolio shifts (which could be much more moderate under fixed rates). Open market operations and occasional revisions in discount rates should be sufficient for this purpose and massive direct intervention would only be necessary in times of financial crisis. Once such parities are established and deemed credible by financial circles, the inflation rates of the countries in terms of tradable goods would gradually (but steadily) converge to a common rate through international commodity arbitrage. Of course, once nominal exchange rates are fixed within a narrow band, successfully stabilizing this now common (PPI) price level would depend on joint monetary policy. The collective supply of national monies would have to be contracted when inflation threatened (and the reverse in response to worldwide deflation). This would require ongoing consultation – as within the EMS today.

To help implement a common monetary policy, breaking out a basket of primary commodities could be a useful early warning indicator of threatened inflation or deflation in the broader PPI, which should remain the primary price-level target of the monetary authorities. Information on primary commodity prices becomes available more quickly than the publication of PPIs, which in turn are more immediately available than are GNP statistics. However, the commodity-basket approach provides a useful indicator for changing the collective money supply only if exchange rates are successfully fixed by relative adjustments in national monetary policies. Only then will there be unambiguous movements in the common price level (the commodity basket) – whether measured in dollars, marks, yen, sterling and so on – for triggering joint monetary action.

The simulation procedure
Once nominal exchange rates among diversified industrial economies are fixed for a sustained period, arbitrage becomes sufficiently strong to align prices of tradable goods. Under the old Bretton Woods system, Figures 7.1 and 7.2 (and Table 7.3) show that the yen/dollar and mark/dollar exchange rates, deflated by national PPIs, were virtually constant from 1960 to 1969. For simulating how fixed rates would have worked in the

Table 7.3 Rates of change in nominal wages and in PPI (% change from 4th quarter to 4th quarter)

	1960–69	1970–80	81	US 82	83	84	85	86
Wages	3.8	8.0	7.6	5.3	3.4	4.1	3.9	0.8
PPI	1.5	9.2	5.9	1.5	1.9	1.3	−0.3	−3.5

	1960–69	1970–80	81	Japan 82	83	84	85	86
Wages	11.3	11.9	5.9	4.4	4.3	4.1	3.8	1.7
PPI	1.2	6.7	0.1	0.2	−1.2	0.3	−1.9	−7.0

	1960–69	1970–80	81	Germany 82	83	84	85	86
Wages	8.0	7.3	4.9	4.7	2.7	2.6	5.1	4.0
PPI	1.1	4.7	6.9	3.8	1.6	2.5	0.9	−3.7

Source: OECD, *Main Economic Indicators.*

1970s and 1980s, therefore, the graphs in Figures 7.3 and 7.4 assume (counterfactually) that the real yen/dollar and mark/dollar exchange rates (deflated by PPIs) remained constant from 1970 to 1986 – the horizontal unbroken lines. The remaining graphs then show residual movements in other relative international prices as if fluctuations in their PPI components had been removed.

The main message from Figures 7.3 and 7.4 is that relative international movements in wages, ULCs, CPIs and GNP deflators can be quite substantial even when international arbitrage effectively aligns tradable goods prices under a common monetary standard. Thus, the internal price-level objectives of each participating Central Bank must be specified consistently with its external obligation to maintain a fixed exchange rate. The safest approach is for each monetary authority to use a broad index of tradable goods prices, something like the PPI, as the measure of its success in stabilizing domestic prices (see McKinnon, 1984, 1988). Consider a counter-example. In aiming for a worldwide price-level stability under a fixed exchange-rate agreement, suppose the German, US and Japanese governments believe they should experience approximately the same zero-growth rate in their GNP deflators. Figures 7.3 and 7.4 then show the possibility of these expectations being inconsistent. If productivity growth in Germany and Japan is high compared to the US (of the magnitude experienced in the 1970s), their GNP deflators would rise

Figure 7.3   Japan–US relative price movements, 1970–86 (simulated with fixed exchange rates and no change in relative producer prices)

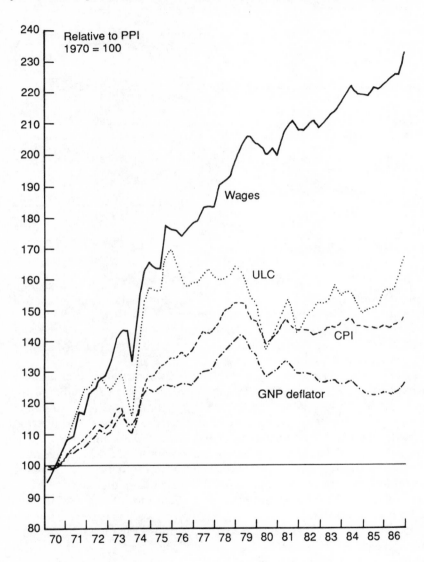

Note: The series on relative producer prices for Japan and the US is simply subtracted from relative wages, unit labour costs, CPIs and GNP deflators. The horizontal solid line simulates unchanging relative PPIs.
Source: OECD, *Main Economic Indicators.*

Figure 7.4 Germany–US relative price movements, 1970–86 (simulated with fixed exchange rates and no change in relative producer prices)

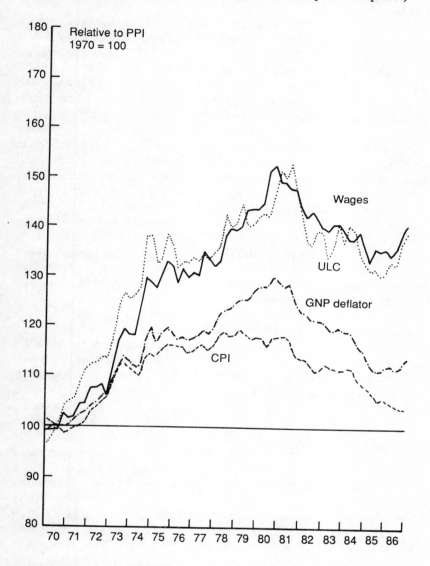

Note: The series on relative producer prices for Germany and the US is simply subtracted from relative wages, unit labour costs, CPIs and GNP deflators. The horizontal solid line simulates unchanging relative PPIs.
Source: OECD, *Main Economic Indicators.*

relative to that of the US. More generally, in the 1970s and 1980s, both relative CPIs and GNP deflators move somewhat differently – but not consistently so – from their relative PPIs.

In addition to fixed exchange rates, suppose further that the (correctly defined) common price level is anchored: the hypothetical exchange-rate agreement succeeds in adjusting aggregate money growth so as to stabilize the common PPI of the US, Japan and Germany. Figures 7.5, 7.6 and 7.7 then simulate how the absolute levels of wages, ULCs, CPIs and GNP deflators would have moved within each of the countries had their individual PPIs not changed from 1960 to 1986. The most striking aspect of the three figures is how little divergent price movement there is within the slowly growing US (Figure 7.5) in comparison to rapidly growing Japan (Figure 7.6). Wages and even the CPI increase very fast in Japan and hardly at all in the US; Germany (Figure 7.7) is somewhat between these extremes. However, much of this divergent price movement in Japan comes from her rapid real economic growth in the 1960s and early 1970s. It is best not extrapolated forward at that extraordinary pace into the 1990s. In the wage and price series for Japan in Figure 7.6, the extraordinary downward spikes in 1973–74 and 1979–80 should not be taken literally. They reflect the sharp upward increase in producer prices (the *numéraire*) associated with worldwide inflation under an unstable international monetary standard.

Prices, wages and productivity growth
Under the proposed regime of a constant average price level for tradables and fixed exchange rates, the relative price of individual tradable goods can, and will, change in response to real shocks. High productivity growth will drive down the absolute (and relative) price of microelectronic integrated circuits, whether measured in yen, marks or dollars. Similarly, a disruption in Mid-East oil supplies will raise the relative and absolute price of petroleum products – even though the average price of all tradable goods in the system remains fairly constant. However, across-the-board changes in one country's tradable goods *vis-à-vis* those of another country are ruled out; that is, changes in a country's terms of trade, induced by an unexpected (and possibly reversible) exchange-rate fluctuation, would be avoided. In fact, one of the primary goals of our proposal is to restore the role of observable nominal prices as accurate signals of real relative scarcity within the integrated world economy. Under floating exchange rates, by contrast, it is harder to distil real signals from noisy prices; confused agents tend to react less (and with a longer lag) to permanent changes in real relative scarcity.

The net trade balance need not go to zero under PPP – nor are changes

Figure 7.5 *United States: absolute price movements, 1960–86 (simulated with unchanging producer prices)*

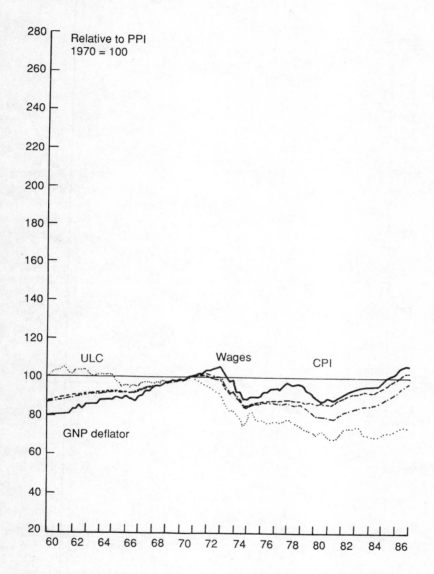

Note: The series on American producer prices is simply subtracted from those on American wages, consumer prices, GNP deflators and unit labour costs.
Source: OECD, *Main Economic Indicators.*

Figure 7.6   Japan: absolute price movements, 1960–86 (simulated with unchanging producer prices)

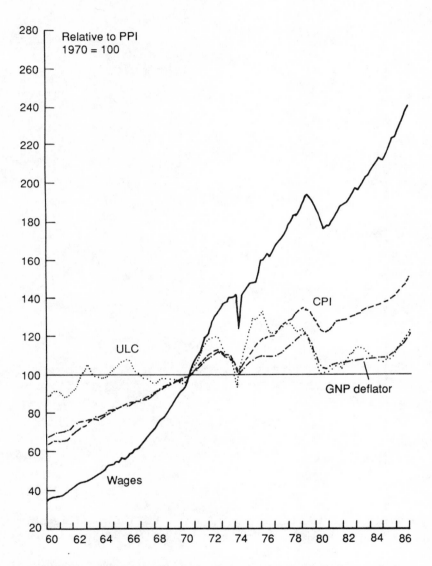

Note: The series on Japanese producer prices is simply subtracted from those on Japanese wages, consumer prices, GNP deflators and unit labour costs.
Source: OECD, *Main Economic Indicators.*

Figure 7.7 West Germany: absolute price movements, 1960–86 (simulated with unchanging producer prices)

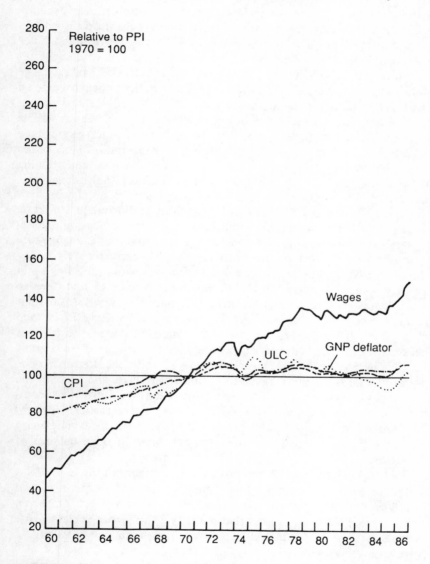

Note: The series on German producer prices is simply subtracted from those on German wages, consumer prices, GNP deflators and unit labour costs.
Source: OECD, *Main Economic Indicators.*

in any country's terms of trade necessary to adjust its trade balance. With a high degree of financial integration when nominal exchange rates are fixed, the continual opening and closing of gaps between saving and investment would cause absorption changes that automatically generate trade deficits or surpluses – as the current large US fiscal deficit led to a trade deficit of the same order of magnitude. To preserve overall balance in international payments, these trade deficits or surpluses would be offset by inflows or outflows of financial capital – provided the official exchange parities remained credible. 'Correcting' trade deficits then becomes a fiscal rather than a monetary problem.

Although the average (common) price level of tradable goods will be kept constant, movements in the prices of non-tradables can diverge across countries. In the short or intermediate run, non-tradable prices would be gradually bid up in countries absorbing capital and running trade deficits (and vice versa in trade surplus countries). In the longer run, trends in money-wage growth in each country will reflect ongoing productivity differentials and little else but all such real adjustments would be more gradual and far smoother than under the current floating regime, without any sudden inflations or deflations arising out of exchange-rate misalignments or overshooting. Such a regime held approximately during the Bretton Woods period. Under fixed exchange rates in the 1950s and 1960s, Japanese money-wage growth was about three times (and German more than twice) than in the US (Table 7.3), in rough proportions to their relative trends in productivity. At the time when countries' PPIs moved closely together (Figures 7.1 and 7.2), internal money growth was necessarily much higher in Japan and Germany than in the US to support their higher growth in money wages and GNP. Under the Bretton Woods dollar standard, the Bank of Japan's monetary policies and those of the Bundesbank were (largely) endogenously determined by their commitments to fixed exchange rates. Neither had to aim consciously for very high growth in domestic money wages; it arose from the expansionary monetary policies necessary to prevent surpluses in their balance of payments.

The breakdown of the common monetary standard in the early 1970s undermined the pressure to gear domestic monetary expansion and increases in money wages to each country's productivity growth. From 1975 to 1986, Table 7.4 shows that actual US money-wage claims rose faster than those in Japan and Germany (101 per cent versus 93 and 71 per cent, respectively). For the same 1975–86 period, Table 7.4 also simulates how the countries' wages would have grown under a common monetary standard with fixed exchange rates had the common (PPI) price level remained stable. The residual wage growth, after subtracting actual

Table 7.4   Actual and hypothetical nominal wages (1975 = 100)

		1975	1980	1986	Annual average growth (1975–86)
United States	actual	100	150	201	6.3%
	hypothetical	100	98	117	1.4%
Japan	actual	100	150	193	6.0%
	hypothetical	100	116	157	4.1%
Germany	actual	100	135	171	4.9%
	hypothetical	100	112	123	1.9%

Note: Hypothetical wages are calculated assuming that tradables (PPI) prices are constant. Thus, they approximately reflect gains in labour productivity in the absence of inflation. *Source:* Wages and PPI from OECD, *Main Economic Indicators*.

PPI inflation from each country's actual wage inflation, approximately measures differential increases in productivity. In such a stable price environment, Table 7.4 indicates that US wages *should* have grown only 17 per cent – compared to hypothetical growth of 57 per cent in Japan and 23 per cent in Germany – over this 12-year period. By 1983–84, actual wage inflation in the US had slowed sharply, but so too had that in Japan and Germany. Indeed, the sharp appreciation and overvaluation (by our PPP criterion) of the yen in 1986–87 was perverse: the forced deflation in the Japanese economy slowed actual growth in money (yen) wages far below their hypothetical long-term trend consistent with constant tradable-goods prices and stable exchange rates.

From the 1975–86 simulated data, Table 7.4 indicates that the appropriate trend in Japanese wage growth should be about 4.1 per cent per year under the presumption that tradable goods prices remain constant. Actual money-wage growth in Japan in 1986 was only 1.7 per cent (Table 7.3) and indicators are that it slowed further in 1987. On the other hand, growth in US money wages in 1986–87 was only slightly higher than its long run hypothetical norm of 1.4 per cent. Thus, to prevent wage trends from diverging from the underlying long-term productivity changes, there was room in 1987–88 for monetary expansion in Japan and to a lesser extent in Germany – with balancing monetary restraint in the US in order to anchor the common price level. However, as spot exchange rates in financially integrated economies are highly sensitive to relative monetary policies, such cooperation is only possible if the three governments allow the yen/dollar and mark/dollar exchange rates to be nudged upwards toward their PPPs.

References

Balassa, B. (1964), 'The purchasing power parity doctrine re-examined: a reappraisal', *Journal of Political Economy*, **72**, 584–96.

Cassel, G. (1918), 'Abnormal deviations in international exchanges', *Economic Journal*, December.

Cassel, G. (1922), *Money and Foreign Exchange After 1914*, London: Macmillan.

Dornbusch, R. (1986), 'Purchasing power parity', *New Palgrave Dictionary of Economics*.

Frenkel, J. and M. Mussa (1980), 'The efficiency of foreign exchange markets and measures of turbulence', *American Economic Review*, **70**, May.

Isard, P. (1977), 'How far can we push the Law of One Price?', *American Economic Review*, December.

Komiya, R. (1967), 'Non-traded goods and the pure theory of international trade', *International Economic Review*, **8**, June.

Levich, R. (1986), 'Gauging the evidence on recent movements in the value of the dollar', in *The U.S. Dollar: Recent Developments, Outlook and Policy Options*, Federal Reserve Bank of Kansas City.

Lindbeck, A. (1979), 'Imported and structural inflation: the Scandinavian model reconsidered', in A. Lindbeck (ed.), *Inflation and Employment in Open Economies*, Amsterdam: North-Holland.

Marston, R. (1986), *Real Exchange Rates and Productivity Growth in the United States and Japan*, NBER Working Paper No. 1922.

McCloskey, D.N., and J.R. Zecher (1976), 'How the gold standard worked: 1880–1913', in J.A. Frenkel and H.G. Johnson (eds.), *The Monetary Approach to the Balance of Payments*, Allen and Unwin.

McKinnon, R.I. (1974), 'A new tripartite monetary agreement or a limping dollar standard?', *Essays in International Finance*, No. 106, Princeton, NJ.

McKinnon, R.I. (1984), *An International Standard for Monetary Stabilization*, Institute for International Economics, Washington.

McKinnon, R.I. (1988), 'Monetary and exchange rate policies for international financial stability: a proposal', *Journal of Economic Perspectives*, **2**, 83–103.

Meese, R. and K. Rogoff (1983), 'Empirical exchange rate models of the 1970s: do they fit out of sample', *Journal of International Economics*, February.

OECD, *Main Economic Indicators* (various issues).

Ohno, K, (1987), 'Estimating purchasing power parities: the price pressure method', in K. Ohno, *The Exchange Rate and Prices in Financially Open Economies*, PhD dissertation, Stanford University, California.

Triffin, R. (1964), 'The evolution of the international monetary system: historical reappraisal and future perspectives', *Studies in International Finance*, No. 12, Princeton, NJ.

Comment by Charles Goodhart

This chapter has two separable aspects. First, it provides a *positive* description of various alternative ways of estimating purchasing power parities – particularly when various pressures have driven actual exchange rates away from their PPP levels for many years so that it is not possible to assert (with any confidence) that some recent year represents a base period at which PPP held. The second facet of the chapter involves a more *normative* argument to suggest that, if the three major countries of the world wish to coordinate so as to hold their exchange rates closely in line, then they could reasonably do so on the basis of a slightly modified, jointly estimated and agreed PPP basis, leading to an approximation of conditions prevailing in a single currency area.

Let me first address the positive issue for which McKinnon and Ohno provide a number of criteria. First, they consider which indices are theoretically preferable; this would suggest PPI or ULC. Second, they examine which index shows the greatest tendency towards mean reversion, which suggests the PPI since there are disturbingly large trends in the relative ULC series. Third, they try to find a 'best' estimate by a combination of averaging and judgment and, finally, they use a regression method adopted by Ohno to identify PPP on the assumption of the existence of certain pre-specified forms and speeds of relative price adjustment. The bottom line of this exercise for the authors is that all methods lead to an estimated PPP exchange rate of some 180–222 yen and around 2 Deutschmarks to the dollar. Given the inertia in the domestic wage spiral, they advocate a somewhat lower target range for exchange rates to allow for convergence at say 160–180 yen and 1.9–2.1 Deutschmarks to the dollar.

Some significant concerns arise here. The authors are naturally concerned about the marked deviation of ULCs from PPIs. They suggest (slightly cavalierly, since they present no evidence) that measurement error might lead to an understatement of Japan's cost competitiveness relative to the US. The particular measurement error to which they point is the bias caused by the introduction of new products. What worries me is that such sources of measurement error could also bias the PPI estimate of competitiveness so that even this underestimates Japan's competitiveness. What is ultimately at stake here is the difficulty in accepting that the 'equilibrium' PPP yen–dollar rate really would require a 25–33 per cent appreciation of the dollar from its present level. The Japanese appear to be able to work economic miracles, beyond the ken of western economists, and amongst these miracles could be the ability to defy the gravitational pull of PPP. My second concern relates to Ohno's price-pressure method for estimation of PPP exchange rates. What worries me is that the sequence and relative speeds of interaction of price and labour unit costs is assumed to follow a somewhat tightly constrained time path as set out in equations (7) and (8). If, however, we were to run an unconstrained vector autoregressive process (with domestic prices, unit labour costs and exchange rates as arguments) I doubt whether these equations would emerge as the parsimonious form statistically accepted by the data.

Turning to normative matters, suppose we accept, as a working hypothesis, the estimates of the authors for PPP. If I understand the authors' views, they propose that, if as an essential precondition, internal measures were taken to adjust domestic demand into line with domestic supply, then the dollar should be nudged higher relative to the yen and the Deutschmark – in order to bring international competitiveness into line and to restrain inflationary pressures in the US and deflationary pressures in Japan and Germany. Perhaps! However, I am sceptical both of the political process and of our knowledge of the relevant parameters, including the PPP estimates. Thus I would be happy enough to see the dollar stabilize, preferably without the need for outside official support, and I would regard any proposal for nudging it in either direction now as being both premature and potentially dangerous.

I have increasingly come to share with McKinnon and many others the feeling that recent misbehaviour of the foreign-exchange markets has been such as to lead to a presumption in favour of managed stability. McKinnon seems to feel that such stability would come easiest and be best maintained on an approximate PPP basis. I have my doubts about that position. The first best solution, I feel, especially in a European context, would be a single currency union – though this union should be accompanied by measures to overcome imperfect market (especially labour market) adjustments in the form of regional fiscal policies, imaginative retraining policies, and other supply-side measures. Given the observed weakness of PPP as a gravitational force during recent decades, I doubt whether it would be necessary (and certainly not sufficient) to establish the initial fixing of relative exchange rates particularly close to PPP in order to provide for successful establishment of a currency union. There are many other, more-problematic, political issues to overcome.

If we cannot achieve an effective currency union (perhaps because of continuing labour market rigidities) so that countries maintain monetary independence and policies, then we must remain in a world of political realignments. In this world, the domestic desideratum is usually a particular target rate of growth of nominal income or of inflation. In this latter case, the question raised is how much extra inflation, or reduced real growth, each major country would be prepared to accept in order to maintain more stable exchange rates. In this respect the recent (March 1988) experience of the UK was perhaps illuminating. The implications, in terms of lower interest rates, faster monetary growth (and, hence, of higher immediate inflation), of pegging to the Deutschmark proved unacceptable to the Prime Minister. We moved, temporarily at least, to a policy of balancing the effect of exchange-rate appreciation against interest-rate cuts in order to have a broadly constant impact on nominal incomes.

What we need, in effect, is an internationally cooperative resolution of conditions in which 'too fast' nominal income growth accompanies an appreciating exchange rate, or vice versa. Frankly, what I find hard to see is the role, if any, PPP calculations would play in this kind of exercise, except peripherally. The very fact that exchange rates can move into (and stay in) massive misalignment for years at a time implies that detailed and sophisticated PPP estimates may well be of long-term academic interest, but they are hardly of immediate, short-term policy relevance.

8 The international monetary system: An analysis of alternative regimes

Marcus H. Miller and John Williamson

At the beginning of the 1970s the OECD countries were on a *de facto* Dollar Standard, in which the US selected its monetary policy with a view to domestic stability and other countries pegged to the dollar, with the right to change their peg at their unilateral discretion. By 1973, the Dollar Standard had collapsed, giving way to a regime of floating exchange rates coupled with national money-supply targets, a regime long advocated by Friedman (1953, 1968). Since the Plaza Agreement of September 1985, however, the US has made the external value of the dollar an explicit target of policy. The coordination of international macroeconomic policies was sought in order to help secure a reduction of its external deficit. These developments prompt two questions – first, is a change in the international monetary system really called for rather than simply a change in, for example, US fiscal policy; and, second, if so, what are the alternatives?

It is not the purpose of the present chapter to debate the first question with those who maintain 'if it ain't broke, don't fix it', as the case for reform of the system has been developed in some detail elsewhere (see Williamson, 1985). What we offer instead, on the second question, is a simple exercise in positive economics in which the floating rate regime of 1973–85 is compared with alternatives. These alternatives are indicated in Table 8.1, which classifies systems on two criteria; namely, whether they are hegemonic or not, and how exchange rates are determined. Thus the international system prevailing from 1973 to 1985 which appears in the first column is classified as 'symmetric', in contrast to the hegemony under Dollar Standard, which appears in the second row of the second column.

The focus of this paper is on regimes without hegemony, and the alternatives to floating with monetary targets that are considered are, first, McKinnon's proposals for fixed exchange rates, and, second, Williamson's system of target zones for real exchange rates. McKinnon's proposal of 1984 was designed both to ensure symmetry in the operation of the IMS and to put the control of inflation on an explicitly monetarist footing. The

Table 8.1 International monetary systems compared

	Floating rates with national money supply targets	Fixed exchange rates	Managed exchange rates
Symmetry	OECD 1973–1985	McKinnon's Proposals	Williamson's Target Zones
Hegemony	—	Dollar Standard 1968–73	EMS 1979–

plan was to have key-currency members (US, Germany and Japan) agree to a target for their combined monetary growth, which was to be pursued under fixed exchange rates by national DCE targets and symmetrical non-sterilized intervention. McKinnon's confidence that the variations of velocity observed at the national level were due to currency substitution and so would cancel out at the global level (and be adequately neutralized by the intervention policy) was challenged *ex ante* (Dornbusch, 1983) and also eroded by subsequent experience. As a result, in a later version of his proposal, McKinnon (1986) shifted to the 'classical' position that monetary policy at the global level should aim directly at price stability, rather than at the control of a monetary aggregate. He has thus addressed two issues arising under fixed exchange rates – how to make the determination of monetary policy more symmetric and, subsequently, how to cope with the observed instability in the demand for money.

Under neither of McKinnon's proposals do the mechanisms which keep inflation at bay at a national level involve control of a domestic monetary aggregate. In the absence of portfolio shocks, monetary policy will require keeping interest rates in line with those elsewhere (and controlling domestic credit expansion in the first case). The mechanisms are rather the longer-run effect on expectations of belonging to such a currency union, together with the immediate impact of union-wide interest rates, and more directly the impact on trade and employment of allowing prices to rise relative to those in partner countries. With nominal exchange rates fixed, inflation differentials will change real exchange rates in ways which shift demand from inflationary countries towards non-inflationary countries (while the level of the 'global' interest rate will act so as to stabilize inflation in the union as a whole).

Under the regime of floating-with-money-supply-targets, the experience of the US and the UK was not that the nominal exchange rate simply adjusted to offset inflationary differentials so as to keep real exchange rates fairly stable (as Friedman had implied would be the case) but that real exchange rates showed prolonged deviations from equilibrium. It is this feature that Williamson's target zones are designed to remedy: on the assumption that fiscal policy is not allowed to crowd out the desired (high employment) balance of payments, domestic interest rates (and foreign currency intervention) are to be aimed at keeping the real exchange rate with a band ± 10 per cent of the equilibrium level implied by the balance of payments target.

Williamson's plan resembles McKinnon's proposal in assigning domestic monetary policy to an external objective; in this case, however, the requirement to stabilize the real exchange rate will, in the absence of portfolio shocks, require real interest rates to be kept reasonably in line with those in partner countries. This policy assignment has been severely criticized by Adams and Gros (1986) for leaving domestic inflation out of control. As we show below, however, the combination of assigning monetary policy to this external objective and fiscal policy to domestic money-income target is not open to this criticism – indeed, at a formal level, the mechanism for checking domestic inflation resembles that which operates under the McKinnon plan.

At a global level there is a good deal in common between the Williamson and McKinnon plans. Whereas McKinnon proposed that 'global' interest rates be set so as to stabilize aggregate money or aggregate prices, the proposal in Edison, Miller and Williamson (1987) is that nominal income be the target.

Since 1979, Germany, France, Italy, the Benelux countries and Denmark have created a regional monetary system (EMS) with agreed nominal parities, which have, however, been adjusted *ex post* to accommodate most of the inflation differentials emerging between them. It has recently been argued by Giavazzi and Giovanni (1987) that the EMS is in effect a regional currency standard, a hegemony led by Germany, with limited independence permitted by extensive capital controls in France and Italy, and so it is entered in the second row of Table 8.1. The EMS, as such, is not analysed in this paper, because it is not symmetric.

The framework of analysis
The formal framework used to assess alternative proposals is a simple two bloc model with goods prices which adjust more slowly than the exchange rate which is determined by rational expectations in the foreign-exchange market, *cf*. Dornbusch (1976). Inflation expectations are captured simply by an augmenting Phillips curve with terms measuring long-run inflation under the regime in question, *cf*. Buiter and Miller (1981). The formal analysis of the two country floating-rate case is essentially that developed in Miller (1982) to which 'fads', as Poterba and Summers (1987) describe them, have been added, while treatment of the fixed-rate case is derived

from Buiter (1986). The stochastic specification closely follows recent contributions by Fukuda and Hamada (1986) and Aoki (1987), and we are grateful to have had access to the PRISM package developed by Currie and his colleagues for the stochastic analysis.

In this chapter, we use asymptotic or steady-state variances (obtained under the assumption of rational expectations) to study the performance of monetary and fiscal policy rules without falling foul of the Lucas critique, as advocated by Taylor in the *European Economic Review* (1985). For a comprehensive stochastic treatment of various monetary-policy rules – chosen optimally but subject to a 'time consistency' constraint – the reader is referred to McKibbin and Sachs (1986).

The equations which constitute the model are listed in detail in Table 8.2 and the notation is given thereafter. The structure is doubtless familiar so it can be quickly summarized. First comes the condition for money-market equilibrium (the LM curves) which are subject to stochastic, serially-uncorrelated, disturbances ε_m, ε_m* (asterisks are used to denote variables involving the foreign country). Output in each country depends on the *ex ante* real interest rate, the real exchange rate, fiscal stance, output overseas and a stochastic shock (ε_g, ε_g*). As shown in the third line, inflation reflects domestic demand pressure and also long-run inflation expectations under the regime in question (represented by the term π). The inflation process is also subject to white noise errors ε_p, ε_p*.

The specification of the foreign-currency arbitrage condition contains a novelty as the usual assumption of 'uncovered interest parity' is modified in that expected changes in the nominal exchange rate are set equal to the interest differential plus the change in an exogenous, autoregressive

Table 8.2 Model equations

Home country	Foreign country
Money $m - p = ky - \lambda i + \varepsilon_m$	$m^* - p^* = ky^* - \lambda i^* + \varepsilon_m{}^*$
Goods $y = -\gamma E[r] + \delta c + s + \eta y^* + \varepsilon_g$	$y = -\gamma E[r^*] - \delta c + s^* + \eta y + \varepsilon_g{}^*$
Price $Dp = \phi y + \pi + \varepsilon_p$	$Dp^* = \phi y^* + \pi^* + \varepsilon_p{}^*$

Currency arbitrage	$E[De] = E[i - i^*] + E[Df]$
Poterba/Summers fad	$Df = -\psi f + \omega$

where
$$r \equiv i - Dp \qquad\qquad r^* = i - Dp$$
$$E[r] = i - \phi y - \pi \qquad E[r^*] = i^* - \phi y^* - \pi^*$$
and $\quad c = e + p^* - p$

Technical note: Strictly speaking solutions of stochastic differential equations have no derivatives, so the use of the differential operators is inadmissable. Nevertheless for linear systems with constant coefficients, asymptotic moments can be obtained by treating the system as if it were continuously differentiable (see, for example, Jazwinsky (1970, Ch. 4)).

Table 8.3   (a)   Global economy

Money	$m_a - p_a = ky_a - \lambda i_a + \bar{\varepsilon}_m$
	$\Rightarrow i_a = \lambda^{-1}(p_a + ky_a + \bar{\varepsilon}_m - m_a)$
Goods	$y_a = -\gamma(i_a - \phi y_a - \pi_a) + s_a + \eta y_a + \bar{\varepsilon}_g$
Prices	$Dp_a = \phi y_a + \pi_a + \bar{\varepsilon}_p$

with the notation

$$y_a \equiv \frac{y + y^*}{2} \text{ for variables and } \bar{\varepsilon}_m \equiv \frac{\varepsilon_m + \varepsilon_m{}^*}{2}$$

for stochastic shocks.

Table 8.3   (b)   International differences

Money	$m_d - p_d = ky_d - \lambda i_d + \hat{\varepsilon}_m$
Goods	$y_d = -\gamma E[r_d] + 2\sigma c + sd - \eta y_d + \hat{\varepsilon}_g$
Prices	$Dp_d = \phi y_d + \pi_d + \hat{\varepsilon}_p$
Arbitrage	$E[De] = E[i_d] - \psi f$
Fad	$Df = -\psi f + \omega$

where

$$E[r_d] = i_d - E[Dp_d] = i_d - \phi y_d - \pi_d$$
$$c = e - p_d$$

with the notation

$$y_d \equiv y - y^* \text{ for variables and } \hat{\varepsilon}_m = \varepsilon_m - \varepsilon_m{}^* \text{ for}$$
stochastic shocks.

Notation

y	real output, measured relative to capacity (in logs)
i	short-term nominal interest rate
E[r]	*ex ante* short-term real interest rate, $i - E[Dp]$
r	*ex post* real interest rate, $i - Dp$
c	real exchange rate in logs, $(e + p^* - p)$: increase indicates higher competitiveness for home country
s	index of fiscal stance, scaled to have unit effects on log output
p	domestic price index, in logs
m	money supply, in logs
n	nominal income target, in logs
π	augmentation term systematically affecting price changes
f	fad, see Poterba and Summers (1987)
ε, ω	white Gaussian noise processes; $N(0, \sigma_\varepsilon^2)$, $N(0, \sigma_\omega^2)$ respectively
Dp	inflation
D	differential operator
E	expectations operator

'fad'. The idea comes from Poterba and Summers (1987), who show that the existence of such 'fads' is consistent with the behaviour of US stock prices. Adding such a 'coloured noise' process to asset prices violates the usual assumption of market efficiency – but, as Poterba and Summers also show, the tests used (successfully) to establish market efficiency have very low power against such fads.

Since the parameters in each country are identical, the dynamic (and stochastic) analysis can be conducted separately in terms of 'averages' and 'differences', *cf.* Aoki (1981). The global economy (averaged) looks like a closed economy, see Table 8.3(a), and does not involve the exchange rate. The latter is determined only by the system of differences given in Table 8.3(b). While it may seem rather contrived to work in terms of these artificial variables, the gain in analytical simplification is worthwhile. First, we look at the global economy (in the next section) before going on to examine the determination of exchange rates, inflation, etc. under the three alternative regimes.

The global economy

Thanks to the assumption of symmetry, the analysis of global aggregates is very straightforward. The focus here is on the different nominal targets proposed as guidelines for world monetary policy, starting with the world money supply target, m_a, growing at the rate μ_a (McKinnon).

Substituting world interest rates i_a from the first line of Table 8.3(a) into the world IS curve of line two, we obtain

$$y_a = \frac{1}{\Delta_a}(-\gamma\lambda^{-1}p_a + \gamma\lambda^{-1}m_a + \gamma\mu_a + s_a - \gamma\lambda^{-1}\bar{\varepsilon}_m + \bar{\varepsilon}_g) \qquad (1)$$

where $\Delta_a = 1 + \gamma\lambda^{-1}k - \phi\gamma - \eta$, and π_a has been set equal to μ_a as in Buiter and Miller (1981), i.e. the inflation process is

$$Dp_a = \phi y_a + \mu_a + \bar{\varepsilon}_p. \qquad (2)$$

To simplify matters a little, we set $m_a = \mu_a = s_a = 0$, i.e. the world money stock is fixed and fiscal policy 'neutral', so output is determined only by prices and aggregate shocks to velocity and demand, as shown at the top row of Table 8.4. On combining this with the inflation process (2), the asymptotic or unconditional variance of price is determined (see Annex 8.1) as,

$$\sigma_{p_a}^2 = \frac{1}{2|\rho_s|}\left\{\rho_s^2\sigma\frac{2}{\varepsilon_m} + \left(\frac{\phi}{\Delta_a}\right)^2\sigma\frac{2}{\varepsilon_g} + \sigma\frac{2}{\varepsilon_p}\right\} \qquad (3)$$

given that the shocks are independent. The speed of adjustment, ρ_s, appearing here is found from Table 8.4, column 2. Note that the variance of price includes the variance of velocity multiplied by half this speed of adjustment (in absolute value).

These results so obtained for a money supply target are easily modified to reflect a change on target variable. For convenience, we assume that the McKinnon price-level target is for stable prices and Williamson's is for stable nominal income – and take the growth of potential GNP to be zero. Now the rules for interest-rate setting involved in pursuing these targets

Table 8.4   Determinants of output (y) and the speed of adjustment (ρ_s)

	Output	Speed of adjustment
Averages		
Global	$y_a = \dfrac{1}{\Delta_a}(-\gamma\lambda^{-1}p_a - \gamma\lambda^{-1}\bar{\varepsilon}_m + \bar{\varepsilon}_g)$	$\rho_s = -\phi\gamma\lambda^{-1}/\Delta_a$
Economy		$\Delta_a = 1 + \gamma\lambda^{-1}k - \phi\gamma - \eta$
Differences		
1 Floating with money targets	$y_d = \dfrac{1}{\Delta_1}\{(-\gamma\lambda^{-1} + 2\delta\theta)p_d - \gamma\lambda^{-1}\bar{\varepsilon}_m + \bar{\varepsilon}_g\}$	$\rho_s = \phi(\gamma\lambda^{-1} + 2\delta\theta)/\Delta_1$ $\Delta_1 = 1 + \gamma\lambda^{-1}k - \phi\gamma + \eta$
2 McKinnon	$y_d = \dfrac{1}{\Delta_2}(-2\delta p_d + \bar{\varepsilon}_g)$	$\rho_s = -\phi 2\delta/\Delta_2$ $\Delta_2 = 1 - \phi\gamma + \eta$
2a McKinnon with fiscal activism	$y_d = \dfrac{1}{\Delta 2_a}(-(2\delta + \zeta\alpha)p_d + \bar{\varepsilon}_g)$	$\rho_s = -\phi(2\delta + \zeta\alpha)/\Delta_{2a}$ $\Delta_{2a} = 1 - \phi\gamma + \eta + \zeta\beta$
2 Williamson	$y_d = \dfrac{1}{\Delta}(-\sigma p_d + \bar{\varepsilon}_g)$	$\rho_s = -\phi\sigma/\Delta_3$ $\Delta_3 = 1 + \sigma + \eta$

Notes: 1.   The denominators (indicated by $\Delta_a, \Delta_1, \dots$) in the first column are given in detail in the second column.
2.   The speed of adjustment refers to ρ_s, the stable root characteristic of the system averages or differences for the regime in question.

can be written as simplified versions of the inverted LM curve used above; specifically

McKinnon II $i_a = \beta_M p_a$ i.e. $k = 0$, $\lambda^{-1} = \beta_M$ and $\sigma\dfrac{2}{\varepsilon_m}$ is omitted,

and Williamson $i_a = \beta_w(p_a + y_a)$ i.e. $k = 1$, $\lambda^{-1} = \beta_w$ and $\sigma\dfrac{2}{\varepsilon_m}$ is omitted.

These parameter substitutions will alter the speed of adjustment and the term Δ_a appearing in equation (3) but one can see that both these rules, like McKinnon's monetarist rule, involve a feedback of interest rates on price level (the integral of past inflation). They omit the noise caused by using money-supply targets to achieve this feedback (as $\sigma2/\varepsilon_m$ is omitted).

Floating with national monetary targets

In this section, we analyse the behaviour of the real exchange rate when each country adopts a fixed-target growth rate for its money supply (not necessarily the same) and allows its currency to float freely. With identical coefficients of the separate national economies, the exchange rate depends only on 'differences', including the differences of shocks (denoted $\bar{\varepsilon}_m, \bar{\varepsilon}_g, \bar{\varepsilon}_p$ where $\bar{\varepsilon}_m = \varepsilon_m - \varepsilon_m{}^*$), together with the fad process.

On the assumption that the 'augmentation' term in the price equation is the domestic rate of monetary growth, i.e.

$$Dp = \phi y + \mu + \varepsilon_p \qquad \text{and} \qquad Dp^* = \phi y^* + \mu^* + \varepsilon_p^*$$

then

$$Dp_d = \phi y_d + \mu_d + \hat{\varepsilon}_p \qquad \text{and} \qquad E[Dp_d] = \phi y_d + \mu_d. \qquad (4)$$

Since inflation (and the inflation differential) may persist, it is convenient to deflate each nominal money stock by the domestic price level, so $\ell \equiv m - p$, $\ell^* = m^* - p^*$ and $\ell_d = \ell - \ell^*$. As the evolution of real balances depends on the rate of inflation relative to the rate of monetary growth, so, using equation (4), note that

$$D\ell_d = -\phi y_d - \hat{\varepsilon}_p. \qquad (5)$$

The behaviour of the real exchange rate reflects both the inflation differential and the determinants of the nominal exchange rate. So, using equation (4) again, we find (on taking expectations of both sides) that as

$$Dc = De + Dp^* - Dp = \quad \text{so} \quad E[Dc] = E[i_d] - \psi f - \phi E[y_d] - \mu_d. \qquad (6)$$

Equations (5) and (6) show how the evolution of real balances (ℓ_d) and the real exchange rate (c) depend on both income and interest differentials. Solving for the latter (using the goods and money-market relationships from Table 8.3(b)) and adding the autoregressive fad process

$$Df = \psi f + \omega \qquad (7)$$

yields the stochastic differential equations for this regime, as follows:

$$
\begin{bmatrix} D\ell_d \\ E[Dc] \\ Df \end{bmatrix} = \frac{1}{\Delta}
\begin{bmatrix}
\phi\gamma & 2\phi\lambda\delta & 0 \\
1 + \eta & 2\delta(\phi\lambda - k) & -\Delta\psi \\
0 & 0 & -\Delta\psi
\end{bmatrix}
\begin{bmatrix} \ell_d \\ c \\ f \end{bmatrix}
$$

$$
+ \frac{1}{\Delta}
\begin{bmatrix}
-\phi\gamma & \phi\lambda & \phi\gamma\lambda & \phi\gamma\lambda & -\Delta & 0 \\
-(1 + \eta) & \phi\lambda - k & 0 & \lambda(1 + \eta) & -\Delta & 0 \\
0 & 0 & 0 & 0 & 0 & \Delta
\end{bmatrix}
\begin{bmatrix} \hat{\varepsilon}_m \\ \hat{\varepsilon}_g \\ s_d \\ \mu_d \\ \hat{\varepsilon}_p \\ \omega \end{bmatrix}
\qquad (8)
$$

where $\Delta = -k\gamma - \lambda(1 - \phi\gamma + \eta)$ and is assumed to be negative.

Figure 8.1   'Fads', dynamics and asymptotic probability contours

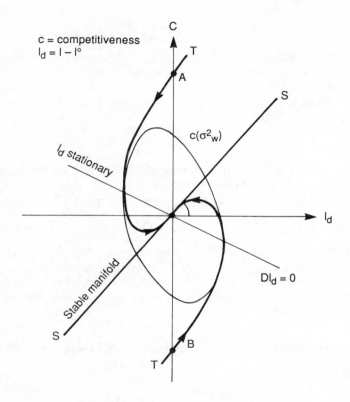

Since the nominal exchange rate is a forward-looking variable, stable behaviour is observed only on the stable manifold (i.e. the subspace of this system associated with the stable roots which we denote as ρ_s and $-\psi$). The stable dynamics of this system and the role played by the serially-correlated fads changing the more orthodox account are most easily seen from Figure 8.1. In the absence of fads, the dynamics of adjustment in this Dornbusch-style model would lie on the line marked SS in the figure. Where there is 'overshooting', the slope of this line will be greater than one – since a shock to the money stock will have a greater than unit effect on the exchange rate, *cf.* Dornbusch (1976) Appendix.

However, the serial correlation of the fad process adds another stable root, and (in the diagrammatically convenient case where $-\psi = \rho_s$) the stable trajectories leading to equilibrium have the shape shown by the line TT. These trajectories are symmetric around the origin but not around SS. The reason is that a fad which by raising the value of the domestic currency cuts competitiveness (so that c lies beneath SS) slows down the adjustment of real balances towards the origin, while a fad which increases competitiveness (putting c above SS) gives rise to forces which speed up the adjustment of ℓ_d towards equilibrium.

Also shown in the figure is the (asymptotic) probability contour revealing points of equal probability in the long run. As the orientation of the ellipse demonstrates, the pattern of correlation between ℓ_d and c arising from such fads is negative. The reason is made clear by observing that, from a point such as A, a large part of the subsequent expected trajectory is in the North West quadrant, and conversely for movements from point B, which orients the ellipse in the fashion shown. This negative correlation appears to be independent of the respective sizes of $|\rho_s|$ and $|\psi|$.

In the absence of the fads, the probability distribution of outcomes for c and ℓ_d lies along the stable manifold (and the isoprobability 'contours' become two points on SS). Under the convenient assumption that the rates of monetary growth are the same (so we can write $\mu_d = m_d = 0$), then $\ell_d = -p_d$ and on the stable manifold, $c = \theta \ell_d = -\theta p_d$, i.e. competitiveness is simply relative prices multiplied by the coefficient θ (which measures the degree of overshooting). Under these assumptions, the determination of output is shown in line 2 of Table 8.4 and the formulae of Annex 8.1 may be used to calculate asymptotic moments.

As was observed earlier, the regime of floating-with-money-supply targets led to much greater fluctuations in real exchange rates than many economists had expected. The above account is inevitably something of a caricature but it suffices to show how the combination of sluggish prices, shocks to economy and inefficiency on the foreign exchange market are, in principle, capable of generating substantial fluctuations in the real exchange rates.

Fixed exchange rates
The combination of a fixed exchange-rate regime with perfect capital mobility is usually taken to ensure that nominal interest rates are equalized across countries, which would mean eliminating the fad process included earlier to characterize the behaviour of the floating exchange rate. Of course, if the fad were to be treated as a phenomenon which has nothing to do with the exchange rate regime *per se* – but is, for example, a 'safe-haven' portfolio shift – then it would be perfectly possible to incorporate the effects of such fads on interest differentials under fixed exchange rates. For present purposes, however, we assume that the fad is eliminated by the change of regime.

Under a fixed-rate regime, 'competitiveness' is measured by the ratio of nominal prices, $c \equiv p^* - p = -p_d$, and its evolution reflects differential inflation. Under the reasonable assumption that the augmentation term π_d will also go to zero, the inflation differential is as in equation (4) above, except that $\pi_d = 0$, *cf.* Buiter (1986).

The determination of output differences (after substitutions reflecting the assumption of zero interest differentials, constant nominal exchange rate and the inflation process) is given in the line labelled 'McKinnon' in Table 8.4. Using the values for Δ_2 and ρ_s shown here, the asymptotic variance of the real exchange rate may be calculated as

$$\sigma_c^2 = \sigma_{p_d}^2 = \frac{1}{2|\rho_s|} \left(\frac{\phi 2\sigma_{\varepsilon_g}^2}{\Delta^2} + \sigma_{\varepsilon_p}^2 \right) \tag{9}$$

assuming for convenience that $\hat{\varepsilon}_g$ and $\hat{\varepsilon}_p$ are independent and $s_d = 0$.

Thus the real exchange rate depends on shocks to the goods market and on differential inflation shocks but not on the money-market disturbances represented by ε_m, which are accommodated so as to keep interest rates equalized. What keeps relative prices in line in the long run – and so keeps the asymptotic variance of the real rate from diverging – is the negative feedback effect of past inflation differentials on the current output and inflation differentials; the country which has had more inflation is less competitive and loses demand for that reason.

It is of course possible to add a fiscal-policy response to external developments. Thus if

$$s_d = -\xi\beta = -\xi(-\alpha p_d - \beta y_d),$$

where β is the balance of trade, the parameters are modified as shown on the next line of Table 8.4, labelled 'McKinnon with fiscal activism'.

Stable real exchange rates with domestic nominal income targets

Finally we turn to the case where real exchange rates are stabilized and fiscal policy used to support the anti-inflationary stance of policy. For reasons discussed earlier, we treat the fad as a characteristic of free floating which disappears with the change of regime. (Once again, however, behaviour of this sort which reflects portfolio shifts can, if necessary, be included.) We consider in detail a regime where the real exchange rate is kept constant; this is, of course, a limiting case since Williamson's target zones are 20 per cent wide! Nevertheless it is of interest in view of the argument that limiting movements in the real rate will necessarily destabilize inflation, see Adams and Gross (1986).

Assume first that nominal interest differentials are set equal to the anticipated inflation differential (reducing to zero the *ex ante* real interest differential), i.e.

$$i_d = \phi y_d + \pi_d. \tag{10}$$

Let fiscal policy be used to pursue a nominal income target (n, n*) with fiscal stance being adjusted in proportion to the deviation from target, i.e. $s = \sigma(p + y - n)$, $s^* = -\sigma(p^* + y^* - n^*)$ so

$$s_d = -\sigma(p_d + y_d - n_d). \tag{11}$$

The nominal-income targets are designed to accommodate non-inflationary potential income growth; as we are, for simplicity, ignoring the growth of potential output in this chapter, the two targets n and n* will be constant (and their differences n_d can be set to zero by choice of units). For the same reason, the term π_d appearing in (10) can be set to zero, just as in McKinnon's monetary union – except here it is the commitment to nominal income targets that is to achieve this result. Relative output demand is usually affected by (*ex ante*) real interest differentials and the real exchange rate but the former is zero (by assumption); the latter will also be constant (as a corollary). The reason is simply that the real rate differs from equilibrium by the integral of expected future real interest differentials, which are set to zero by policy.

So relative output depends only on relative prices and demand shocks as shown in the last line of Table 8.4, which is formally very similar to the preceding calculations for the fixed nominal exchange rate, the main difference being that here only relative fiscal stance and not the real exchange responds to past inflation differentials (represented in integral form by p_d). Since the inflation process is unchanged, the formula for the unconditional variance of inflation will be as for (9) above, except that now $\rho_s = -\phi\sigma/\Delta_3$ and $\Delta_3 = 1 + \sigma + \eta$.

How can one square the striking correspondence between the output and inflation behaviour and that derived for McKinnon's monetary union (where surely inflation was under control) with the basic conclusion of Adams and Gros (that assigning monetary policy to real things destabilizes inflation)? The answer lies in the fact that in the extended target-zone system being analysed here, a fiscal-policy rule is used in conjunction with the monetary-policy assignment. If this is deleted, so σ goes to zero, then indeed the asymptotic variance will go to infinity – the Adams and Gros point.

Summary and conclusions

When the Dollar Standard came to an end, macroeconomic policy became *ipso facto* more decentralized and, by and large, policy-makers adopted national monetary targets to fight inflation and floated exchange rates to offset inflation differentials. However, the velocity of money was highly variable while deviations from purchasing power parity were both pronounced and prolonged. The alternative systems examined here attempt to cope with these developments.

In seeking to stabilize exchange rates, they both seek to coordinate monetary policy across countries but without returning to a Dollar Standard. In the belief that variations in velocity were due to 'currency substitution', McKinnon initially proposed that world interest rates be set so as to attain an aggregate money-supply target. Even in aggregate, however, velocity has proved too fickle. Both McKinnon's revised plan to use this price level as a target and Williamson's choice of nominal income are ways of avoiding shocks to velocity while retaining the crucial monetarist principle that monetary stringency be progressively increased in response to inflation.

At the national level, McKinnon proposes to fix nominal exchange rates while Williamson seeks to stabilize real exchange rates within a relatively wide band : in neither case are monetary targets recommended. The adoption of such policy rules may avoid the fads which appear to characterize floating exchange rates, although this is still an open question. Even aside from this important issue, there are crucial differences between the regimes, as illustrated for example in Table 8.5, where the long-run variances of prices and output – in the face of supply and demand disturbances – are shown for various regimes.

For brevity, we consider only the variances arising from supply-side shocks, shown in columns (4) and (5) of the table. It is apparent that, for

Table 8.5 Asymptotic variances of price and output under various regimes: supply and demand shocks only

| | Key parameters values | | | Asymptotic variances | | | |
| | | | | Supply side shocks[1] | | Demand shocks[2] | |
	a^3 See Table 8.4	Δ See Table 8.4	ρ_s $\dfrac{-\phi a}{\Delta}$	σ_p^2 $\dfrac{1}{2|p_s|}$	σ_y^2 $\dfrac{a}{2\phi\Delta}$	σ_p^2 $\dfrac{\phi}{2a\Delta}$	σ_y^1 $\dfrac{1}{\Delta^2}\left(\dfrac{a\phi}{2\Delta}+1\right)$
Averages	(1)	(2)	(3)	(4)	(5)	(6)	(7)
(1) Money or Nominal Income Target	0.25	0.9	−0.139	3.60	0.28	1.11	1.32
(2) Price Level Target (With $\beta = \gamma^{-1}$)	0.25	0.65	−0.192	2.60	0.38	1.54	2.59
Differences							
(3) Floating with Money Target	1.18	1.1	−0.536	0.93	1.07	0.19	1.05
(4) McKinnon's Proposal	1.0	0.85	−0.588	0.85	1.18	0.29	1.79
(5) Williamson's Target Zones	0.5	1.6	−0.156	3.2	0.31	0.31	0.42

Notes:
1. Supply side shocks are disturbances to the inflation equation.
2. Demand side shocks are disturbances to the demand equation.
3. a is the parameter appearing in equation (1) of Annex 8.1.
4. Asymptotic variances are given as a multiple of the variances of the shock indicated.
5. Parameter values used: $\eta = 0.1$, $\gamma = \phi = \delta = \sigma = 0.5$, $\theta = 0.93$, k = 1, $\lambda = 2$.

the illustrative parameters used here, the product of price and output variances is a constant in the face of supply-side shocks; the regimes are trading off variations in prices and output. In row 1, one can see that for both a world money-supply target (as originally proposed by McKinnon) and for a global nominal-income target (pursued with an equally active use of interest rates), the variance of prices exceeds that of output. (If one were to include shocks to the velocity of money as well, they would increase the variances associated with the money-supply rule, leaving those for the nominal-income target unchanged). However, targeting the price level directly, as McKinnon has more recently recommended, does, even without fiscal activism, reduce price variance (row 2) – at the cost of higher output variance.

Turning now to the country-specific inflation shocks, one sees, in rows 3 and 4, that the fluctuations in relative prices and of relative output levels are much closer together. The reason is that, in an open economy, the movement of the real exchange rate adds an extra channel to monetary policy. In addition to the direct effect of real interest rates on aggregate demand, the real interest rate will influence the trade balance via its effect on the real exchange rate. Interestingly, however, the 'gold standard' results appearing in row 4 – where the country with high inflation sticks to a fixed exchange rate and suffers a loss in competitiveness – are much the same as those for free floating with money supply targets (row 3). The intuitive reason for this is that if, as here, the exchange rate does not significantly overshoot under floating and if the money target is constant, then the floating nominal exchange rate will be pretty stable too – absent the fads. (In practice, the variance of exchange rates seems to have exceeded what can be explained in terms of variation in economic fundamentals: this is why we have included fads in the foreign-exchange markets, which affect the behaviour of the floating exchange rate but disappear when the rate is fixed or managed.)

Under both these regimes, international competitiveness will fluctuate as relative prices move but the nominal exchange rate remains stable. As can be seen from the last row, moving nominal rates so as to keep competitiveness constant does stabilize output but it means that prices become more volatile. Indeed, the outcomes begin to look more like those for the closed economy, which makes sense as the monetary authorities act so as to prevent real exchange rates from moving as they have in the previous two cases.

In the remainder of the table, the variances arising from demand shocks are also shown for the several regimes. A more complete treatment would, of course, include other shocks and a consideration of their joint distribution but this illustration gives some idea of the way in which the different exchange-rate regimes seek to spread the burden of checking supply-side inflation. (See also Frankel, 1983.)

The options with regard to exchange-rate policy are no longer simply whether to use monetary policy so as to fix the exchange rate or to let it float freely. This chapter has shown that schemes to manage the exchange rate, involving both monetary and fiscal policy, give distinct and equally coherent answers to the issues involved in choosing of an exchange regime.

Annex 8.1
Given

$$y = \frac{1}{\Delta}(-\mathrm{a}p - \mathrm{b}\varepsilon_m + \varepsilon_g) \tag{1}$$

$$\mathrm{D}p = \phi y + \varepsilon_p = -\frac{\phi}{\Delta}\mathrm{a}p - \frac{\phi}{\Delta}\mathrm{b}\varepsilon_m + \frac{\phi}{\Delta}\varepsilon_g + \varepsilon_p \tag{2}$$

so $\rho_s = -\phi a/\Delta$, then the asymptotic variance of price is

$$\sigma_p^2 = \frac{1}{2|\rho_s|} \left\{ \frac{\phi^2}{\Delta^2} (b^2\sigma_{\varepsilon_m}^2 + \sigma_{\varepsilon_g}^2) + \sigma_{\varepsilon_p}^2 \right\}$$

$$= \frac{\phi}{2a\Delta} (b^2\sigma_{\varepsilon_m}^2 + \sigma_{\varepsilon_g}^2) + \frac{\Delta}{2\phi a} \sigma_{\varepsilon_p}^2 \tag{3}$$

assuming that the disturbances are independently distributed. For (1) and (3), the asymptotic variance of output is

$$\sigma_y^2 = \frac{1}{\Delta^2} (a^2\sigma_{\varepsilon_p}^2 + b^2\sigma_{\varepsilon_m}^2 + \sigma_{\varepsilon_g}^2)$$

$$= \frac{1}{\Delta^2} \left\{ \frac{a\phi}{2\Delta} b^2\sigma_{\varepsilon_m}^2 + \left(\frac{a\phi}{2\Delta} + 1 \right) \sigma_{\varepsilon_g}^2 + \frac{a\Delta}{2\phi} \sigma_{\varepsilon_p}^2 \right\}. \tag{4}$$

The asymptotic covariance of price and output is simply

$$\sigma_{py} = -\frac{a}{\Delta} \sigma_p^2. \tag{5}$$

Note:
Where the balance of trade is governed by $B = -\alpha p_d - \beta y_d$, then the unconditional covariance of B is

$$\sigma_B^2 = \alpha^2\sigma_{p_d}^2 + \beta^2\sigma_{y_d}^2 + 2\alpha\beta\sigma_{p_d y_d}.$$

References

Adams, C. and D. Gros (1986), 'The consequences of real exchange rate rules for inflation: Some illustrative examples', *IMF Staff Papers*, **33**, 439–76.
Al-Nowaihi, A., P. Levine and A. Fontenelle (1985), 'The PRISM computer package for the simulation of continuous and discrete time stochastic rational expectations models: A user's guide', Mimeo, Queen Mary College.
Aoki, M. (1981), *Dynamic Analysis of Open Economies*, Academic Press.
Aoki, M. (1987), 'Decentralized monetary rules in a three country model and time series evidence of structural dependence', Mimeo prepared for Conference of Money and Banking, Aix-le-Provence.
Buiter, W. (1986), 'Macroeconomic policy design in an interdependent world economy', *IMF Staff Papers*, **33**, 541–82.
Buiter, W. and M.H. Miller (1981), 'Monetary policy and international competitiveness: The problems of adjustment', *Oxford Economic Papers*, **33**, suppl.
Buiter, W. and M.H. Miller (1982), 'Real exchange rate overshooting and output cost of bringing down inflation', *European Economic Review*, **18**, 85–123.
Dornbusch, R. (1976), 'Expectations and exchange rate dynamics', *Journal of Political Economy*, **84**, 1161–76.
Dornbusch, R. (1983), 'Flexible exchange rates and interdependence', *IMF Staff Papers*, **30**.
Edison, H.J., M.H. Miller and J. Williamson (1987), 'On evaluating and extending the target zone proposal', *Journal of Policy Modelling*, **9**, 199–224.

Frankel, J.A. (1983), 'The desirability of a dollar appreciation, given a contractionary US monetary policy', *NBER Working Paper*, No.1110.

Friedman, M. (1953), 'The case for flexible exchange rates', *Essays in Positive Economics*, University of Chicago Press.

Friedman, M. (1968), 'The role of monetary policy', *American Economic Review*, **58**.

Fukuda, S.I., and K. Hamada (1986), 'Towards the implementation of desirable rules of monetary coordination and intervention', *Growth Center Discussion Paper*, Yale University.

Giavazzi, F., and A. Giovanni (1987), 'Models of the EMS: Is Europe a greater Deutschemark area', in R. Bryant and R. Portes (eds) *Global Macroeconomics*, Macmillan.

Jazwinsky, A.H. (1970), *Stochastic Processes and Filtering Theory*, Academic Press.

Levine, P., and D. Currie (1985), 'Optimal feedback rules in an open economy macromodel with rational expectations', *European Economic Review*, **27**, 141–63.

McKinnon, R.I. (1984), *An International Standard for Monetary Stabilization*, Institute for International Economics.

Miller, M.H. (1982), 'Differences in the policy mix and consequences for the real exchange rates', in S. Honkapohja (ed) *Money, Inflation and Economic Policy*, Y. Jahnsson Foundation, forthcoming.

Poterba, J.M., and L.H. Summers (1987), 'Mean reversion in stock returns: Evidence and implications', mimeo, NBER.

Williamson, J. (1985), *The Exchange Rate System*, Institute for International Economics (revised).

Realistic options and relevant extensions.
Comment by Michael Jones

Miller and Williamson take a new look at an old issue. They view international monetary regimes as operating procedures for monetary (or, perhaps, fiscal) policies – that is, money-stock targets or nominal or real interest-rate targets at either the global or national level – and compare regimes according to the volatilities they generate for key macroeconomic variables. Related works in this area date back to Stein (1963) for exchange-rate management, and to Poole (1970) for intermediate targeting. The large literature is surveyed by Marston (1985). The contribution of this chapter, shared with recent studies by McKibbon and Sachs (1986) and Fukuda and Hamada (1988), is to shift the analysis to a dynamic world of several countries in which regimes matter for the pace at which a shocked system moves back to steady state. This extension is important. Nominal price rigidity and the forward-looking nature of exchange rates introduce employment and inflation dynamics into virtually all models with interesting policy implications. In addition, policy rules which lessen the immediate impact of shocks could be undesirable for the long run if these rules deny the economy its ability to shed shocks over time. As it turns out, many intuitions derived from the older literature (especially Poole) carry over into the dynamic framework. However, his confirmation does not diminish the usefulness of the analysis, which neatly extends the popular sticky price IS/LM model to a continuous-time, stochastic setting. Each of us, no doubt, will find objectionable some features of the specification. For example, the motion of nominal prices (the model's key dynamics) is governed by a Phillips curve, unaugmented by inflation expectations of either a forward or backward-looking variety. Also, asymptotic variances are imperfect proxies for the objective functional common in dynamic control. These and other simplifications limit the relevance of the regime comparisons but they make the model tractable and the conclusions transparent.

The regime comparisons

Let me highlight the underlying logic and identify some troubling features of the illustrative computations. Consider, first, the management of the global economy – the average system. Here we find that setting interest rates on the basis of the price level rather than nominal income will make interest rates respond more powerfully to price-level changes (that is, increases in the price-level lower output on impact) but less powerfully to goods market shocks (which affect output but not the price level on impact). In turn, under the price-level rule, price changes affect output (and hence inflation) strongly and the speed of convergence of the global economy is rapid. As a consequence, the price-level rule gives favourable asymptotic properties in the face of Phillips curve shocks but, despite the slower adjustment pace, the nominal income rule is preferable for goods market shocks. Targeting monetary aggregates places third in the comparison for, given the unitary income elasticity of money demand assumed here, money targets are just a noisy way of tying interest rates to nominal income, the noise being velocity of money shocks. In essence, the interest-rate rules work better because they exploit more contemporaneous information. This difference, however, seems artificial. The very point of intermediate targets is that reliable information on ultimate objectives is not contemporaneously available. In particular, nominal income cannot be an immediate target. More realistic depictions of policy options would have the money stock (the control) feedback on the price level (the only state variable); or, to preserve some contemporaneous feedback, the monetary authority might 'lean with or against the wind' of the interest-rate surprises which would happen under a money target. Formally, these rules can be written as $i_a = \beta(P_a + KY_a + \bar{\varepsilon}_M)$, with β greater than $1/\lambda$ representing leaning with the wind and β less than $1/\lambda$ representing leaning against the wind. For rules of this latter sort, the classic Poole results remain valid – that is, the global authority should lean against the wind of interest-rate surprises when velocity shocks are important; lean with the wind when goods market shocks are important; and, when aggregate supply shocks predominate, leaning against the wind buys output stability at the cost of price instability.

Turning to the differenced system, we find that a fixed nominal exchange rate is equivalent to a nominal interest peg; and that free floating (no foreign exchange market intervention) is equivalent to a targeted difference in money-growth rates. Thus, as emphasized by Fukuda and Hamada, Poole's results again apply to the fixed/floating comparison under goods and money-market shocks. Since nominal exchange-rate fixing inevitably requires equal growth of national money in the long run, the speed of adjustment under the two regimes is similar. This result nicely supports the view that the stagflationary shocks of the 1970s would not have been accommodated more smoothly under fixed exchange rates.

The novelty here is the analysis of a third option; namely, real exchange-rate targets. By fixing the real exchange rate, we achieve impressive reductions in output volatility. However, by eliminating any of the price level on output (and hence inflation), we turn the difference in national price levels into a random walk, in the absence of fiscal support. In my view, the significance of the latter result – the need for a 'nominal anchor' – is overdone. While the nominal price level has infinite variance, all real variables and the inflation rate have finite asymptotic variances. Indeed, since the real system under real exchange-rate targets has essentially an infinite speed of convergence, real variables are comparatively stable and the inflation rate is quite predictable. I simply cannot find an obvious connection between welfare and the variance of the price level. The former result is also overstated: since the real exchange rate is the only state variable whose level or motion affects output, fixing it is bound to stabilize output. Few critics of real exchange-rate targets would deny this point but, also, few would accept the realism of the model's constant long-run real exchange rate. Instead, critics argue that the long-run real exchange rate is itself a moving target, influenced by fiscal policy and by a variety of real shocks which cannot be observed contemporaneously. Since there is some unavoidable real exchange-rate variability (and since the current arrangement is not strict money targeting, not free floating, and involves a fiscal/monetary mix), we must view the Miller–Williamson comparisons as something of a caricature. At a minimum, the model should incorporate some permanent shocks to goods markets or aggregate supply, which would move the long-run real exchange rate over time.

Relevant extensions

Although I have quibbled with some of the detailed features of the regime comparisons, I am in strong agreement with the basic methodology: regimes matter for macroeconomic performance in a multi-country, dynamic setting; how they matter provides the criterion for regime selection. Let me close with three suggestions for the future research needed to translate their methodology into prescriptions.

First, as the comparisons show, there is no dominant regime: (given preferences), the best rule depends on the pattern of shocks. At this time, we do not know much about this pattern. Our ignorance is not from lack of effort; instead, shocks are the residuals of structural equations of the world economy and there is no consensus on what this structural model is. Some would even argue that the regime itself affects the pattern of shocks – as Miller and Williamson suggest by supposing fads are peculiar to free floating.

Second, the current non-system exhibits a diversity of exchange arrangements. Since these policies have been chosen in non-cooperative fashion, there is no presumption that they are optimal. This diversity does, however, illustrate important asymmetries in national preferences, shocks and structures. These asymmetries prevent the crisp, analytical distinction between global aggregates and differenced variables. More importantly, these asymmetries change the nature of the exercise from finding unanimously best rules to finding the range of Pareto-optimal rules. Under asymmetries, this range can be broad, perhaps encompassing several combinations of the rates analysed here.

Third, the McKinnon proposal would make national monetary policies totally subservient to international rules. The Williamson proposal (supplemented by a global interest-rate agreement) would, as well, completely determine national fiscal stances. Since Miller and Williamson implicitly seek simple rules which approximate policy rules in a first-best cooperative equilibrium, all relevant policies should be exploited. This precise, all-encompassing set of rules is unlike any international regime we have seen – or are likely to see, given the national asymmetries and lack of consensus on predominant shocks just described. Instead, the realistic options involve regime rules in some spheres of policy but unregulated, non-cooperation in other spheres of policy. Second-best considerations make the benefits of different rules non-obvious in this context. Rogoff (1985), Jones (1987) and others show plausible circumstances under which a partial movement towards fully cooperative policies (across countries and over time) can worsen welfare. These results caution us against an incremental approach to reform and direct us to stake out the feasible and Pareto-superior middle ground of reform options.

References

Fukuda, S.-I., and K. Hamada (1988), 'Towards the implementation of desirable rules of monetary coordination and interventions', in Y. Suzuki and M. Okabe (eds.), *Toward a World of Economic Stability*, University of Tokyo.

Jones, M. (1987), 'IMF surveillance, policy coordination and time consistency', *International Economic Review*, **28**, 135–58.

McKibbon, W. and J. Sachs (1986), 'Comparing the global performance of alternative exchange arrangements', *Brookings Discussion Papers in International Finance*, **49**, August.

Marston, R.C. (1985), 'Stabilization policies in open economies', in R. Jones and P. Kenen (eds.), *Handbook of International Economics II*, Amsterdam: Elsevier.

Poole, W. (1970), 'Optimal choice of monetary policy instruments in a simple, stochastic macro model', *Quarterly Journal of Economics*, **84**, 197–216.

Rogoff, K. (1985), 'Can international monetary policy coordination be counterproductive?', *Journal of International Economics*, **18**, 199–218.

Stein, J. (1963), 'The optimum foreign exchange market', *American Economic Review*, **53**, 184–402.

9 The future of the international monetary system

Sidney Dell

Precarious as the present state of the international monetary system may be (or non-system, as some would describe it), it is as well to keep in mind the fact that there are even greater economic perils facing the international community. These are due to the conflicts and tensions between the major powers on questions of macro-management of the world economy, the large current trade imbalances and the protectionism to which they give rise, and above all the failure of the international community to develop a rational long-run strategy for dealing with the world debt crisis, as a result of which the Third World has been in a state of persistent economic depression for most of the present decade and no end of the problem is in sight. We cannot enter into these matters because our agenda concerns the system, not the behaviour of the members of the system. But one has to be careful not to blame the system for the policy errors of its members. No doubt the system should be designed in such a way as to make it easier for members to follow harmonious policies aiming at full employment but no system can overcome a fear of the consequences of full employment.

It is the fear of full employment, or of high levels of employment, that is at the root of many of the current problems of the world economy. Propositions of doubtful validity relating rates of inflation to levels of employment are invoked to justify policies that discourage growth and development in the industrial countries and that create a world economic environment in which it is impossible for the great majority of developing countries to adjust to their present problems under conditions of adequate growth. It is unlikely that the problems of the IMS can be solved except in the context of an expanding world economy that would accommodate the adjustments facing industrial and developing countries alike without imposing intolerable burdens on any of them.

Any enquiry into the future of the IMS has to start with assumptions about the kind of world in which it will be expected to function. The Bretton Woods system was based on the assumption that various forms of malfunctioning of the world economy can be corrected by governments if they take the right kind of steps. There was a considerable variety of opinion as to what those steps should be, but there was a general presumption that solutions were in the hands of governments. This presumption came under fire in the 1970s and 1980s and the view has gained ground that the market knows best, not the governments, and the best thing governments can do is to be guided by the market and to create conditions under which the market will be able to operate with as little interference as possible. With deregulation of the private sector, as many activities of the public sector as possible should, on this view, be turned over to private enterprise. These policies appear to command wide public support in most of the industrial countries.

The exchange rate system
The IMS has provided little comfort for those espousing these views. It is generally agreed that floating exchange rates have not brought with them the advantages that were expected. According to the IMF (1984), the short-term variability of nominal exchange rates for the seven major currencies was about six times greater under floating rates than during the last decade of adjustable par values. Exchange speculation has been destabilizing, not stabilizing as had been predicted. Even more serious, exchange-rate misalignment has also been at least as great, if not greater, as during the Bretton Woods period. For example, in the second quarter of 1985 the real effective exchange rate of the US dollar was over 50 per cent above the level implied by purchasing power parity (IMF, 1987, p. 4). As the Group of 24 (G-24, 1985, para. 62) pointed out, much of the medium-term movement in real exchange rates reflects not the changing pattern of competitiveness but rather inconsistencies in the fiscal and monetary policies pursued by the major industrial countries.

Even those most staunchly opposed to government interference in the marketplace found themselves compelled to advocate such interference to correct what they regard as market errors or imperfections. Thus US Treasury Secretary Baker told the IMF on 30 September 1987 that 'We have agreed that we should be concerned about the predictability and stability of exchange rates'; and statements by several ministers of the Group of Ten (G-10), including Baker, to the effect that the decline of the dollar had gone far enough implied agreement that, in the absence of such statements and the tacit threat of coordinated exchange intervention by Central Banks, the markets would be likely to force the dollar down below long-run equilibrium levels.

As a result of the failure of the floating exchange-rate system, much attention has been given to the possibility of setting up a target-zone system that would seek to avoid the destabilizing uncertainties of floating rates without reintroducing the rigidities of a par value system. The G-24 has given tentative support to this proposal, urging that it be carefully studied. The proposal also has support within the G-10 but the majority of G-10 members oppose it on several grounds, including the difficulties likely to be experienced in achieving consensus on the determination of the zones and the danger of focusing attention on exchange rates rather than on the root cause of misalignment – namely the divergence of macro-economic policies. There is a good deal of substance in the latter point – perhaps more than the G-10 majority itself would allow. The issue is not simply the choice between fixed and floating-rate systems or between these two systems and some hybrid that tries to combine the perceived virtues of both. The issue is whether the heavy emphasis placed by the inter-national community and the IMF on the importance of adjustment through exchange-rate changes is justified by the experience gained. Already in 1977, Kaldor (1978, p. xxi) reached the conclusion that 'Unless the next few years bring some large and dramatic changes, the experiment of securing a more balanced relationship in the trade between industrial countries through exchange rate variations must be adjudged a failure.' He based this conclusion partly on the fact that despite a 40 per cent reduc-tion in the effective exchange rate of sterling since 1972, imports claimed a growing share of Britain's domestic absorption of manufactures while Britain's share in world exports of manufactures continued to decline. Similarly, a 31 per cent gain in the cost-competitiveness of the US over a similar period failed to stem the growth of import penetration or the decline of the US share in world export markets for non-military goods.

More recent experience strongly confirms Kaldor's conclusion. The exchange rate of the US dollar declined more than 50 per cent from its peak against the mark and the yen but the balances of payments of the Federal Republic of Germany, Japan and the US have been remarkably sluggish in their response. Not only are the relevant elasticities inherently low (and the time-lags inherently lengthy) but the two surplus countries have, by various means, been able to slow down shifts in trade balances, for example, by accepting reductions in export profit margins. At the same time, it is reported that many US exporters prefer to see their profit margins raised rather than undertake the additional effort of expanding the volume of sales at more competitive prices. Thus, in the 1970s and 1980s alike, even drastic changes in the exchange rates of the major indus-trial countries have not affected their balances of payments as quickly or as decisively as expected. The countries that are in surplus today are the same countries that were in surplus in the 1970s and, indeed, in the 1960s.

Many analysts (e.g. McKinnon) believe the recent decline of the dollar has not had the results expected because of the overriding influence of the US budget deficit on the trade deficit. This belief derives from the accounting identity whereby gross private savings must equal the sum of gross private investment, export surplus and budget deficit. Consequently, at any given level of private savings and private investment, there is a direct relationship between the external balance and the budget deficit. However, a mere accounting identity cannot reveal either the nature of the interaction between the components of gross private savings or the direction of causality. Nor can private savings and private investment be taken as invariant with respect to the budget deficit and trade deficit – especially since, under conditions of less than full employment, private savings are passive. Moreover, the larger the economy and the smaller the ratio of exports and imports to national income, the less likely it is that one will find a strong relationship between the external balance and the macro-economy. In the case of the US, of the 42 years from 1946 to 1987, 28 were years in which there were budget deficits according to the national-income definition. Only in five of these 28 years – from 1983 to 1987 – were budget deficits accompanied by external deficits on goods and services. Finally, the secular loss of market share both at home and abroad by the US manufacturing industry over a period of decades is not simply a question of price but results from long-run structural factors. It is not plausible to attribute all this change to the budget deficit.

My conclusion is that the elimination of the US budget deficit is neither a necessary nor a sufficient condition for the correction of the deficit in the US balance of payments. It is, of course, possible that a reduction in the US budget deficit, by depressing employment and income, would have led to a sufficient reduction in US imports to improve the external balance. However, even this is quite uncertain because of the impact of a fall in US imports on the world level of activity and, hence, on the world demand for US exports. It was, moreover, supposed to be one of the advantages of the floating rate system that this would increase the degree of freedom of major countries to follow domestic macropolicies of their own choosing. If countries cannot protect themselves against rising unemployment even through drastic depreciation of their currencies, what is the point of exchange-rate flexibility?

The effectiveness of market forces and of the price mechanism in changing the current-account balance at given levels of income has been greatly overestimated, with the result that too much has been expected of the exchange-rate system. Owing to the inefficiency of markets, the range of exchange rates compatible with any given current-account balance in the short and medium term appears to be quite wide, so that the actual level of the rate tends to be determined by factors unrelated to long-run equilibrium. Indeed, since the system is continually in flux, the long-run equilibrium itself presents a moving and elusive target.

Lamfalussy (1987, p.36) raises the question whether the downturn of the dollar in 1985 occurred because the market finally realized the current-account imbalances were becoming unsustainable or because the authorities intervened to help bring it about. His answer is that we shall never know, though it is arguable that without intervention the decline would have been delayed. If he is right on the latter point, as seems likely, market forces were much weaker and concerted intervention much more effective in changing the trend of exchange rates than was generally anticipated. If purchasing power parity is any guide (which, however, seems less and less plausible) the dollar's decline has gone much too far because on that basis the dollar should, according to McKinnon, be worth about 200 yen instead of the current 125. It also seems to follow from Lamfalussy's point that so long as the major governments are in broad agreement on the level and pattern of exchange rates, they have no reason to fear being overwhelmed by disruptive capital movements. The mere fact that inter-country capital movements are far larger than the flows across the exchanges resulting from current transactions does not necessarily mean that the former will always determine the direction of exchange-rate changes. The market does not, in general, have at its disposal information that would provide a firm anchor for medium or long-term exchange-rate expectations, so the direction of the market at any particular time depends on predominantly short-term and speculative influences that could readily be overcome by evidence of strongly concerted intervention by the major industrial-country authorities.

Capital controls could, of course, reinforce any chosen configuration of exchange rates. For all the globalization of capital markets that has taken place, the viability of the European Monetary System (EMS) depended significantly on the capital controls maintained by the weaker members of the system (IMF, 1987, p. 15). Apart from direct capital controls, it is also possible to regulate capital flows by various tax devices. A tax on international financial transactions as proposed by Tobin (1978, pp. 155, 158–9) would, as pointed out by Keynes (1936, pp. 159–60) in connection with a similar proposal at the domestic level, mitigate the predominance of speculation over enterprise.

The foregoing considerations, particularly the stickiness of current-account balances in the face of exchange-rate changes, imply that a return to an adjustable peg system is feasible so long as the macroeconomic policies of the major countries are not too far out of line with one another. On the other hand, if there are major divergencies in the policies of these countries, no other system (whether based on target zones, objective indicators for macroeconomic policies, or strengthened surveillance within the existing system) would be a significant improvement over the present exchange-rate arrangements. The latter approaches involve major uncertainty as to the commitment of governments to more stable exchange rates. Particularly in the case of the soft version of the target-zone proposal, the lack of firm official commitments to prevent exchange rates from moving beyond the zonal limits would be a clear incentive for exchange markets to repeatedly test the limits – in the expectation that, sooner or later, the governments would give way. Since the markets have little or no basis on which to determine medium or long-term trends in exchange rates, volatility and misalignment would persist. A more stable exchange-rate system probably cannot be achieved without a clear and widely publicized commitment by the major industrial countries to a particular pattern of exchange rates and to the measures of concerted intervention required to defend that pattern.

The importance of reducing the enormous risks to long-term investment that result from steep unforeseen changes in exchange rates is, in itself, a sufficient reason for giving high priority to greater stability. Since there is probably not much to choose between a target-zone system and an adjustable peg from the standpoint of the degree of policy harmonization required for the success of each, it may be worth going the extra distance toward the adjustable peg instead of selecting a 'halfway house' that may turn out to be neither the one thing nor the other (Akyuz and Dell, 1987, pp. 39–44).

Towards a world Central Bank

It is sometimes suggested that the establishment of a world Central Bank would go a long way towards providing remedies for the ills of the IMS. While this would take many years to accomplish, the setting of the objective together with step-by-step approaches towards its realization are viewed as a helpful direction in which to proceed. The basic difficulty, however, is that just as a national Central Bank is an instrument of a politically unified government so too a world Central Bank would depend on a high degree of international political unification – that is to say, on some kind of world central government. The monetary policies of a world Central Bank could never be relied upon to affect all countries equally and acceptance of such policies by those countries experiencing consequences less favourably than others would depend on a degree of international solidarity that is not to be found in a world of separate sovereign states. Thus the view that the establishment of a world Central Bank would make for a better IMS solves the problem by assuming it away! We need to find a solution for a world of independent sovereign states, having diverse and often conflicting interests and objectives.

If the IMF has aspirations towards becoming a world Central Bank in due course, it received a rude shock at the time of the Jamaica Agreement in 1976. The IMF historian (De Vries, 1985, ch. 37) described this development:

> Jamaica signaled a turning point in the Fund's history in yet another way. The Fund's regulatory functions and its role as custodian of international monetary arrangements were de-emphasized. Increased attention was to be devoted to the role of the Fund as a provider of financial assistance, especially to its developing members.

In proposing a realistic approach to the possible evolution of the IMF towards a world Central Bank, Cooper (1987) was well aware of the *de facto* curtailing of Fund responsibilities in the Jamaica Agreement. Taking a time-horizon of 20 years, he postulated a world of sovereign states with autonomous national monetary policies and national currencies floating against one another, but a world with an increased perception of economic interdependence and the need for coordination of various aspects of economic policy. This perception would lead to 'heavy management of exchange rates and acceptance of the implied restraints on the exercise of full monetary autonomy'.

Cooper's key assumption was that world reserves can influence world economic activity, at least for a time. A more generous level of world reserves would, he suggested, result in less restrictive economic policy by member countries, and vice versa. He traced the possible evolution of the IMF toward the standing of a world Central Bank as a lender of last resort, a source of international liquidity, a contributor to global economic stabilization and to the management of exchange rates, and the provider of an 'intermediating arrangement for making key economic decisions' through a strengthened Interim Committee. These were quite modest objectives when they were first suggested by Cooper in 1983 but the trend of the present decade has, for the most part, been in a quite different direction. Major shareholders of the IMF have continued the trend begun in the Jamaica Agreement by cutting back the existing functions of the IMF still further.

As a realist, Cooper recognized that any prohibition on increments to foreign currency reserves was highly improbable but he counted on the IMF to contribute to the growth of international reserves, particularly *net* reserves. The G-10, however, now questions the need for SDRs on the grounds that any creditworthy country can borrow whatever reserves it needs and – by implication – that any uncreditworthy country had better put its house in order so as to allow it to join the ranks of those able to borrow reserves when necessary. Similarly, in regard to stabilizing the world economy, Cooper saw a possibility that the IMF could adjust the volume of SDR creation and the conditionality required of borrowers in a countercyclical manner and enlarge the compensatory financing facility (CFF) 'with little or no conditionality' so as to be able to cope with the effects of severe recessions, if necessary, by lending SDRs through the facility. Here again the trend of Fund practice has been exactly the opposite. No SDRs have been issued since 1981, access to Fund resources has been reduced, and the conditionality of Fund lending has been progressively tightened without regard to prevailing world economic conditions. Worst of all, the whole character of CFF has been so altered that it no longer lends itself to use as a countercyclical instrument: CFF is now little more, in effect, than a fifth credit tranche carrying upper credit tranche conditionality (Dell, 1985). Thus most of the proposals for a gradual evolution of IMF responsibilities that seemed modest and realistic when Cooper put them forward in 1983 now appear unrealistically radical in the context of 1988. Major reversals of the policies of the Federal Republic of Germany, Japan and the US would be required to put the IMF back into a position from which advances along the lines of Cooper's ideas could be contemplated.

It may be useful to examine the background of these matters in greater depth. The fact that the IMF has been converted into an agency that deals mainly with the balance-of-payments problems of developing countries is well known. What is, perhaps, less clearly recognized is the progressive shift in the direction of Fund activities even within this field, so as to limit IMF assistance as much as possible to high-conditionality programmes, to the detriment of other programmes that ought to have been expanded rather than contracted. Moreover a major step towards the collective management of international liquidity has been sharply reversed.

The role of the SDR

The major G-10 countries see no future for the SDR but the group is sharply divided on this subject. The majority of the members of the G-10 (1985, para. 74) recognize that severe strains in liquidity conditions have built up in the system – strains that are reflected in the decline of reserves in relation to imports and foreign debt, the lopsided distribution of reserves, and the rise of barter trade. Major industrial countries, however, take the position that international liquidity embraces not only monetary authorities' actual holdings of reserve assets but also credit arrangements permitting the acquisition of reserves from private and official sources.

Thus, it is contended, countries may obtain reserves from financial markets provided they maintain their creditworthiness. It is, however, admitted by the G-10 that the terms on which reserves are supplied by the market are affected by the financial policies of reserve-currency countries. Some members of the G-10, moreover, consider that arrangements for the provision of liquidity have not been optimal or conducive to gradual adjustment toward non-inflationary growth. They also point out that sudden and marked shifts in the terms and conditions on which international liquidity is made available, late recognition of (and abrupt response to changes in) creditworthiness, and the very limited access that certain groups of countries have to market borrowing are factors that cannot be ignored.

The position of the major countries is not very persuasive on this matter. The overwhelming majority of developing countries have never been in a position where they could rely on access to private or official sources for acquiring reserves. Such access, therefore, simply has not entered into any assessment of their needs for reserves. A number of developing countries did reach the position during the 1970s where they could borrow from financial markets to supplement reserves. Such building up of reserves was considered essential in strengthening their credit standing and hence their borrowing capabilities. However, such ready access to the financial markets disappeared with the onset of the debt crisis, thereby disrupting their reserve planning at the very time they could least afford such disruption.

A significant indicator of the shortage of reserves in non-oil developing countries (and of the importance they attach to strengthening their position in this respect) is the fact that, from the end of 1982 to the end of 1984, they increased their reserves by more than $25 billion although this meant an even sharper curtailment of imports of goods of which they were greatly in need. These facts are relevant to the argument that developing countries would immediately spend any SDRs allocated to them. There is no reason why they should not do so if circumstances so require but this evidence shows the developing countries are well aware of the benefits as well as costs of holding reserves. If, therefore, reserve needs were not satisfied through allocations of SDRs, the burden of further attempts to strengthen reserves would have to fall on additional compression of imports.

The refusal of the major industrial countries to agree to issue SDRs is a violation of the Articles of Agreement, which require all member countries to cooperate with the Fund in making the SDR 'the principal reserve asset' in the IMS (Article XXII). It also creates a serious imbalance between those countries that are able to borrow reserves and those that are compelled to earn their reserve holdings through additional curtailment of imports, at a time when the Fund and the World Bank are in full agreement that the most important constraint on the heavily-indebted developing countries is a shortage of imported goods. Nothing these countries can do in the immediate future could restore their ability to borrow from private markets. Moreover if (as implied in the reasoning of the major G-10 countries) the level of reserves held by creditworthy countries is demand-determined, and if such countries can borrow whatever reserves they need whenever they need them, the question arises as to why the holdings of non-gold reserves by the industrial countries rose rapidly and continuously during the present decade.

Stated fears of SDR-induced inflation lack credibility. Even if developing countries spent their entire allocations of SDRs on imports from developed countries, the demand pressure generated by such means would be minimal. Fund staff estimates show that, if all SDRs received by developing countries were fully transferred to developed countries and reflected in their monetary base, a total allocation of, say, SDR 10 billion to all countries would increase this base by less than 2 per cent, which is smaller than the spread between the upper and lower limits of money-supply targets in many developed countries. In 1981, the Fund staff put forward options for SDR allocations ranging from SDR 4 billion to SDR 19 billion a year, taking the position that none of these magnitudes would be sufficient to generate inflationary pressure of demand. Since 1981, inflationary pressures have subsided so that there would be even less danger of excessive demand under present conditions.

The G-10 (1985, paras 71–2) stated that developments in the IMS have lessened official interest in an internationally issued and administered reserve asset. They suggest that 'the expansion of international financial markets has provided a feasible and efficient source of reserves for many countries, and the emerging multi-currency reserve system has reduced dependence on a single currency in international settlements and reserve holdings.' They go on to say that 'The Deputies recognize that these developments have affected the rationale for the SDR, including the objective of placing the SDR at the center of the system as the main reserve asset.' In arguing that the availability of borrowing facilities supersedes the need for SDRs, however, the G-10 forgot their own report of 7 July 1966 (para.7(d)) which read, in part, as follows:

> In the past the need for international liquidity has been met by improving credit facilities as well as by additions to reserves. In the future, credit facilities can no doubt continue to play a constructive role, but their use can be only a partial and temporary substitute for reserves which are at the full disposition of the country holding them.

Regardless of what the G-10 Deputies now say about the adequacy of credit facilities in supplying reserve needs, the governments of the countries they represent are as mindful as ever of the superiority of reserves that are at the *full* disposition of the country holding them. Notwithstanding the fact that dollars have not been officially convertible into gold since 1971, and despite the volatility of the market price of gold, the central banks of the industrial countries kept gold as a major reserve asset. In fact gold, valued at market prices, amounted to over 45 per cent of the total value of the reserves of industrial countries at the end of 1986, only slightly less than the 47 per cent recorded at the end of 1970, just before the dollar's link to gold was broken. The same considerations that prompt the G-10 industrialized countries to maintain an asset (gold) that is at their full disposition within their reserves also apply to developing countries. Consequently it is of the highest importance for these countries to be able to benefit from SDR allocations, the SDR being (in some respects) a substitute for gold that is free of the costs and risks associated with gold. If the G-10 were to maintain that no new allocations of SDRs should take place either now or in the foreseeable future, this position would be tantamount to asserting that, unless developing countries are prepared to use their own resources to buy gold, they are not entitled to the benefits of acquiring reserve assets that would be at their full disposition and not subject to the goodwill of any one country.

To sum up, the best way of meeting the liquidity requirements of developing countries is through adequate annual allocations of SDRs. The G-24 points out that the allocation of SDRs to developing countries would not only meet the unfulfilled absorptive capacity of developing countries but also reduce the pressures on the industrial countries to accommodate an improvement in the current-account balances of developing countries. In other words, allocations of SDRs to developing countries would yield benefits to the international community as a whole since they would reduce the need for developed countries to accept import surpluses of goods from the developing countries in payment of their debt service.

Countercyclical functions of the IMF?
At a meeting of the UN Sub-Commission on Employment and Economic Stability held in 1949, Harrod expressed regret that, in their replies to a questionnaire addressed to them by the UN Secretary-General, almost all governments stated that if faced with unemployment and balance-of-payments difficulties as a result of declining exports, they would resort to important restrictions. This, said Harrod, implied disregard of the ideas of international cooperation developed at Bretton Woods. If necessary, international arrangements should be strengthened so that governments

would gain confidence in their effectiveness and not feel compelled to resort to import restrictions. For example, the resources of the IMF should be increased and its tasks broadened through the addition of central banking functions. Kalecki, representing the Secretary-General, commented that the IMF's reply to the questionnaire indicated that it did not have the resources required to resist a major economic downturn. The IMF representative at the meeting concurred with Kalecki's view. Subsequently, the resource base of the IMF was greatly expanded (though less than in proportion to world trade) but the idea that the IMF had a counter-cyclical role to play in the world economy never made much headway until the establishment of CFF in 1963. Even then, the rationale for CFF was not directly addressed to countering worldwide recession but was virtually limited to compensatory lending to countries experiencing shortfalls in export earnings for reasons beyond their control. Such shortfalls were, of course, a likely accompaniment to a setback in business activity in some or all of the developed countries and supporting commodity markets was, after all, one of the methods available for dealing with such setbacks. However, CFF was not intended as a means of sustaining the level of demand in industrial countries.

The first facilities oriented directly towards countercyclical activity by the IMF were the oil facilities of 1972–73, which were intended to prevent the increase in oil prices of that period from triggering a worldwide recession. The conditions laid down for the drawings on the oil facilities were totally different from any that the Fund has ever required before or since. In fact, the conditions came close to the semi-automaticity of drawings envisaged by Keynes and many others during the negotiations that preceded the Bretton Woods Conference. Countries drawing on the facility were expected to sustain appropriate levels of economic activity and employment (while minimizing inflation) and not to impose new, or intensify existing, restrictions on trade and payments. It is of considerable interest to recall the reasoning that was used to explain this strategy – embodying an approach that would probably not command a consensus in the IMF of today. In a note presented to the Committee of Twenty in January 1974, the Managing Director stated that, in the short run, the group of oil-importing countries would have to accept the deterioration of the current account in its balance of payments since attempts to eliminate the additional current deficit caused by higher oil prices through deflationary demand policies, import restrictions, and general resort to exchange-rate depreciation would serve only to shift the payments problem from one oil-importing country to another and to damage world trade and economic activity (IMF, 1974, p. 26).

The adoption of this countercyclical programme was due, in large measure, to the insight and determination of the Managing Director, Witteveen, who carried the day against the strong opposition of US Treasury Secretary Shultz and, to a lesser extent, of the Federal Republic of Germany. Gold (1979, p. 3), in explaining the conditions under the oil facilities, pointed out that there was, at that time, no fixed relationship between the resources made available by the Fund unconditionally or on the basis of mild conditionality and the resources for which stronger conditionality was applied. In the case of the oil facilities, he said, the Fund wished 'to deter hasty adjustment by such measures as competitive devaluation or restrictions that members would have been tempted to adopt in order to deal with balance-of-payments difficulties caused by the increased costs of imports of oil.' The opposing forces were, however, too strong for Witteveen to be able to carry his programme forward in the manner he desired. At the 1974 annual meetings, he called for increased official recycling of funds from oil exporters to oil importers and for a substantial increase in recycling through the Fund. His position was supported by developing countries as well as by a number of developed countries. The UK Chancellor of the Exchequer Healey argued for the investment of a significant proportion of oil revenues in international organizations in exchange for some type of asset issued by the Fund. France and Italy also favoured increased recycling by the Fund. The US, however, considered that the recycling function should be undertaken by commercial banks to the greatest extent possible, continued to favour collective action by the industrial countries in resistance to OPEC policies, and proposed a 'financial safety net' for the industrial countries. In the event, agreement was reached on a relatively small second oil facility so that the great bulk of the recycling was carried out by the commercial banks. This proved to be a most unfortunate decision since it led to the excessive build-up of commercial bank debt, with the debtor-countries absorbing the entire interest-rate risk, that has brought the development of many countries in the Third World to a halt in the 1980s and perhaps beyond.

Since 1980, the low-conditionality options referred to by Gold appear to have been closed off. Particularly noteworthy is the 1983 decision of the Fund's Executive Board with regard to CFF, which appears to have changed the character of the facility on a permanent basis, removing by far the largest single source of low-conditional IMF resources. In so doing, the Board acted in a manner entirely inconsistent with the Fund's own traditional doctrine that cases in which balance-of-payments deficits are temporary and self-reversing should be handled by financing and not by adjustment. As a Fund pamphlet (Guitián, 1981, p. 4) points out:

Deficits stemming from adverse transitory (external or internal) factors typically call for temporary resort to financing. Mechanisms have been devised in the Fund and elsewhere to cope with situations of this sort – the Fund's compensatory financing and buffer stock facilities and the European Community's STABEX Fund are examples of such mechanisms.[1]

In order to be able to deal effectively with the many different kinds of balance-of-payments problems, the Fund needs to be able to deploy an array of resources ranging from unconditional to highly conditional, depending on circumstances. Moreover, the Fund's resources need to be adequate for all these purposes so the ratio of Fund quotas to world imports needs to be restored to the level envisaged at Bretton Woods – equivalent to something of the order of 16 per cent of world imports, compared with the present ratio, which is less than 6 per cent.

A commodity link
Another useful element in providing countercyclical protection for the IMS would be to establish a policy link with commodity markets. On 30 September 1987, US Treasury Secretary Baker startled his audience at the annual meetings of the World Bank and Fund by saying 'the United States is prepared to consider utilizing as an additional indicator in the coordination process, the relationship among our currencies and a basket of commodities, including gold. This would be simply an analytical tool helpful as an early-warning signal of potential price trends.' Dornbusch ridiculed this proposal as a mere political gesture towards those who favour the gold standard but the proposal could be interpreted differently and, as such, there are perfectly sound arguments in its favour. It will be recalled that Kaldor, Hart and Tinbergen submitted a paper to the first Conference of UNCTAD in 1964 in which they set out the case for an International Commodity-Reserve Currency. The key point of the paper was that the most effective development of the IMS would lie not along the lines of a further extension of the key currency system, nor in the creation of a world paper currency, nor in the revaluation of gold, but in the monetization of real assets other than or in addition to gold. They proposed that the IMF create its own currency, which should be convertible both into gold and into a bundle of the 30 or so principal commodities in world trade. This would make it possible to create a world currency reserve which would expand in line with the production and use of primary products for the supply of these products is the ultimate constraint on world economic growth. By the same token, such a scheme would provide an effective instrument for stabilizing the terms of trade between primary products and manufactures. (See Hart's treatment in Chapter 15 below.)

Kaldor recognized that there were certain practical difficulties in the scheme. In a later article (*Lloyds Bank Review*, July 1983), he advocated instead the scheme recommended by Keynes during World War II for worldwide price stabilization by means of buffer-stocks for as many commodities as possible. Kaldor argued that a buffer-stock scheme linked to the use of SDRs would provide the world with a basic money unit that would be stable in terms of basic commodities. The existence of an international reserve currency that was stable in terms of commodities would, he felt, exert a strong dampening effect on wage-induced inflation. A critical element in this approach was that a commodity-reserve currency (or a commodity-stabilization scheme financed by SDRs) would lead to the stabilization of the world economy as a whole. It would, moreover, secure the highest sustainable rate of economic growth for the world as a whole – that is, the highest rate of world industrial expansion permitted by the growth of supplies of primary products. Kaldor was sceptical about the viability of an international paper currency without commodity backing – not because he saw any theoretical necessity for commodity backing but because he foresaw that the world's bankers would never feel really comfortable with an unbacked paper currency at the international level and that they would prefer to hold one or more of the key currencies such as the dollar. On this he proved to be absolutely right: as noted earlier, the G-10 has now openly raised the question whether the SDR has any future as an international reserve currency.

It is a long way from Kaldor's modified scheme to the Baker proposal for a commodity-price indicator but they have something important in common. They both acknowledge the merits of stabilizing commodity prices and recognize that sharp movements (upwards or downwards) in the general level of commodity prices are indicators of potential economic trouble ahead. Kaldor would rely on a mechanism linked to a commodity-based SDR to provide the impulses needed for stabilization while Baker, by implication, would see a shift in commodity prices as a signal, along with other signals, for increasing or decreasing the world level of effective demand. There is an important place for ideas along these lines in a reform of the IMS.

Surveillance
Considerable attention has been devoted in recent years to the development of IMF surveillance over the macroeconomic policies of its members. Both the G-10 and the G-24 dealt at length with this subject in separate reports published in 1985. The G-10 recognized that, during the period of floating exchange rates, 'surveillance has not been as effective as desirable in influencing national policies and in promoting underlying

economic and financial conditions conducive to exchange rate stability . . . [Some] countries appear to have been able on occasion to sustain policy courses not fully compatible with the goals of international adjustment and financial stability' (para. 36). They therefore presented proposals for strengthening surveillance (both bilateral and multilateral) and pointed out that effective surveillance implies the assessment of all policies affecting trade, capital movements, external adjustment and the effective functioning of the IMS. Such strengthened surveillance, they suggested (para. 38), would require enhanced dialogue and persuasion through peer pressure, rather than mechanically imposed external constraints. Some members of the G-10, however, consider that an element of constraint would also be required as well as greater publicity for policy conclusions reached as part of the Article IV consultation process.

While the G-10 appears to have accepted that surveillance of the major countries is more significant for the international community as a whole than surveillance of the developing countries, paragraph 41 of their report notes the existence of other institutions of more limited membership having a role in the surveillance process, notably the OECD. While this paragraph acknowledges that the central role of the IMF in surveillance should be preserved, the reference to OECD and other bodies implicitly conveys the view that the Fund's role *vis-à-vis* the industrial countries is not, and should not be, necessarily the decisive one. There are suggestions that the IMF should have the task of preparing documents analysing these external repercussions of national policies of G-10 countries while the G-10 ministers and governors and Working Party No. 3 of the OECD should use the IMF documentation in assessing the appropriateness of the policies of members. Problems in the trade field would be taken up by GATT in cooperation with the IMF.

There is a good deal of common ground between the G-10 and G-24 reports but the latter goes further in certain important respects. First, the G-24 report (1985, para. 77) considers that

> Surveillance, to be effective, should be explicitly recognized as surveillance of the international adjustment process . . . The design of such an international adjustment process, based on coordinated national economic policies, must aim at sustained growth of output, employment, and trade of all countries and ensure adequate real resource transfers to developing countries.

This clearly goes considerably beyond anything that the G-10 has thus far contemplated. Second, multilateral surveillance and bilateral (Article IV) consultations should form two stages of the surveillance process, rather than two parallel operations. One stage should involve multilateral discussions and negotiations to be conducted on a regular basis (within the framework of the IMF) about a mutually consistent set of objectives and a set of policies to achieve collectively these objectives. The aim might be to search for a set of outcomes (objective indicators or targets) that appear to be sustainable in the medium term and desirable to all parties. This, says the G-24, 'should be quite feasible when the multilateral surveillance exercise is limited to a few major industrial countries, such as the key currency countries.' The other stage would involve a comparison between actual outcomes and these recommended targets or indicators, and a discussion of what measures would be appropriate when the two differ. The G-24 (para. 78) consider that this stage might be conducted most efficiently on a bilateral basis as part of Article IV consultations. Multilateral surveillance should also take place in the IMF Board, which should examine 'the international repercussions and interactions of national policies of the major industrial countries' and should recommend 'a set of policies and the likely outcomes or performance indicators' (para. 79).

Despite the G-10 and G-24 reports, there is vagueness and confusion about the content and boundaries of surveillance, as well as about where responsibility lies. One source of vagueness is the Fund's mandate, under Article IV 3(b), to 'exercise firm surveillance over the exchange rate policies of members' – a responsibility that is, in theory, concerned largely with avoiding exchange-rate manipulation. However, the Fund's management has taken a far broader view of its authority (a position supported by the G-24) and the opening sections of its annual reports and studies of the world economic outlook deal with overall trends and macroeconomic policies. This approach has not been challenged by any of the Fund members but, since it has not been formally endorsed, some loopholes remain. A second source of uncertainty is the extent of Fund responsibility in this field, especially *vis-à-vis* regional groupings. In April 1986, the IMF's Interim Committee indicated tentative agreement to the use of objective indicators in improving multilateral surveillance but, in the following month, the seven summit countries went further, asking their Finance Ministers to 'review their economic objectives and forecasts collectively at least once a year . . . with a particular view to examining their mutual compatibility'. Given the trend since the Jamaica Agreement, whereby Fund responsibilities and resources have been progressively cut back under the pressure of the industrial countries, is it likely that the major countries aim at an intensification of Fund surveillance of the policies of its members? Perhaps so, but then there is at least some inconsistency between the erosion of Fund authority in the one area and its enhancement in the other.

The mere fact that policies of the major economic powers are confronted in more than one inter-governmental forum does not raise any difficulty so long as there is one ultimate authority (to which the other fora channel their conclusions) and so long as conflicts do not arise between any one forum and another. Since the IMF has a relatively large number of members, it makes sense that problems arising among the major countries are discussed between them in any forum they choose. The question is one of substance, not form. Is the G-5 or G-7 simply preparing the ground for the wider airing of surveillance issues in the IMF or are they reaching decisions that can be reported to the IMF but are not subject to change in that body? It has been reported by participants in both fora that, on the one hand, discussions of surveillance issues in the smaller groups have been less extensive and profound than in the Fund, but that, on the other hand, the major industrial countries regard the Fund's responsibility as being more in the nature of consultation than of supervision.

Kenen (1987, p. 1447) raises an important question regarding the G-24's integration of multilateral surveillance and bilateral (Article IV) consultations with major industrial countries. As he points out, the Summit countries assigned the whole process to their own officials although the Fund's Managing Director was to continue participating in their discussions. Here differences between outcomes and targets may not be due exclusively to one country's policies and should therefore be pursued in a multilateral framework but, if that multilateral framework is predominantly the G-5 or the G-7, the Fund's role in surveillance becomes a distinctly secondary one and the chances are that, as in many other matters, the developing countries will simply be presented with *faits accomplis*.

The problems for the present and future are clear. First and foremost, there is the question of how to persuade the major industrial countries that insistence on national economic sovereignty and associated prerogatives will, if pressed too far, be disastrous for all. Secondly, as noted at the outset, the problems of the IMS can be solved only in the context of an expanding world economy. Finally, there is the problem of how to reconcile the oligarchic propensities of the Summit countries with the insistence of the developing countries that they are now a sufficiently important factor in the world economy to have their views taken effectively into account. None of these problems is new – the system has been wrestling with them for many years without much indication of significant progress.

Conditionality and the design of Fund-supported programmes
There has been widespread criticism of the design of Fund-supported programmes and the conditionality that goes with them. It is often suggested that developing countries are opposed to IMF conditionality in principle but this is quite wrong. The opposition is to the form and character of the

conditions applied, not to the principle *per se*. What can and should be questioned is the view, now predominating among the major industrial countries, that virtually all balance-of-payments lending should be at high conditionality (a view that is completely inconsistent with IMF experience and the Articles of Agreement). The Articles require the Fund to establish adequate safeguards for the temporary use of its resources (Article V(3)(2)) but they also make clear that maladjustments in balances of payments should be corrected without resorting to measures destructive of national or international prosperity (Article I(V)). The case for counter-cyclical Fund policies, as already stated above, necessitates an array of resources from unconditional to highly conditional, depending on circumstances.

Dissatisfaction with Fund-supported programmes is not limited to developing countries. The address of US Treasury Secretary Baker to the annual meetings of the IMF and World Bank in October 1985 stressed the importance of ensuring that adjustment under Fund-supported programmes would be combined with growth. In so doing, Baker was saying implicitly that the programmes of austerity and economic contraction (characteristic of the IMF in the past) were no longer acceptable either to the developing countries or to the industrial countries. The principal criticism of these programmes by developing countries is that:

> [I]rrespective of the causes of balance of payments difficulties, the Fund generally has insisted on heavy reliance on demand management policies for correcting maladjustments in external payments. Thus, developing countries have been required to curtail demand as a means of adjusting to changes in the external environment – such as the decline in growth of world trade, changes in energy prices, the declines in the availability of finance, soaring interest rates, and exchange rate variations, among others – even though these factors were already constricting their growth. (G-24, 1987, para. 21)

The policies of expenditure reduction prescribed by the Fund have led to substantial losses of output and sharp curtailment of investment even in export industries. These losses have often been aggravated by import compression while expenditure-switching policies involving devaluation have added considerably to inflationary pressures. Moreover, some studies have shown that Fund programmes almost invariably require much more severe constraints on the level of demand than would be necessary to attain their balance-of-payments objectives – resulting in widespread non-compliance and continuous breakdowns and revisions of the programmes.

If the adjustment-with-growth objectives of the Baker Plan are to be attained, Fund-supported programmes must be designed quite differently. Where the availability of finance for balance-of-payments support is very limited – as it usually is – and no effort is made to raise additional funds, the programmes emerging from the Fund's financial exercises will almost inevitably be sharply deflationary, imposing declines in both output and investment. If the Fund is to take the growth objective seriously, it has to assess the external capital requirements of growth-oriented adjustment programmes and then participate actively in mobilizing the financial support needed over and above what the Fund itself can provide. At times of pressure on Fund resources, the Fund should be entitled to borrow from governments or even from capital markets. Adjustment programmes that go beyond demand compression and seek to effect structural changes (for developing new export capabilities and efficient substitutes for imports) inevitably call for more investment which, in most developing countries, has a high direct or indirect import content in the form of capital goods, intermediates, raw materials and other essential supplies.

The content of conditionality raises a whole spectrum of difficult problems. Since the external and internal transactions of any economy are closely interrelated, policies to deal with domestic economic problems usually have implications for the balance of payments. This consideration is held to justify involvement of the IMF in the domestic policies of its members. At the same time, it would be absurd to suppose that the World Bank and the IMF have the capability to direct the affairs of the developing countries from Washington. Moreover, in a democratic society, those who run the economy are expected to be answerable to political constituencies while the World Bank and the IMF only report to their member governments. There is, therefore, a strong case for limiting conditionality to the balance of payments. The World Bank and the IMF have a legitimate stake in balance-of-payments adjustment and, even if that implies examination of domestic policy variables, there is no need for such variables to form part of their conditions for lending.

Limiting conditionality to the balance of payments does not dilute performance requirements. On the contrary, such conditionality can be every bit as tough as that conditionality addressed to monetary targets. With the failure of money-demand functions to perform in a predictable manner, one never really knows the effects on the balance of payments when the economy achieves (or fails to achieve) a particular monetary target. With a balance-of-payments target, the Fund and its member countries would know exactly where the borrower stands – when additional measures are needed and when they can be relaxed. Contingency mechanisms must be built firmly into Fund-supported programmes so that conditionality provisions can be reviewed in the event that there are any changes in the external conditions affecting a country's adjustment for reasons beyond its control. In particular, the failure of a programme to generate the rate of growth that had been anticipated should automatically trigger a reconsideration of the entire programme and, if necessary, the provision of supplementary resources.

One aspect of conditionality that went largely unnoticed until UNICEF drew attention to it is the effect of adjustment programmes on vulnerable groups within the population, particularly children. UNICEF reported rising levels of malnutrition and increases in morbidity in many parts of the world beginning in the early 1980s. Adjustment programmes, said UNICEF, were transmitting and usually multiplying the impact on the poor and the vulnerable. UNICEF advocated a policy of 'adjustment with a human face' – a conscious commitment to the protection of basic human welfare as part and parcel of adjustment programmes, sustaining in particular the minimum nutrition levels of children and other specially vulnerable groups (Cornia *et al.*, 1987). The IMF and World Bank expressed their full support of the objectives of the UNICEF drive but it is too early to tell whether this support is being translated into the requisite modifications of the lending programmes of these institutions.

The debt overhang
Views differ as to how much the world debt crisis is due to systematic factors as against the improvidence of individual countries and governments, but several points should be non-controversial. First, as noted earlier, it was a unanimous decision of the entire Fund membership that countries should accept the deficits resulting from the first oil shock and avoid attempts at deficit reduction that would merely have the effect of shifting the burden elsewhere. Secondly, the policy of recycling petrodollar surpluses through the commercial banks rather than through the multilateral financial institutions was disastrous. The multilaterals would probably have exercised better control of their lending programmes than the commercial banks did and they would not have transferred the entire interest-rate risk to the borrowers. Finally, the IMF is now deeply involved in the world debt problem in a capacity that is often difficult to reconcile with the need for the Fund to be regarded by all its members as an objective and independent entity, able to take an impartial view of the relations between debtors and creditors.

Apart from these considerations, the magnitude of the debt problem, its role in causing a widespread and long-lasting economic depression in the Third World, a perverse net transfer of resources from low-income to high-income countries, a blocking of the normal channels of trade and stimulation to protectionism in the industrial countries, and (above all) the continuing increase in total volume of debt – all these factors must be a source of anxiety for those concerned with the future security of the IMS. By one means or another, the debt overhang must be greatly reduced if it is not to constitute a persistent threat to the IMS. Also the reduction cannot come about through repayment of the entire debt, either now or in the future, unless the industrial countries step up their rates of growth and import demand to the levels that prevailed during the Bretton Woods period – something that is quite feasible but is beyond reach for political reasons in the foreseeable future.

Given this situation, there is no alternative to a programme of massive debt relief for official and market borrowers alike. Thus far, proposals for such relief have failed to win support in the quarters that have the power of decision in this field. One reason is the mistaken impression that debt relief would make it more difficult to secure a return to voluntary lending by the commercial banks – although, in the absence of debt relief, there is no plausible scenario for the return of voluntary lending.[2] The second reason is that the governments of the creditor-countries are not prepared to face public opinion with the acknowledgement that these countries must bear their fair share of the burden of debt relief.

Failing effective action, there is nothing but trouble ahead for the IMS. The Fund will find itself increasingly embroiled in conflict with member countries whose peoples will be insisting that their governments emulate the behaviour of the governments of developed countries that often escaped their debt obligations under much less severe political and economic pressure than is now being experienced by the developing countries. As Tarshis (1987) pointed out, the Allies' treatment of Germany after World War I was, in regard to reparations, incomparably more lenient than that now meted out to the developing country debtors. The repudiation of reparations by Germany in 1933 was used by the formerly allied European countries in partial justification for defaulting on their war debts to the US. There was no doubt some substance in this contention – although stronger justification could be found in the devastating effects of the US depression, the surge of US protectionism in the Smoot–Hawley Act of 1930, and the sudden drying up of US capital outflows. If the outright defaults of the industrial countries in the 1930s can be defended, then certainly the circumstances of today call for debt relief on a scale sufficient to permit a resumption of investment and growth in the Third World.

Problems of universality
Recent changes in the economic policies of the Soviet Union obviously raise the question of its participation in the international monetary and trading systems and of membership in the IMF and GATT. Many

obstacles to such participation and membership may be eased as the new policies gather momentum. The USSR participated actively in the Bretton Woods Conference and would have been entitled to claim membership both in the IMF and in the World Bank but was unwilling to supply some of the information required under the Articles of Agreement, such as the level of gold and foreign-exchange reserves. Now its readiness to provide the military information needed under the recent Agreement on Intermediate-range Nuclear Forces and to permit inspection in that context suggests that the earlier unwillingness to release economic information may likewise be modified. Despite participation at Bretton Woods, the USSR would have to apply for membership of the IMF and World Bank and would then go through the normal procedures to be accepted by the Boards of Governors. A liberalization of its international economic policies would probably not have much effect on the functioning of the IMS. The rouble exchange rate appears to be pegged to a basket of Western currencies in a fairly conventional way.

Throughout the international monetary crisis of the past 20 years, the USSR has not created any difficulties for the system and is even less likely to do so in the event of improved East–West relations in the political and military fields. It favours a major role for gold in the system but this is, presumably, the point of view of a gold producer rather than of a socialist country as such. Very few members of the IMF support a return to the gold standard but a role for commodities (including gold) in the macromanagement of the world economy has been suggested by Baker, as noted earlier. Certain questions would arise if the USSR sought membership in the IMF. It is unlikely to avail itself of the Fund's conditional credit facilities because of an unwillingness to subject itself to the requirements of conditionality. Regarded by private capital markets as creditworthy, the USSR would, in the absence of some major catastrophe, utilize the borrowing facilities available in those markets in the event of a need for balance-of-payments support. Under conditions of détente, it might also borrow from other governments on favourable terms. There is no reason to think that it would have any difficulty with the SDR arrangements of the Fund or that it would itself cause difficulties for those arrangements.

One possible difficulty is that, under Article VIII of the Articles of Agreement, no member of the Fund may impose restrictions on the making of payments and transfers for current international transactions. However, many new members (including Poland) have availed themselves of the transitional arrangements in Article XIV, whereby a member 'may, notwithstanding the provisions of any other articles of this Agreement, maintain and adapt to changing circumstances the restrictions on payments and transfers for current international transactions that were in effect on the date on which it became a member.' The USSR could also, presumably, claim Article XIV status, although it would be expected to make some effort to move to Article VIII status in due course. In principle, the Fund may (under Article XIV, Section 3) require a member to move from Article XIV to Article VIII status but this provision has never been invoked and there is no reason to think that it would be invoked in the case of the USSR.

More significant in the long run, probably, is the problem of accommodating a country as important as the USSR in the procedures and decision-making process of the Fund. Under the system of weighted voting in the Bretton Woods institutions, formal challenges to the dominance of the major powers have been rare. Although the developing countries could, in principle, muster a collective veto on many of the Fund's decisions requiring qualified majorities, in practice issues are never allowed to reach that stage. Instead negotiations continue until the requisite degree of consensus is achieved. Occasionally, however, a proposal favoured by the industrial countries has been dropped for lack of support by the developing countries. A successful application by the USSR would, of course, result in the assignment of a quota to that country, insufficient to give the USSR a veto on any Fund decision. However, the USSR would almost certainly seek to join the US, UK, Federal Republic of Germany, France, Japan, Saudi Arabia and China in having the right to appoint an Executive Director to the Executive Board and might well make its willingness to join conditional on the granting of this request.

Inevitably, the present members of the IMF would be concerned as to how the admission of the USSR to membership would affect the political balance of the Fund. They would have to reckon with the probability that it would have a distinctive point of view on matters coming up for decision. It might be able, from time to time, to mobilize sufficient support from other members to make the achievement of consensus a complex and difficult process. The impact on decision-making in the Fund is, however, ultimately a question of political accommodation that could probably be solved in the long run if the improvement in East–West relations in other fields went far enough.

Democratizing the decision-making process
Cooper's idea of strengthening the Interim Committee could be a step in the direction of democratizing the decision-making process in the IMS. As long ago as 1973, at the annual meetings of the Fund and World Bank, US Treasury Secretary Shultz advanced the view that 'The logic is strong that for the Fund to act effectively, member governments should have

available a forum of workable size within the organization at which responsible national officials can speak and negotiate with both flexibility and authority.' Subsequently the Committee of Twenty (1974, p. 18) recommended the establishment of a permanent and representative Council, with one member appointed from each Fund constituency and with the participation of the Managing Director. The Council, which was to meet regularly, three or four times a year as required, 'will have the necessary decision-making powers to supervise the management and adaption of the monetary system, to oversee the continuing operation of the adjustment process, and to deal with sudden disturbances which might threaten the system.'

Pending the amendment of the Articles of Agreement that was required to set up the new Council, the Board of Governors, in September 1974, established an Interim Committee structured along the lines of the Committee of Twenty. Until the requisite amendment was adopted, the new Committee could have only advisory powers even though it invariably met – and continues to meet – at ministerial level. Decisions remained in the hands of the Executive Board except where the endorsement of the Governors themselves was required under the Articles. It is, however, the Interim Committee that has survived and the Permanent Council that has been shelved. De Vries explains this by suggesting that 'some long-time Executive Directors were concerned about a possible loss of power by the Executive Board' and that some of the Executive Directors elected by developing country members 'regarded themselves as more experienced than their finance ministers who tended to be in office only for short periods'.

A more important consideration for developing countries may have been that they were sceptical of the capacity of the IMF, with its weighted voting, to be even-handed in its treatment of Fund members. They were prepared to accept a strong high-level Council in the Fund if that body were prepared to lean as heavily on the key currency countries as on the weaker members. If, however, this were not to be the case, the developing countries could only lose from a strengthening of Fund machinery. Hence the continuation in being of the Interim Committee might, they thought, be the best compromise. This Committee, with its consensus procedure, gives developing countries a role in the political decision-making process in the Fund without creating the danger of high-level political pressures upon the less powerful countries.

Whether decision-making in the Fund would have become more democratic if the Permanent Council had been established is debatable. Members of the Executive Board, as officials of the Fund separated from their home countries, might tend to be more susceptible to institutional influences than officials coming to periodic meetings from capitals would be. This consideration weighed heavily with Keynes in opposing the US view of the Board as a body of officials earning high salaries and resident at IMF headquarters. He proposed that the Board should not be in permanent session but should provide opportunities for senior officials of the Central Banks and Treasuries to meet together at intervals in 'a truly international body for consultation and cooperation on monetary and financial problems' (Moggridge, 1980, p. 221). The US view of the Board prevailed at the Savannah Conference, prompting the comment from Keynes (p. 227) that 'the strength of the new institutions [i.e. of the World Bank as well as of the Fund] has been impaired both for effective action and for unwise interference alike'. On the other hand, it is unlikely the G-7 countries would have been more inclined towards a sharing of their decision-making powers with other Fund members simply because of the creation of a Permanent Council.

Far from there being any current pressure for the establishment of the Permanent Council recommended by the Committee of Twenty, even the opportunities provided by the existence of the Interim Committee have not been fully utilized. The Committee normally meets only twice a year for one day each time, which is insufficient to allow for serious discussion or negotiation of any major policy issue in depth. Thus the participation of Ministers of Finance and Governors of Central Banks does not mean that major policy issues are given thorough high-level examination. The Committee does make significant recommendations to the Executive Board for action but mainly on the basis of the Board's own submissions. The G-24 would like the degree of the developed country voting dominance (in the Interim Committee and Executive Board alike) to be somewhat reduced but they do not aim at unweighted voting. This, however, is only the formal side of the question. The more important issue for the 1990s is to persuade the G-10 or the G-7 to engage in a meaningful dialogue on the salient problems arising in the international monetary and financial system. Given that the predominant influence on the decision-making process will remain in the hands of the G-7, it is reasonable to expect a growing willingness of the group to consult non-members in advance so that all interests could be taken adequately into account. That would require a great deal more than the perfunctory exchanges of views that take place at the one-day meetings, twice a year, of the Interim Committee.

Notes

1. In April 1988, the IMF adopted in principle a contingency mechanism in combination with CFF to make it possible to 'maintain the momentum of adjustment in the face of

a wider range of adverse external shocks' (IMF, 1988, para. 7). The wider range of shocks, it is understood, may include increases in interest rates on funds borrowed from abroad. While this decision represents an important new departure and a modest enhancement of the range of IMF capabilities to respond to the balance-of-payments needs of its members (severely limited, however, by an increase in access to resources quite inadequate to the scale of demands likely to arise), it does not alter the fact noted earlier that the original character of CFF has been so changed as to prevent its use as a countercyclical instrument with – in Cooper's words – 'little or no conditionality'. This can be seen from the statement by the Interim Committee that '[U]se of the contingency element would be attached to a Fund-supported adjustment program' (ibid.). It is indeed a curious example of IMF logic that, under this formula, country A would be required to adopt strict measures of adjustment simply because country B, the source of a past variable-interest rate loan to A, decides for domestic reasons having nothing to do with A to raise interest rates – even temporarily. Indeed, B's need to raise interest rates could conceivably be the result of mismanagement of aggregate domestic demand. The fact that A was not responsible would in no way relieve it of the need for strong measures of adjustment in return for a contingency drawing, while B would be under no compulsion to adjust unless it was forced to seek IMF assistance – something that is not very likely if B happens to be an industrial country.

2. Portes (1987) has pointed out the proposition that debt relief would block debtors' access to international capital markets for an indefinite period is contradicted by the historical evidence. Countries obtaining debt relief have not suffered subsequent loss of access to capital markets to any greater extent than the countries that met their commitments in full. On the contrary, under the right conditions debt relief tends to increase creditworthiness, not reduce it.

References

Akyuz, Y. and S. Dell (1987), 'Issues in international monetary reform', in *International Monetary and Financial Issues for the Developing Countries*, UNCTAD.

Committee of Twenty (1974), *International Monetary Reform: Documents of the Committee of Twenty*, IMF.

Cooper, R.N. (1987), 'The evolution of the international monetary system toward a world central bank', in *The International Monetary System, Essays in World Economics*, MIT Press.

Cornia, A.C., R. Jolly and F. Stewart (eds.) (1987), *Adjustment with a Human Face: Protecting the Vulnerable and Promoting the Growth*, Oxford University Press.

Crocket, A. and M. Goldstein (1987), *Strengthening the International Monetary System: Exchange Rates, Surveillance and Objective Indicators*. IMF Occasional Paper No. 50.

Dell, S. (1985), 'The fifth credit tranche', *World Development*, February.

Dell, S. (1986), *The World Debt Problem: A Diagnosis, Report to the Group of Twenty-Four*, UNCTAD/MFD/TA/33.

De Vries, M.G. (1985), *The International Monetary Fund 1972–78*, Vol. 1, IMF.

Gold, J. (1979), *Conditionality*, IMF Pamphlet Series No. 31.

Group of Ten (1966), *Communiqué of Ministers and Governors and Report of Deputies*, July.

Group of Ten (1985), 'The functioning of the international monetary system', *IMF Survey*, Supp., July.

Group of Twenty-four (1985), 'The functioning and improvement of the international monetary system', *IMF Survey*, Supp., September.

Group of Twenty-four (1987), 'The role of the IMF in adjustment with growth', *IMF Survey*, Supp., August.

Guitián, M. (1981), *Fund Conditionality*, IMF Pamphlet Series No. 38.

International Monetary Fund (1974), *Annual Report 1974*.

International Monetary Fund (1984), *Exchange Rate Volatility and World Trade*, Study by the Research Department, IMF Occasional Paper No. 28.

International Monetary Fund (1988), *IMF Survey*, 18 April, 114–17.

Kaldor, N. (1978), *Further Essays on Applied Economics*, London: Duckworth.

Kaldor, N. (1983), 'The role of commodity prices in economic recovery', *Lloyds Bank Review*, July.

Kenen, P. (1987), 'What role for IMF surveillance?', *World Development*, December.

Keynes, J.M. (1936), *The General Theory of Employment, Interest and Money*, London: Macmillan.

Lamfalussy, A. (1987), 'Current-account imbalances in the industrial world; why they matter', in *International Monetary Cooperation: Essays in Honor of Henry C. Wallich*, Princeton, NJ.

Moggridge, D. (ed.) (1980), *The Collected Writings of John Maynard Keynes*, Vol. 26, London: Macmillan and Cambridge University Press.

Portes, R. and B. Eichengreen (1987), in *Threats to International Financial Stability*, R. Portes and A.K.Swoboda (eds), Cambridge University Press.

Shultz, G.P. (1973), 'Statement by the Governor of the Fund and World Bank for the United States', *Summary Proceedings of the Annual Meeting of the Board of Governors*, 1973, IMF.

Tarshis, L. (1987), *German Reparations and the Debt of the LDCs*, mimeo.

Tobin, J. (1978), 'A proposal for international monetary reform', *The Eastern Economic Journal*, 3, July/October.

Comment by Michael Dealtry

In his comments on the SDR, Dell puts forward the view that the refusal of the industrial countries in recent years to agree to issue SDR is 'a violation of the Articles of Agreement [of the IMF] which require all member countries to cooperate with the fund in making the SDR the principal reserve asset in the IMS'. There is one important stand in the argument of some industrial countries on this matter to which Dell does not refer. It is that 'in all its decisions with respect to the allocation . . . of the Special Drawing Rights the Fund shall seek to meet the long-term global need, as and when it arises, to supplement existing reserve assets', (Article XVIII of the Fund's Article of Agreement).

In recent years, while a large number of developing countries have been short of reserves, industrial countries, and some LDCs too, have not been in that position. Indeed at the present time a number of countries' reserves are more than adequate and, in addition, those countries are in a position to add to their reserves, if they so wish, by borrowing in the international markets. Consequently, it can be, and has been, argued that the shortage of reserves in recent years has not been global in nature. The failure of what can be generally agreed to be a global shortage of reserves to emerge is in part the result of creditworthy countries' ability to borrow reserves in the market. This may or may not be a good thing but it is a fact. It is a feature of the IMS that did not exist at the end of the 1960s, when the SDR facility was created, and it perhaps suggests that the facility itself, and the conditions for using it, may need to be re-examined in the light of the changes that have occurred over the past 20 years in the way in which additional reserves are created in the system.

10 External impacts of the United States' financial policies

Peter M. Oppenheimer

Discussion of the external impacts of the United States' financial policies is of interest for several reasons. Although the United States' GNP is today a considerably smaller fraction of non-communist world's GNP than it was in the 1950s and 1960s, it remains by far the largest single national product in the system. Moreover, despite the lower GNP share of the US, the influence of the United States upon the global conjuncture has generally been perceived as larger in the past 15 years than in the previous 20 years. The most important single reason for this perception is the international integration of credit markets, which, since the early 1970s, has greatly magnified the global impact of US monetary conditions in particular. It is true that the principal exchange rates in the system have floated during this period, ostensibly allowing monetary trends in different currency areas to diverge. However, so far as large countries are concerned, the scope for such divergence is limited in practice.

There have also been some fairly major and clear-cut shifts in US policy during the past 15 years. Monetary policy eased in the aftermath of the first oil price shock (1974–75), enabling the United States to lead the world recovery from recession in the second half of the 1970s. Then came the sharp tightening of money, combined with the shift to money-base regulation, initiated by the Federal Reserve under Volcker in autumn 1979. Other countries followed suit (or, in the case of the UK, were actually ahead of the US) in imposing restrictive policies to curb inflation. This monetary stringency, together with the second oil shock of 1979–80, brought about the world recession of 1980–82. The US monetary squeeze was subsequently relaxed in two main stages. The first stage occurred after August 1982 in response to the world debt crisis. The second stage followed during 1985 in response to the dollar's overvaluation and the mounting protectionist pressures which this was generating. At least until 1985, the relaxation of monetary policy was more cautious and partial than in 1975. The main policy stimulus to the US economy came this time from fiscal policy, that is, from the Federal budget deficit created by the combination of Reagan's tax cuts and higher defence outlays. The years 1981–84 then saw the United States running a policy mix of easy budgets and tight money. Like the easy monetary policy of 1975–78, the fiscal stimulus put the United States out in front in recovering from the 1980–82 recession. The final reason for interest in the US financial policies is that European policy-makers, including the EEC Commission, have maintained a more or less continuous stream of complaints since the early 1970s (indeed since the early 1960s) about these financial policies, blaming them for a large share of Europe's own economic difficulties. Without commenting on the political aspects of these complaints, it is interesting to assess the cogency of the economic reasoning involved here.

In order to analyse the external impacts of the US policy, we distinguish between target variables and transmission mechanisms. The main target variables are real GNP and its fluctuations; inflation; international payments balances; and real interest rates. As regards transmission mechanisms, at least four channels should be distinguished; namely, Keynesian expenditure flows (with approximately constant relative prices); competitiveness effects of real exchange-rate movements; terms-of-trade effects of real exchange-rate movements; and portfolio balance effects. Not all target variables are of equal welfare significance, and the boundary between target variables and transmission mechanisms is somewhat arbitrary. For instance, real interest rates are of concern not so much in themselves but rather because of their implications for capital accumulation and growth and for the financial viability of debtors. Also, the transmission mechanisms may interact in various ways. For instance, changes in portfolio preferences will affect exchange rates and hence competitiveness and the terms of trade.

The basic theoretical apparatus for analysing external aspects of fiscal and monetary policies is the Mundell–Fleming model and its extensions, including contributions by Mundell, Branson, Corden, Dornbusch, Mussa and others. The core of this model assumes a small country, whose policies have negligible global repercussions. The terms of trade are externally given and portfolio preference considerations are ignored – so only the first two transmission mechanisms are considered. Furthermore, the country's economic situation and policies are usually assumed to be unsynchronized with the rest of the world (for example, the country experiences recession while the world at large is in a boom). In addition, the model makes the 'Keynesian' assumptions of constant money wages and a margin of unemployment.

US policies plainly have a global impact so the small-country assumption must be dropped. Also, consideration should be given to prior economic trends and policies in other countries in so far as they affect the global context in which the US operates. Admittedly, this point could be applied to the small-country version as well. Synchronized national policies would significantly alter the analysis. It is not possible, for instance, for all currencies to depreciate at the same time. The constant money wage assumption also cannot easily be maintained. Countries seek the best possible combination of high employment and price stability. This does not mean that one has to assume an identifiable Phillips curve trade-off, even in the short run, between unemployment and inflation. It does mean that one or other target may, at certain times, receive overriding priority from policy-makers, depending on the economic situation and on the government's social welfare function.

The dollar exchange rate has been on a floating basis since the early 1970s. In the Mundell–Fleming framework, the first general effect of dropping the small country assumption is to lessen the significance of the exchange-rate regime for policy impacts in the home country. Both fiscal and monetary policy have 'closed-economy' impacts on the home country under both fixed and floating exchange rates. Their magnitude may, of course, vary and some of it is achieved indirectly via repercussions upon global economic conditions and other countries' policies. The second point is that attention must be given to the *direction* of the home country's policy impact upon the outside world. An expansionary impetus at home may exercise either an expansionary influence ('positive transmission', to use Corden's terminology) or a restrictive one ('negative transmission') upon other countries. One possible example of negative transmission cited by Corden would be a US economic upswing which raises world oil or other commodity prices. This development would boost income and expenditure in commodity-exporting countries but it would call forth restrictive impacts and policies in Western Europe and Japan.

The usual Mundell–Fleming classification of policy actions distinguishes between 'pure' fiscal policy (a change in government expenditure or tax rates with money stock constant) and 'pure' monetary policy (either open-market operations or some form of 'outside' money creation, such as a one-shot budget deficit). Corden, though not precisely departing from this approach, treats the 'pure' policy cases as different mixtures of transmission mechanisms. He begins by distinguishing between pure 'locomotive' and 'capital-market' transmission mechanisms. The former is characterized by a change in US output and employment but without an imbalance on current external payments. The latter involves the opposite; namely, an external imbalance but no change in US output or employment, with the monetary-fiscal policy mix being geared to achieve this result.

Corden's main reason for adopting this approach appears to lie in the major importance which he attributes to the terms-of-trade transmission mechanism. This mechanism tends in general to work in opposite directions in the 'locomotive' and 'capital-market' cases. The need to equilibrate the US current balance of payments at a higher output level is assumed to worsen the US terms of trade and improve that of the foreign country, say Germany, thereby allowing a *ceteris paribus* increase in German real wages, which implies a favourable (leftward) shift in the German Phillips curve. Now it is true that the Mundell–Fleming model neglects this line of transmission and that it could, in principle, be important once allowance is made for target real wages or other forms of real-wage inflexibility. Similarly, it is true that Mundell's extension of his model in 1963 to the large-country case maintains rather rigidly Keynesian assumptions in the monetary domain – constant nominal money supply and average price level in the foreign country, even in the face of an exchange-rate movement. Corden points out that various standard Mundell–Fleming results no longer hold when these assumptions are relaxed. In my opinion, however, it is necessary to apply a little dose of Friedman's positive methodology here. A full taxonomy of alternative assumptions produces a hopelessly wide and unenlightening range of possible results. Empirical research or empirical judgements are called for to decide which set or sets of assumptions appear to give insight into actual events.

In this spirit, it must be said that the practical importance of the terms-of-trade/real-wage mechanism is unclear. The US monetary expansion of 1975–78 may be taken as an example. According to Corden, US monetary expansion – by depreciating the dollar – will bring a twofold improvement via both locomotive and capital-market effects in Germany's terms of trade and, thereby, it acts in an expansionary way. Mundell, on the other hand, argues that DM appreciation will have a contractionary effect in Germany, a case of negative transmission. This arises through Germany's loss of competitiveness, coupled with the fall of interest rates which ensures equilibrium in the money market despite a fall in money income. Any positive effect arising from the higher US income and employment is too small to alter the net outcome for Germany.

The two positions of Corden and Mundell may be reconciled by pointing out that Corden's expansionary effect presupposes that German policy-makers respond to the inward shift of the Phillips curve by taking steps to boost economic activity; whereas Mundell's agreement takes German policy to remain unchanged, which it obviously need not do and in 1978–79 actually did not do. German monetary and fiscal policy – and even more strikingly Swiss monetary policy – was at that time shifted to a more expansionary tack. The German government also took the initiative towards establishing the EMS as from March 1979 in the hope that this might cause higher portfolio demand for non-dollar assets to be spread more widely in future and be less concentrated on the DM. However, the perception in Germany and Switzerland at the time of the dollar depreciation/Euro-appreciation was closer in spirit to Mundell than to Corden. Appreciation was seen as a threat to the export competitiveness and even to the viability of European corporations and not as a welcome opportunity to move up the Phillips curve. This perception was also in the spirit of Dornbusch's 'exchange-rate overshooting' analysis (*Scandinavian Journal of Economics*, 1976), which itself is based on Mundell's model. A flexible exchange rate allows a country to opt out of global inflation fully only if its currency is not subject to severe overshooting. If it is so subject, then the stickiness of domestic money wages may oblige the country to participate in world inflation to some extent in order to curb the overshooting.

I turn now to the specific impacts of US financial policies in the 1980s. The US policy mix that developed in the first half of the decade was one of tight money and easy budgets. The tight money came first, beginning in autumn 1979, a good two years before the emergence of the Reagan budgetary stimulus. It had two immediate effects on financial variables: it raised interest rates worldwide and it started the dollar exchange rate on its upward path. The second effect, unlike the first, was expansionary for other countries *via* the competitiveness mechanism (and disregarding the terms-of-trade aspect). As it happens, other industrial countries were no longer seeking much of a demand stimulus. On the contrary, they joined enthusiastically in tightening money, especially after the second oil price shock of 1979–80, in order to put an end to high inflation. Still, aside from the United Kingdom in the first flush of Thatcherism, the monetary squeeze on non-dollar currencies was not enforced to the point of halting the recovery of the dollar. After all, other countries had been very concerned about the undervalued level to which the dollar had sunk in 1977–78 and were keen to see this reversed.

World recession and high real interest rates triggered the debt crisis some 2½ years later in August 1982. This gave a further upward push to the dollar of some two years' duration through the portfolio-preference transmission channel. Bankers and, to some extent, trade creditors in the United States and elsewhere shifted their lending preference away from Third World loans towards US securities and credit markets. During these years (1982–84), European policy-makers complained about high real interest rates emanating from the United States (which they charged with discouraging investment and harming employment) and about the ever-rising dollar (which they charged with obstructing the cure of inflation in Europe). The strictures on the rising dollar can be rationalized *à la* Corden by reference to terms-of-trade/real-wage effects. Yet the complaints were one-sided since they overlooked the stimulative effects on Europe's competitiveness of exchange-rate depreciation.

At the same time, from 1982 onwards, the US fiscal deficit entered the picture. This imparted a major Keynesian direct stimulus to the US economy, helped, to be sure, by the price-stabilizing impact (in US dollar terms) of the rising exchange rate. The US entered a new economic upswing with a rapid two year take-off far more vigorous than in other industrial countries. Externally, the indirect impact was to reinforce the global shift of portfolio preferences in favour of the United States and hence further strengthen the dollar. The portfolio shift also facilitated the partial easing of US monetary policy by exercising some downward pressure on US security yields. In the early years, this was probably more important than the opposite effect stemming from the increased flow supply of US government debt. The Europeans, of course, argued that the US budget deficit was principally responsible for keeping real interest rates at historically high levels and for the continued upward pull on the dollar. How well founded were these complaints? I have noted that, by engendering the US economic upswing, the budget deficit indirectly enhanced the attraction of the United States to portfolio managers and foreign corporations, thus swelling the desired capital inflow. But can one identify any direct transmission channel, including upward pressure upon interest rates?

We should distinguish here between nominal and real appreciation. Even if the fiscal deficit caused no nominal appreciation, it might have been responsible for a real appreciation; that is, but for the deficit, prices of US non-traded goods might have risen less (or fallen more) relative to traded goods at any unchanged nominal dollar exchange rate. Thus there are two questions. Did the fiscal deficit cause the continuing nominal dollar appreciation in 1982–85? Even if it did not, was significant upward pressure generated on US wages and other non-traded prices? As regards the nominal appreciation, US nominal interest rates, and the positive differential between them and non-dollar rates, were conspicuously lowered after the onset of the debt crisis. In general, the fiscal deficit showed no sign of generating upward pressure on US interest rates until 1987. Up to that year, the rearrangement of international portfolio – together with the savings surpluses of the non-US world (mainly Japan and Germany, but also including others such as the United Kingdom and Switzerland) – produced an inflow of funds to the US greater than was needed to clear the currency market at a constant dollar rate. Possibly the rest of the world's surplus savings might have been smaller in the absence of the economic stimulus coming from the US 'twin deficits' but possibly not – in which case absence of the US fiscal expansion might have caused the dollar to appreciate more (not less) than it actually did.

As for the budget deficit having perhaps inflated prices of US non-tradables, this looks implausible in the light of continuing spare capacity within the US economy throughout the first half of the 1980s and, especially, the conspicuous absence of wage push. Average real wages in the US remained stable while, in Europe, they were increasing by 2–3 per cent a year. In short, I suggest that the US fiscal stimulus had little upward impact on dollar interest rates or the dollar exchange rate. The rising exchange rate, for its part, had – up to 1985 – the effect partly of lowering overall US inflation and partly of dampening or offsetting the domestic expenditure-increasing impetus of the budget. From the outside world's point of view, the rising dollar provided the key stimulus to recovery through the competitiveness-transmission mechanism. The budget deficit could be viewed as a back-up facility. Had the dollar not risen, much the same income stimulus would have been imparted to the outside world but somewhat later in time and chiefly through Keynesian demand flows rather than through competitiveness effects.

Since 1985, the dollar's strength has been reversed while the US 'twin deficits' have remained. This is a further indication that the budget deficit was not, in any direct way, responsible for the strong dollar. Essentially the dollar was brought down, after some initial nudges from monetary authorities, by a reversal of the portfolio-preference mechanism, especially on the part of non-US investors. The dollar's decline had a prompt and substantial effect on the US economy. Concern about long time-lags and overlapping J-curves under floating exchange rates is misplaced. A recent paper by Meade of the Federal Reserve provides explicit support for this view, showing *inter alia* that the US trade balance in 1987 would have been a lot worse if the exchange rate had remained high *ceteris paribus*. The impact has been on the internal balance, causing the United States' GNP in 1987 to stand 1 per cent or more higher than it otherwise would have done. Export volume gained from the lower dollar but faster expansion of business investment as well as consumption boosted imports. In other words, the internal effect of dollar depreciation has been symmetrical with that of dollar appreciation, lifting economic activity and, so far to a lesser extent, price inflation in the United States. Correction of the current external deficit is still waiting on effective action to narrow the budget deficit.

This assignment of policy impacts – the exchange rate to internal balance, fiscal policy to external – has been adumbrated in the US by McKinnon in particular. A decade and a half ago it was mistakenly put forward in relation to the UK by the so-called 'New Cambridge Group' under Godley. If it turns out to be correct for the current US situation, this is not because it rests on any fundamental law of economics, but simply because US savings/investment behaviour happens to fit it. The financial or savings surplus of the US private sector (households plus corporations) has been low and relatively stable over the business cycle, so that any excess financial deficit of the combined government sector has fed through promptly to the current balance of payments. There is no guarantee that this pattern will remain unchanged for the foreseeable future, although it may do so.

While dollar depreciation boosted US economic activity in 1986–88, we should also note the counterpart transmission mechanisms affecting other countries. Diminished competitiveness *vis-à-vis* the US has been largely offset by stronger import demand and, at the same time, the terms-of-trade/real-wage effect noted by Corden had facilitated more expansionary domestic policies. As of 1987–88, only Japan and – to a lesser extent and less appropriately – the UK achieved a significant acceleration of domestic demand. Absence of inflation in Germany has, however, remained conspicuous along with Germany's external current surplus so the opportunity for stimulus is undoubtedly there. In the longer run, global equilibrium may or may not require further depreciation of the dollar. At the present time, a change in world savings/investment patterns – increased financial saving in the US, diminished financial saving in Germany and Japan – is a more evident need which should be directly addressed.

A word remains to be added on real interest rates. If we deny the US budget deficit any disproportionate or unique role in keeping up interest rates, how do we explain the persistently high level of real interest rates worldwide into the late 1980s? The initial upward jump at the start of the decade was certainly due to monetary policy but this cannot apply to their persistence after seven or eight years. For one thing, monetary policy has not remained tight and, for another, it is implausible to attribute to monetary action such a prolonged effect upon a non-monetary variable. I do not think that we have a complete answer to the conundrum but inflationary expectations – and especially the long lag of those expectations or anxieties behind the realities of the day (a case, on the face of it, of emphatically non-rational expectations) – seem to be an important element.

In the 1970s, real interest rates were negative because price expectations seemed obstinately unwilling to catch up with reality. In the 1980s, the same obstinacy appears in reverse, and real rates were slow to decline to their historical norm. This development is particularly unfortunate from the standpoint of the world debt problem. It is an argument for some more generous form of assistance or relief to major sovereign debtors (quite apart from any remaining threat to world financial stability arising from the debt issue). The situation is as if creditor-countries had succumbed to a kind of collective moral hazard: having lent huge sums at initially low or negative real rates, they are happy to see those rates pushed up as high as possible, short of actually provoking default. Problems also arise in relation to economic growth and stability in the industrial countries. In the US and the UK, though not on a major scale in other countries, the rapid growth of credit in the later 1980s has gone first and foremost to finance not fixed investment but higher outlays on consumer durables. From a British standpoint, I must say that whatever may be done in international markets, there is a good case for reimposing administrative restrictions such as minimum down-payments upon the growth of consumer credit, which seems largely undeterred by real borrowing rates of over 20 per cent. Yet the phenomenon of high real rates has also been just as conspicuous in countries like Japan and Germany, where consumer credit is not extensive and where government borrowing, albeit large absolutely, is modest in relation to the flow of household and corporate savings.

References

Corden (1987), *Inflation, Exchange Rates and the World Economy*, 3rd edn, Chapter 11. See also earlier papers.
McKinnon, R.I. (1988), *Journal of Economic Perspectives*, 2.

Comment by L.D.D. Price

I find much to agree with in Oppenheimer's chapter, particularly the notion that the effects of US policies cannot be judged without considering how other governments and Central Banks will react. Even if it is no longer the hegemon, the effects of US policies on other countries are still so large that they are bound to react to them in deeds and words. There may often be a degree of ambivalence in these reactions. For instance, Europeans and others have rightly bemoaned the twin deficits and low private savings in the US, while quietly welcoming the demand stimulus from strong US growth as their own economies were depressed for much of the 1980s. How countries react to US actions obviously varies over time. As Oppenheimer points out, Corden is able to show that a monetary expansion in the US will have an expansionary effect in Germany because he assumes that the German authorities will respond as they did in the 1978 Locomotive episode. Clearly times change. Consider the reactions to the huge increases in foreign-exchange reserves of many countries which followed the support operations for the dollar, first in 1970–71 and then over the last two years. In 1971, many countries found themselves with adequate foreign-exchange reserves for the first time since before World War II and so they were free of the balance-of-payments constraint which they had long regarded as inhibiting the growth of their economies. The policy reactions to this situation contributed to the worldwide spending boom of the early 1970s and ultimately to a sharp upsurge in inflation. In contrast, there is little sign of the countries which have been amassing reserves over the last two years being tempted to follow similarly expansionary policies. Some countries might perhaps be taking a slightly more cautious line if their reserve position were less comfortable, but some key countries remain quite resistant to suggestions that they could take a less restrictive stance, despite high levels of unemployment and in some cases large current-account surpluses.

Turning to the continuing problem of the large US current-account deficit, I share Oppenheimer's agnosticism as to whether longer-run global equilibrium may or may not require further real depreciation of the dollar. It is clear that the US balance of payments is reacting to the depreciation of the dollar since 1985 and some effects of that improvement in competitiveness are no doubt still to come. However, with capacity utilization already high and unemployment low in the US, further progress must require some slowing in the growth of domestic demand below that of productive potential. There may be little room for further domestic demand growth during the remainder of 1988 if the current-account deficit is to be no higher than $130 billion at an annual rate at the beginning of next year. This is by no means a recipe for stagnation for it should be consistent with GNP growth at around 2 per cent per annum both this year and next as the trade deficit is reduced. If the balance of payments were not to improve at least to that degree, there must be some risk that financial markets would come to see the present position as unsustainable.

Comment by Michael Dealtry

I find myself in broad agreement with what Oppenheimer says in his chapter, so my remarks on it will be more in the nature of comments than criticisms. I take as my starting point his remark that one reason for examining the external impacts of US financial policies is that since the early 1970s, European policy makers have 'maintained a more or less continuous barrage of complaints' about US policies and have blamed them for a large share of Europe's own economic difficulties. There is a good deal of truth in this, although to speak of a barrage of complaints is perhaps putting the matter rather strongly. Such complaints, in fact, were not unknown before the period which his chapter covers. One notable example, from the beginning of the 1970s, was some European countries' reluctance to accept an adequate devaluation of the dollar against other currencies in December 1971, at the Smithsonian meeting of the Group of Ten. Four years before, the Europeans had been asking the United States to correct its external deficit but when, in August 1971, the US authorities indicated their willingness to accept a new structure of exchange rates between the principal currencies, some other G-10 countries fought hard to limit the devaluation of the dollar. In the event the dollar was devalued against gold by only 7.9 per cent and while some other G-10 countries at the same time revalued against gold by amounts ranging from 2.8 to 7.7 per cent, two countries, whom I will not name, could not fully accept even the modest devaluation of the dollar but themselves devalued against gold by 1 per cent.

In the third part of his chapter, Oppenheimer says that after 1982 Europeans were complaining that the US budget deficit was the principal factor responsible for keeping real interest rates at historically high levels and for the continued upward pull on the dollar's exchange rate and he discusses how well founded these complaints were. I agree that the budget deficit, by engendering the economic upswing in the US that began in 1982, put upward pressure on the dollar's exchange rate through increasing the attractions to foreigners of adding to their stock of investments in the USA. At the same time, however, it also seems to me that the budget deficit, by giving rise to an unusually high public sector borrowing requirement at a time when private credit demand was following an upward cyclical path, directly influenced the level of US interest rates and contributed to the dollar's devaluation. On the other hand, I believe that there was also a channel through which the budget deficit probably tended to limit the appreciation of the dollar's exchange rate. By stimulating economic activity in the US, it contributed to the emergence of large deficits on the current account of the US balance of payments, and these payments deficits provided extra dollar liquidity to the rest of the world.

Given foreigners' strong demand for US assets at that time, in the absence of the US budget deficit that demand would probably have caused the dollar to appreciate even more than it did.

Finally, I would like to comment on the remark that while a further depreciation of the dollar may be needed in order to achieve a better global equilibrium, the most pressing need now is for a change in world savings and investment patterns. Such a change is certainly needed; but I also believe that orderly financing by the market of continuing US current-account deficits, while the adjustment process is proceeding, means that the principal industrial countries should continue to resist further downward pressure on the dollar's exchange rate, should that occur. I would add that the present strength of US export performance, and the major improvement in the international competitive position of the US which that strength demonstrates, reinforces the case for following a policy of trying to stabilize the dollar.

11 Some reflections on the LDC debt crisis
Kari Levitt

The basic facts of the LDC debt problem are well known. There is general agreement on its proximate or immediate causes and there is widespread recognition that these debts cannot – indeed should not – be paid in the full measure of their face value. There is also agreement in opinion-setting quarters that measures must be taken to ensure new financing and to restore normal patterns of international capital movements from rich or mature creditors to new developing countries. There is less agreement concerning the underlying or basic reasons for the severity and persistence of the crisis which has particularly affected both the poor countries of sub-Sahara Africa and middle-income, semi-industrialized countries, most of them in Latin America. It was widely believed that the recovery of the industrialized world from the deep recession of 1981–82 combined with heroic adjustment measures undertaken by debtor countries in the early 1980s would enable them to 'export' themselves out of the crisis. Not so! The situation has substantially deteriorated since 1985 and the cost of stalled development rises exponentially with every year that passes.

The World Bank has recently warned that developing countries with acute debt problems face the risk of prolonged stagnation in real per capita income, greater poverty and more social unrest unless the leading industrial countries can correct the disequilibria in international payments imbalances created by their uncoordinated macroeconomic policies (See *World Development Report 1988*, p. 13). The industrialized world as a whole has been running a current-account deficit of $30–60 billion per annum with the rest of the world ($50 billion in 1987). The developing world is being forced to adjust to this perverse situation by import compression and measures to increase exports in an unfavourable international environment of severely declining real commodity prices and reduced capital flows. As a result of the excess of debt service over new capital flows, the developing world has been forced to generate large trade surpluses ($28 billion in 1987) and net transfers of resources to the industrialized countries of the order of $30 billion a year (see Table 11.1).

There is increasing disagreement concerning the policies which should be pursued by developing countries to decrease vulnerability to external

Table 11.1   Public and private long-term debt and financial flows in developing countries, 1980–86 (US$ billions)

Long-term debt and financial flows	1981	1982	1983	1984	1985	1986[a]	1987[a]
Debt disbursed and outstanding	498.0	556.9	639.4	713.8	783.6	870.7	930.5
Disbursements	124.3	116.6	99.1	92.3	88.7	85.7	90.0
(From private creditors)	91.4	84.2	66.5	58.6	57.3	47.5	49.0
Debt service	89.1	98.7	92.1	99.7	109.5	116.4	119.0
Principal repayments	47.5	49.7	44.7	46.8	54.8	60.8	64.0
Interest	41.7	48.9	47.2	52.8	54.7	55.6	55.0
Net transfers	35.2	17.8	7.1	− 7.3	− 20.8	− 30.7	− 29.0

Note: The 109 countries reporting under the Debtor Reporting System (DRS). Data for Poland are included only from 1984 onward.
  [a] Preliminary for 1986, estimated for 1987.
Source: World Bank, *World Debt Tables*, Vol. I (1987/88), p. xii.

shocks and achieve self-sustaining growth. The record of successes and failures in the developing world raises serious questions concerning the strategies of liberalization favoured by the IMF and the World Bank. There is no evidence that the liberalization measures which regularly accompany programmes negotiated with the Fund – and increasingly also required by the World Bank as a condition of access to structural adjustment loans – have contributed either to stability or to efficiency. Indeed, there is evidence to the contrary, particularly with respect to financial liberalization.

India, China and other poor countries relying principally on their own resources have escaped the devastating effects of uncontrolled incorporation into the disordered system of world trade and capital flows of the 1980s. The contrast with the experience of sub-Sahara Africa and Latin America gives strong grounds for reflection on the wisdom of accelerated integration into the nexus of world trade and payments, as advocated by the IMF and the World Bank. (For comparative performance, see Table 11.2.)

We suggest that the ultimate reason for the severity and intractability of the debt crisis is to be found in the disorders of the international system of finance and payments, and that the industrialized countries bear the primary responsibility for high real interest rates, weak commodity prices, increasing protectionist barriers and perverse capital movements. In particular, we point to the ballooning Eurocurrency and offshore international capital markets as a major contributing factor to the debt crisis of the semi-industrialized developing countries. The recycling of the surpluses of the 1970s by commercial banks, widely applauded by

Table 11.2   The crisis of the 1980s: key statistics for highly indebted (HIC) and sub-Sahara African (SSA) countries

1   *Annual growth of GNP per capital (%)*

	1980 GNP per capita (US$)	Population (million)	Average annual growth GNP percentage			
			1965–73	1973–80	1980–84	1987
Industrial countries	10,760	761	3.6	2.1	1.3	2.2
Developing countries	670	3,130	3.9	3.1	0.7	1.8
Low-income countries	270	2,124	2.9	2.5	5.1	3.1
High indebted countries (HIC)	1,770	494	4.5	2.8	− 3.7	− 0.5
Sub-Sahara Africa (SSA)	600	331	3.7	0.7	− 4.9	− 4.6

Source: World Development Report 1988, Table A8.

2   *Key debt statistics, 1987*

	DOD[a] ($US bil)	Nat exports[b] (US$ bil)	DOD as % exports	Interest on debt Official	Private	Debt services as % exports
Developing countries	886.0	27.6	145.3	170	38.9	20.2
Low-income countries	137.7	− 14.9	180.6	3.0	1.9	17.5
HIC	441.4	25.3	300.4	6.7	23.4	35.2
SSA	92.9	− 3.0	263.3	2.1	1.5	25.5

Note: [a] Debt outstanding and disbursed.
   [b] Goods and non-factor services.
Source: World Development Report 1988, Table A14.

3   *Average annual changes in volume of trade (%)*

	Export volumes		Import volumes	
	1973–80	1980–87	1973–80	1980–87
Developing countries	4.7	5.4	5.9	1.1
Low-income countries	4.7	6.8	5.6	6.4
Highly indebted countries	1.1	1.4	5.5	− 6.3
Sub-Sahara Africa	0.1	− 1.6	7.5	− 6.9

Source: World Development Report 1988, Table A15.

4   *Average annual changes in terms of trade (%)*

	1965–73	1973–80	1980–87	1986
Industrial countries	− 1.0	− 3.0	1.5	9.5
Developing countries	0.7	1.6	− 1.8	− 7.3
Low-income countries	1.7	− 2.5	0.2	− 2.0
Highly indebted countries	1.4	3.5	− 2.7	− 14.0
Sub-Sahara Africa	− 8.4	4.8	− 5.0	− 23.5

Source: World Development Report 1988, Table A9.

academic and governmental experts as an example of the efficiency of the private capital market, has proven to be a disaster. The major industrialized countries, who opposed proposals for the establishment of multilateral facilities for the recycling of excess reserves in the 1970s, bear a considerable share of the responsibility.

The Bretton Woods order, within which the process of political decolonization unfolded in the years following the end of World War II, has disintegrated with the end of fixed exchange rates, the internationalization of inflation and the privatization of credit-creation on an international scale. The system – set up in 1944 with the US as the top metropole and the dollar as the undisputed key currency – has become unravelled. Economic and financial power has increasingly been privatized and has become less subject to governmental control. The self-serving fiscal and monetary policies of the US in the Reagan era favoured speculation, unproductive short-term investments and capital flight from developing countries whose 'formal' economies are being ravaged by the burden of unilateral adjustment to a crisis not primarily of their making. The once powerful IMF has largely been reduced to the role of debt collector on behalf of the international banks while the World Bank is increasingly working in tandem with the Fund. Both agencies are underfunded and unduly influenced by economic theories which place an excessive and unrealistic faith in the capacity of market prices to allocate resources efficiently.

The proximate causes of the debt problem
Note the following causes:

— The unprecedented volume of (short maturity) Eurodollar sovereign loans extended by several hundred commercial banks to semi-industrialized developing countries in the belief, shared by creditors and debtors alike, that the high rates of GDP and export growth of the 1970s were sustainable.
— Banking innovations, including floating interest rates, cross default clauses, syndicated loans and the practice of borrowing short to lend long produced handsome profits for the banks, while shifting interest and exchange-rate risk to the borrower.
— Soaring nominal and real interest rates resulting from inflation-fighting policies by the industrialized countries in the early 1980s. Nominal Eurodollar rates reached 16 per cent p.a. in 1981. Real interest rates, which were approximately 3 per cent p.a. in 1965–73 and negative or very low from 1974 to 1980, jumped to levels of 5–8 per cent p.a. in the early 1980s and have remained high.

— The deep recession of 1981–82, created by the macroeconomic policies of the industrialized countries, and the partial nature of the recovery.
— Deteriorating commodity prices. Non-fuel commodity prices (in real terms) fell by 45 per cent from 1977 to 1982. The purchasing power of total exports of Latin America, which had more than doubled in the 1970s, stagnated and declined. In sub-Sahara Africa, the deterioration in real export prices since 1980 has been catastrophic, resulting in a reduction of the purchasing power of total exports of over 50 per cent from 1980 to 1987.
— Last but not least, the reverse stampede of the banks, starting in mid-1982, as private creditors fell over themselves to pull out of situations which had only recently appeared highly attractive. Capital inflows to Latin America, which had been running at levels of $30–40 billion p.a. plummeted to $5 billion in 1983.

Important contributing factors were investment in large projects with long gestation periods which could not be expected to yield returns capable of contributing to debt service when the crisis broke. Even more important, very large sums of money left these countries as flight capital before and after 1982. A considerable amount of this was financed by external borrowing particularly in those countries that had free capital convertibility. Capital flight has been a significant factor in debt-accumulation in Latin America. Thus, estimated flight capital from Argentina during 1972–82 was $31.3 billion. Nearly half of Venezuela's external debt is estimated to be due to capital flight. Total estimated capital flight for seven highly indebted countries was $92 billion or approximately one-third of total official debt of $307 billion. In Latin America, most privately incurred non-guaranteed debt was subsequently 'socialized' and added to the official external debt. After the onset of the debt crisis in 1982, domestic banks which had borrowed abroad on behalf of firms and individuals were bailed out by their Central Banks, who acquired their non-performing domestic assets and their foreign liabilities. Large-scale capital flight and private foreign borrowing continued side by side after the onset of the debt crisis. In Chile, Argentina, Mexico and Venezuela, the private sector benefited from official subsidization of private borrowing and from the assurance that the governments would ultimately assume private debts of their citizens to preserve the countries' international credit standing – or simply to bail them out. The burden of servicing official external debt is not being borne by the same people who benefited and (in the case of flight capital) continue to benefit from the operations of an internationalized capital market, which favours the 'internationalized' elites of the world including the privileged citizens of debtor countries. In usually frank language, the World Bank has commented (*World Development Report 1988*, p. 67):

> 'Capital flight' meant that the costs of stabilization were often inequitably distributed. The rich protected their income and wealth from devaluation and inflation by shifting assets abroad while the poor suffered real wage declines.

The crisis deepens

The situation of the semi-industrialized debtor countries has gravely deteriorated since 1985. The draconian adjustment measures put in place in Mexico and other highly indebted countries have failed to effect an economic turn around. Severe fiscal contractions and steep devaluations improved the external balance at the cost of reduced imports, investment, consumption and social services. Real wages fell in Mexico by 38 per cent from 1981 to 1986, in Brazil by 21 per cent from 1982 to 1984, and in Turkey by 45 per cent between 1981 and 1986. (See *World Development Report 1988*, p. 65.) It is remarkable that debt continues to be serviced.

Growth rates in industrialized countries slowed to an annual average of 2.5 per cent for 1980–87, as compared with 3.1 per cent p.a. for the 1970s and 5.0 per cent p.a. in the 1960s, the last decade of the Bretton Woods era. In spite of severe devaluations, export volumes for the HICs as a whole have increased very little, while real commodity prices (terms of trade) continued their steep decline. The poor countries of sub-Sahara Africa have been particularly severely affected by falling commodity prices throughout the 1980s, with a reduction of 23.5 per cent in 1986 alone. (See Culpepper, 1987, and Table 11.2.) The fall in oil prices brought little relief to oil-importers, while creating a serious crisis for indebted oil-exporters such as Mexico, Venezuela and Nigeria.

In the 17 countries designated as *highly indebted* (most of which are in Latin America), the deep cuts in imports, investment and consumption for 1983 and 1984 have not been restored. Average annual growth rates for the eight-year period 1980–88 for those 17 HICs are summarized as follows, using data from the World Bank's *World Debt Tables*:

- Compression of imports by 6.2 per cent p.a., compression of investment by 4.8 per cent p.a. and compression of per capita consumption by 1.6 per cent p.a.
- All HICs, except Morocco, suffered a compression of imports, in extreme cases at average annual rates of 19 per cent (Nigeria) and 11 per cent (Argentina). Thirteen countries seriously depleted their capital stock over the period, as reflected in the negative growth rate of investment.

- GDP growth approximated industrial country growth rates in only three countries: Brazil 3.4 per cent p.a., Columbia 2.8 per cent p.a. and Morocco 3.4 per cent p.a. For nine countries, GDP growth was negative or insignificantly small, resulting in an average growth rate for the 17 HICs of only 1.0 per cent p.a. This implies a cumulative reduction in GDP per capita for the period.
- Very few countries succeeded in generating a trade surplus. The average annual trade surplus of $24 billion was the result of surpluses in only four countries – two of them oil exporters: Mexico $9.1 billion, Brazil $8.6 billion, Argentina $3.1 billion and Venezuela $3.9 billion. The average annual trade surplus of $24 billion for these 17 countries represents an average growth of exports of only 1.4 per cent p.a.

This situation is not sustainable. These 17 middle-income, semi-industrialized countries (operating at severely reduced levels of imports, negative rates of investment and living standards below those of 10 or 20 years ago) are transferring capital at the rate of $20–30 billion p.a.

In 1985, the developing countries as a whole became net exporters of capital. According to World Bank data in its *World Debt Tables*, debt service of principal and interest ($345 billion) exceeded net capital inflows ($265 billion) by $80 billion during 1985–87, while outstanding debt increased by $216 billion over the same period. These figures pertain to all developing countries, whose total long-term official debt now stands at $931 billion. Capital inflows to developing countries in 1985–87 were running at a mere 40 per cent of average levels in the pre-crisis period of 1978–83. They consisted largely of involuntary rescheduling and refinancing operations and the capitalization of interest by private creditors. There has also been a modest increase in new finance by official creditors. Whereas Latin America has been transferring capital to the industrialized world since 1983 at the rate of $20–30 billion p.a., prior to 1985 these transfers were offset by normal net resource inflows to other parts of the developing world. Now, developing countries as a whole are transferring real resources to the industrialized countries at the rate of $21 billion (1985), $31 billion (1986), and $29 billion (1987). (See Table 11.1.) A compilation from OECD (due to Carey, 1987, p. 21) is presented in Table 11.3 for the original Baker Group of countries. This summarizes the transition from net resource inflows to net resource outflows in billions of dollars. Note the sharply declining net inflows of capital and continuing capital flight.

There is growing recognition, at least in some official quarters, that it is counter-productive in terms of the future stability of the international economic order to permit the debt crisis to continue without providing for an injection of capital sufficient to restart the process of economic growth

Table 11.3   Net financial transfers: original Baker Group of (15) countries. ($ billions)

	1980	1981	1982	1983	1984	1985	1986
1 Net inflow	51	52	42	19	19	15	12
2 Net investment income	−22	−32	−44	−39	−39	−38	−32
3 Net flight capital	−22	−25	−22	−16	−14	−12	−8
4 Net resource flow (1 + 2 + 3)	7	−5	−24	−36	−34	−35	−28

in the major debtor-countries. It should be noted that the smaller developing countries, whose debt is relatively insignificant to private creditors and whose markets are similarly insignificant to industrialized country exporters, do not have the leverage to force the world to address their problems – which are more intractable by virtue of the constraints that their relatively small size places on development options.

The banks make provision to write off bad loans
Over the past number of years, and particularly in 1987, the banks have been making provision for the writing down of non-performing loans to developing countries and are plainly unwilling to engage in new voluntary lending. By mid-1988, it had become clear that the banks are 'finding their way out of the woods' (Terry Shaunessy of Merrill Lynch, Canada, quoted in *Financial Post*, 6 June 1988). Secondary market prices for developing-country loans are reported at discounts ranging from a low of 9 cents (Bolivia) to a high of 58 cents (Chile) per dollar of loan face-value for Latin American debt. Mexican debt is discounted at 47 cents, and Brazilian debt at 39 cents. The obligations of debtor countries, however, have not been reduced. The international institutional framework does not provide for the equivalent of bankruptcy proceedings to restructure the debt of insolvent sovereign borrowers. Unlike domestic practice which provides mechanisms for a negotiated fair settlement between creditors and debtors in the event of a debtor's inability to pay, international debt negotiations are biased in favour of protecting the claims of creditors.

While the banks have made adjustments to reduce their exposure and reduce the risk of significant bank failure which dominated the discussion of Third World debt a few years ago, the situation of the HICs has now reached a point where new financing is essential. The pressures on government budgets are such that agreed adjustment programmes are becoming impossible to implement and stabilization is undermined by pressures to monetize government debt, much of it related to debt service. This situation is further aggravated by increased local currency costs resulting from heavy devaluations.

The World Bank has acknowledged that 'the assumption that resumed voluntary lending would play a significant role in financing adjustment has proved to be a serious weakness in the strategy of managing the debt problems' (*World Debt Tables*, p. xii). The Baker Plan which, in any event, grossly underestimated the volume of new finances required to restart self-sustaining growth in the highly indebted countries was posited on renewed commercial bank lending. This is not forthcoming. (A World Bank model estimated the amount required by the 15 Baker Group countries over a period of four years at $75–100 billion in real 1986 dollars compared to Baker's prior estimate of $40 billion.) The Baker Plan is now dead in the water. The most that can be said for it is that it recognized, in principle, the desirability of 'adjustment with growth' and further recognized that it is impossible without new financing. Special packages have been negotiated for major debtors such as Mexico, Brazil and Argentina. These refinancings and reschedulings can provide no more than temporary relief and they only postpone the day when the debt will have to be written down. The US, however, continues to oppose any writing-down of Third World debt, except possibly in the case of sub-Sahara Africa.

The steps which have actually been taken in the direction of debt reduction and new financing are small and timid. Major industrialized countries have not yet conceded the principle that the costs of adjustment should be shared between creditors and debtors: the governments of these countries, whose official development assistance and official export credit accounts for a very substantial volume of Third World debt, and who ultimately determine the policies of the Fund and the Bank, have kept a very low profile. Among the small and timid steps are the following, as summarized by Culpepper (1988):

- Several donor countries, including Canada, have converted soft loans to African countries into grants. Because these loans had, however, already been rescheduled, the gain to Africa in terms of cash flows is only some $60 million a year.
- Following the 1987 Venice Summit, a recommendation was made by the leaders of the Summit countries that interest rates on officially guaranteed export credit should be reduced, and grace and repayment periods lengthened. Only four countries benefited from the latter concession. No action on interest-rate reduction was taken.
- The capital base of the World Bank was increased in February 1988 to permit the annual lending capacity of the Bank to grow from current levels of $14 billion to some $20 billion by the early 1990s. This measure was not, however, tied to debt relief but rather permitted an increase in lending to non-problem debtors such as China and India.

- At the end of 1987, the World Bank organized a meeting of donors in Africa to coordinate an increase in adjustment financing. Some $3.2 billion in additional funding was pledged to be made available on highly concessional terms to 22 debt-distressed African countries.
- In December 1987, the Fund announced its Extended Structural Adjustment Facility which added $8.4 billion to the existing Structural Adjustment Facility of $3 billion. These facilities are for adjustment programmes in 62 low-income countries, of which 34 are in sub-Sahara Africa.
- As concerns private creditors, the most interesting initiative is the Morgan Debt Conversion Plan which Mexico hoped could reduce its $64 billion commercial bank debt by $10 billion. The result was disappointing in so far as only 139 out of 600 of Mexico's creditor banks participated. The average discount on the accepted bids was 30 per cent and Mexico's debt was reduced by only $1.1 billion.
- In February 1987, Bolivia, which had ceased to service its commercial bank debt in 1985 and whose debt traded in secondary markets at 9 cents on the dollar, negotiated a debt-repurchase scheme with 131 commercial bank creditors to whom it owed some $660 billion. Bolivia, whose debt in 1987 was $4.6 billion, of which $1.4 billion is owed to private creditors, repurchased $308 million of its debt for $34 million. The arrangement was assisted by the Fund. At the end of the operation, this exceedingly poor and semi-bankrupt country reduced its debt of $4.6 billion to $4.3 billion.
- The 1988 Toronto Summit of the Group of Seven rejected a Japanese proposal to securitize commercial bank debt while a Canadian proposal to study the debt problem of the 27 HICs was quashed by the US before reaching the table. The highly publicized 'menu' proposal of debt relief for the poorest countries reflects the failure to obtain US agreement to a concerted programme of action by the major Paris Club creditor-countries. Each of them may, if they so decide, take measures to reschedule, reduce interest or write down official debt to the poorest LDCs, provided that the debtor-countries pay no less than 30 per cent of export earning in debt services. None of them is committed to do so.

The fears for the breakdown of the international banking system arising from Third World debt have receded. Other more menacing cracks in the system have come into view, such as the vulnerability of the stock market. Crisis management has been effective in preventing declarations of default. The developing countries have conducted themselves with a high degree of responsibility – at enormous costs in terms of lost output, depleted capital stock, depressed employment, declining per capita incomes and rising political tensions. The numerous reschedulings and refinancings – at high transaction costs – have postponed the problem. They have not solved it. Given the depleted and ravaged state of the economies of the major debtors and the extent of adjustment fatigue, the next severe economic downturn of the industrialized world is very likely to result in unilateral debt moratoria. Self-congratulations on successful crisis management are distinctly premature.

A minimum programme of urgent measures
The industrialized countries and their private financial institutions must recognize their shared responsibility for the market failure which transformed the sovereign loans of the 1970s into an horrendous albatross hung on the necks of the borrowing party to these commercial transactions. Steps should be taken in three directions. First, the industrialized countries must make available a sufficiently large volume of official funds to enable the debtor countries to repair the damage to their economies and restart the growth process. Second, mechanisms must be found to write down the face value of the debts, just as the banks are writing them down in their books. Third, given the role which the Fund and the Bank have played and will have to continue to play in negotiations with developing countries, there will have to be a new approach to conditionality.

Many suggestions have been made as to the modalities of delivering increased financial resources. These proposals include a new round of SDR allocations and increased official concessional funding. It is highly unlikely that the private banks will resume voluntary lending to debtor countries. Institutional mechanisms will have to be found for adjusting the face value of debt owed to private creditors to its actual market value. There is urgency in making this adjustment before the vulnerable international banking system is subject to new stresses emanating from instability in the industrialized countries, where overdeveloped credit structures pose a perpetual threat to financial stability. Official bilateral creditors have it in their power to reduce or forgive debt. Debt to the Fund and the Bank cannot be forgiven or reduced but additional resources could and should be made available on highly concessional terms.

We now turn to the contentious question of conditionalities. There obviously must be conditionalities on IMF credits beyond those pertaining to their cost and terms of repayment. Current practices, however, have raised serious criticism. The position of the critics is well summarized by Avramovic (1987), who argues that the Fund should be concerned exclusively with a country's ability to turn around its balance of payments while maintaining its capacity to minimize the deflationary effects of adjustment and to determine its distributional impact on social classes and groups.

Conditionalities should not be used, as is currently the case, to impose arbitrary and ideologically-based 'liberalization' policies on countries with payment problems. Nor should targets with respect to domestic credit-creation and fiscal reform be so tight as to produce 'overkill'. Conditionalities should be governed by an assessment of a country's debt-servicing capacity and pertain otherwise only to sound financial management by the borrower government. The distributional impact of IMF adjustment programmes is a particularly sensitive matter because it can strain the political fabric to the point where governments – especially democratic governments – are forced to buy social peace at the cost of rekindling inflation. The limits of the 'social compact' cannot be measured by econometric models or formulae by the Fund's technocrats, whose projections have in any event frequently been wrong.

Specifically, we make the following recommendations:

- The Fund should abandon its insistence on excessively restrictive monetary targets, which result in compression of domestic demand with idle capacity, unemployment and lost domestic savings.
- The Fund should abandon conditionalities pertaining to financial liberalization which exacerbate inflationary trends and sustain excessively high real interest rates. This further damages investment and growth. (There is no evidence relating the rate of domestic savings to the rate of interest: see Khan and Knight, 1985, pp. 14–16.)
- The IMF should abandon conditionalities pertaining to import liberalization in conditions of scarcity of foreign exchange. These encourage the import of luxury goods, result in the bankruptcy of domestic firms and increased unemployment, favour a shift from productive to distributional activity, and place pressure on the exchange rate. In the case of agricultural imports, there can be serious effects on the capacity of countries to feed themselves.
- The IMF should drop its resistance to selective policy measures which governments may wish to apply so as to minimize the deflationary effects of adjustment and to protect the poor from bearing its principal burden.

Conditionality should be primarily focused on debt-servicing capacity and orderly financial management. Increased emphasis on export expansion, improved public enterprise finances, and higher domestic agricultural prices are among the positive contributions which the Fund and the Bank have made to policy formulation in developing countries. Nor can there be any doubt that fiscal discipline is an essential condition for stability and growth. This does not, however, mean that the Fund should dictate the speed and extent of deficit reduction or identify specific categories of expenditures to be cut. Rather it refers to the desirability of ensuring orderly tax administration, effective public expenditure controls, realistic investment plans, anti-corruption drives, control over foreign borrowing, and the accountability and sound management of public enterprises.

Conditionality should not be used to impose economic policy or an economic doctrine on borrowing countries because it happens to be the prevailing view at the Fund or the Bank that 'it is good for them'. Economic policy which affects income distribution, the strategy of resource allocation, the role of government in economic life, the degree and method of involvement in international trade – in short the essential philosophy of public policy – is a matter which does not tolerate uniform treatment or a uniform doctrine or ideology. It was never intended that the Fund should write policy for its members. The same applies to the World Bank's Structural Adjustment Loans. Whereas official statements of the World Bank and the OECD's DAC have recently affirmed the prime responsibility of governments of the LDCs for designing their adjustment and investment programmes and for coordinating aid and financial flows, the Fund is as hard-nosed as ever and a negotiated agreement with it is normally a precondition of access to the Structural Adjustment Facility of the Bank.

A thoroughly disordered world
The Fund is now exclusively engaged in short-term crisis management in developing (and some socialist) countries. It has abandoned its original role and purpose, which was to provide stability to the system of international trade and payments and prevent competitive devaluations, to sustain the level of world economic activity by supplying medium-term finance to countries experiencing a temporary short-fall of foreign exchange, and to suggest measures to correct fundamental disequilibria.

We all know Keynes's warnings about the need for symmetry of adjustment by surplus and deficit countries to ensure stability in the international system of payments. There is, however, a further asymmetry in the system between the country whose national money serves *de facto* as the world's principal reserve currency and all other countries. The former can pay foreign suppliers in its own money or its own securities while other countries have to earn or borrow foreign exchange. The system functioned well in the classical period of imperialism 1870–1914, when Britain was the top metropole and the pound sterling was the key currency. Britain's economy was complementary to that of its peripheries and a vast private bond market maintained foreign lending and domestic investment in counterpoint. Britain's overseas sphere of influence – dominions, colonies and other dependent regions and countries (such as Argentina) – received continuous stimulation in the form of large inflows of capital and a strong demand for their agricultural and mineral exports. As a well-behaved, mature imperial creditor, Britain financed a large import surplus from the back flow of investment earnings throughout the 1920s and 1930s.

The nature of US leadership was bound to be different. The US – as a large continental country, self-sufficient in food and in most other natural resources – did not have the classic complementarity of a metropole with its peripheries. It was and remains a major exporter of agricultural produce. The US has never depended on the stability of international transactions to the degree that a small island with limited natural resources like Britain (or Japan) must do. Its vast domestic market enabled the US to practise strongly isolationist and protectionist foreign economic policies prior to World War II. When the US emerged as the undisputed hegemonic economic power in the 1940s, it was able to finance both domestic and overseas economic activity so the world experienced a long and remarkable era of economic growth. As the dollar came under pressure in the late 1960s (guns and butter: Vietnam and The Great Society), the US opted to avoid the need for politically painful economic adjustment, abandoned the gold-exchange standard and exported its inflationary domestic pressures by financing its payments deficits with its own IOUs, resulting in an eight-fold increase in the value of international reserves from $79 billion in 1969 to $687 billion by 1984 in a brief span of 15 years (see Triffin, 1986). Commodity prices climbed from the late 1960s culminating in the first oil shock of 1973. In retrospect, we can see that the oil price rise of 1979 was but the last phase of a great commodity boom, just as the fall of oil prices from the mid-1980s is but the last phase of a great commodity-price slide. So much for OPEC! The ballooning increase in international liquidity combined with a series of banking innovations designed to 'make idle money work' is the underlying base of the Eurodollar market. We have seen what an unreliable instrument this has been for the purpose of transferring capital from developed to developing countries.

As the US economy experienced increasing difficulties of low productivity and inflationary pressures in the late 1970s, monetary brakes were applied. Interest rates soared and capital poured in to cover both the external deficit and a growing fraction of the budgetary deficits. The US became the world's largest capital importer, a situation which is neither rational nor stable. This truly amazing disorder has many ramifications of which we address only one aspect – the real rate of interest, now at least twice as high as its historically established norm and substantially exceeding the rates of growth of the world economy or export earnings for most developing countries. This poses a very real problem not only to countries and firms carrying a large volume of debt but also to future prospects of real growth in the world economy.

It is likely that the high real rate of interest has been sustained by 'supply-side' tax reductions, which have systematically increased investment income and government deficits and have also increased the demand for funds to finance them. In a disordered world, the deficits feed inflationary expectations which further sustain high interest rates. These, in turn, favour non-productive, quick turnover and speculative investments with lower risks than those of expansion of productive capacity. The model has appropriately been termed the 'Casino economy'. The disorders of the international economic system are matched by the diversity of opinions among economists concerning the directions in which solutions should be sought. We have been offered superficialities masquerading as sophistication, such as 'the monetary approach to the balance of payments' which makes no qualitative distinction between the factors affecting the increase/decrease of foreign-exchange reserves of countries as different as Saudi Arabia, the US or Jamaica.

It may be useful to identify three particular directions in which appropriate solutions have been and will continue to be sought. The discussion which follows identifies these approaches and reviews them briefly from the viewpoint of their significance to developing countries.

The liberal market-oriented approach

This is the model favoured by the dominant international institution in the 1980s. South Korea and Taiwan are held up as examples to be emulated by other developing countries – although it is now understood that these countries function in a *dirigiste* (rather than a liberal) way. Market-oriented policies aim to subordinate national social policies to the discipline of the international market for goods, services and capital. Using the leverage of debt and aid, developing countries are urged to dismantle subsidies protecting vulnerable sectors of the population, privatize public enterprises, open their markets to imported food, remove restrictions on foreign-exchange transactions and dismantle the protection of domestic industry. This model is predicated on the resumption of respectable rates of growth in the industrialized countries and the removal of barriers which impede the entry of cheap labour products into their markets. In the context of slow growth, high unemployment, rising protectionism and restricted availability of development finance, this is a recipe for explosive political tensions and is likely to be counter-productive in so far as investor confidence and non-inflationary macroeconomic management require a measure of social consensus and stability.

The underlying economic theory is 'born-again' neoclassicism and monetarism. The buzz words are 'outward looking development', 'structural adjustment' and 'getting prices right'. In its more extreme form, the new wave orthodoxy has declared conventional development economics to be *dépassé*. It is said to be 'structuralist' and excessively interventionist. This approach implies that there is no qualitative difference between developed and developing countries, only differences in statistical parameters. The conclusion which follows is that market forces, if permitted to function, will clear markets and create an optimal allocation of resources internally within countries and internationally between countries.

The reformist approach of redistribution with growth
The international context of the reformist model favoured by the MacNamara Bank in the 1970s was the assumed continuation of conditions prevailing before the great postwar boom became mired in stagflation. Economic growth was taken for granted and attention focused on measures to assure equitable redistribution. It was conceded that the benefits of growth do not automatically 'trickle down'. At the international level, there were a variety of proposals for reform and innumerable North–South dialogues. Among reform measures advocated were the linking of SDRs to development finance, a substantial increase in official multilateral assistance, the reorientation of aid towards basic human needs and the alleviation of rural poverty, schemes for commodity-price stabilization and the creation of a new multilateral facility to recycle petrodollar surpluses to developing countries, all of which aborted due to the opposition of the major industrialized countries.

At the level of economic theory, the dominant approach of the reform-monger, to use Hirschmann's phrase, was Keynesian – emphasizing the necessity of maintaining the international circuits of production, consumption, trade and investment by assuring an appropriate volume of concessional finance to developing countries to sustain purchasing power in the face of adverse shocks. International reform-mongering has been in retreat in the 1980s. The only area in which reform continues to remain on the agenda is that of the IMS, due to fears for the stability of financial markets. The demise of Keynesianism and the malaise of the model of the 1950s and 1960s has wiped LDC development off the agendas of the industrialized countries.

Self-reliance approach

The destabilizing international environment of the late 1980s may force developing countries to find their best options in a world of major trade and currency blocs. Societies, whether industrialized or developing, must ultimately protect themselves against intolerable social disruptions inherent in a disordered international economic environment with unlimited and unrestrained private capital mobility.

The malfunctioning of the economies of industrialized countries in the 1980s, which has given rise to powerful protectionist forces, is of a minor order compared with the 'adjustments' made by the weaker and more vulnerable peripheries. What was described by Raoul Prebisch as 'the second great crisis of capitalism' could be dismissed by Professor Haberler as only a bad recession. It is only a matter of time before the larger Latin American countries take unilateral steps to limit the level of debt service compatible with the reconstruction of their devastated economies. It is probable that they will seek to reconstitute a Latin American trading bloc with severe capital controls on external payments. The steps currently being taken in western Europe toward the abolition of internal barriers to capital flows and the harmonization of macroeconomic policies point toward the creation of a powerful European bloc, with special relations with historic spheres of influence, including East Europe. The future of the dollar area is as uncertain, but it is clear that the dollar is too unstable to be able to continue to play the role of the world's privileged reserve currency. We appear to be moving in the direction of major currency blocs rather than a reconstituted truly multilateral payments system as envisaged in the original Bretton Woods system.

The developing countries have been making costly adjustments to a disordered external environment, and have virtually no voice in the multilateral institutions which govern its rules of the game. While the industrialized countries – the Group of Seven, the Group of Ten, etc. – are distancing themselves from multilateralism. Capital flows, which normally sustain the purchasing power and productive capacity of newly industrializing countries are moving in perverse directions. In these circumstances, economic policies of developing countries will turn toward the pursuit of decreased vulnerability to external shocks and an increased measure of self-reliance, on an intra-regional basis. Given the openness of most of these countries to trade and capital flows, the prospects for the future of the international regime governing money and payments will have to become a principal determining factor of development strategy.

The 'economics' required to deal realistically with the problems of the developing world will have to be eclectic, structuralist, heterodox and sensitive to the limitations which political, social and cultural realities place on economic options. The situation calls for approaches better described as political, social or ecological economy rather than 'economics' in the conventional sense of the term.

In its extreme form the liberal market approach places a full burden of adjustment to the disordered world economy on the poor and the vulnerable in the debtor countries. While some small steps towards a sharing of the debt burden may result from reforms in crisis management measures, developing countries will have to rely more strongly on their own economic, cultural and intellectual resources.

References

Avramovic, D. (1987), *Conditionality: Facts, Theory and Policy – Contribution to the Reconstruction of the International Financial System*, Paper prepared for the World Institute of Development Economics Research of the United Nations University, Washington, D.C. Revised 7 May.

Carey, R.H. (1987), *Official Financing and Growth-Oriented Structural Adjustment*, Paper prepared for the Joint IMF–World Bank Seminar on Growth-Oriented Adjustment, Washington, D.C., February.

Culpepper, R. (1987), *Forced Adjustment: The Export Collapse in Sub-Sahara Africa*, North–South Institute, Ottawa.

Culpepper, R. (1988), *The Debt Matrix*, North–South Institute, Ottawa.

Khan, M.S., and M.D. Knight (1985), *Fund Supported Adjustment Programs and Economic Growth*, IMF.

Triffin, R. (1986), 'World Money Reform', *Challenge*, **28**, 4–14.

World Bank (1988), *World Debt Tables*, Vol. I, *1987/88*.

12 Macroeconomic adjustment policy issues*
Fred Z. Jaspersen

I shall address some of the issues of macroeconomic adjustment in the middle-income, highly indebted countries, leaving aside the problems being faced by the low-income African countries since these countries face a very different set of circumstances. As you know, the low-income countries have not been making the massive net transfers to creditors that the middle-income countries have made. While many of the low-income countries face serious debt and fiscal problems, the source of their problems and the instruments which they have for dealing with them are quite different from those of the middle-income, highly indebted countries.

Looking at the experience since 1982, it is clear that we overestimated the speed of the adjustment process for the high-debt, middle-income countries. There has been little or no growth in per capita output since the early 1980s. Output per capita for this group of countries is about 8 per cent lower today than it was in the late 1970s. Unemployment continues high in most of them. Depressed per capita consumption, high savings drain for interest payments on external debt, a substantial internal resource transfer from private to public sector so as to finance external debt service payments, and high inflation are common features of the economic landscape in most of these countries. This situation has existed since 1981 and there are no signs of sustainable growth being resumed. These countries continue to be plagued by internal imbalance. Inflation in many countries has accelerated, imports continue to be repressed, real interest rates in a number of them are at historically high levels and investment remains depressed. Conventional creditworthiness indicators (such as the stock of debt to exports and to GDP) are worse than they were in 1982. There have been some years since 1982 in which improvements occurred but the longer-term trend is clear. As a consequence, there are now nine countries in Latin America which are not making interest payments.

Why has there not been more progress? There are two fundamental reasons for this: namely, the external environment has not been sufficiently supportive; and adjustment policies of the high-debt, middle-income countries have not been consistent, comprehensive and sustained.

On the external side, about 85 per cent of the external debt of the highly indebted, middle-income countries is variable-rate debt. Despite a fall in nominal interest rates in international capital markets, real interest rates remain high. Low commodity prices in real terms is a second adverse external factor. While there has been some strengthening of raw material, grains and oil seed prices, this is expected to be temporary. The prices of coffee and cocoa, which are important to the IDA countries, remain depressed at record low levels. Also there have been inadequate capital flows to this group of countries with the result that they have been making net transfers to their creditors of 5–6 per cent of GDP annually. A graphic example of how the adverse external environment has affected the adjustment efforts of these countries lies in export performance. Almost all of the countries have undertaken real devaluations. For the group as a whole, this has resulted in a 40 per cent increase in the volume of their exports since the early 1980s while the value of exports is relatively unchanged.

Inadequate adjustment policies have also contributed to the lack of progress in the high-debt countries, although there have been some outstanding successes. For example, with a steady adjustment programme, Chile succeeded in eliminating internal imbalance, reduced its external imbalance, maintained current interest payments on its external debt, and re-established an adequate rate of economic growth. Thailand also did extraordinarily well and there has been some heroic action in a number of other countries. Note the impressive non-traditional export performance of Mexico and price stabilization performance of Bolivia. In fact, there was substantial progress in most of the heavily indebted countries in reducing fiscal deficits, rationalizing subsidies, and strengthening their international competitiveness through real devaluation of their currencies. In addition, export-promotion regimes have been strengthened while efforts at privatization and restructuring of the financial sector have occurred in some cases. However, these efforts have not been either comprehensive or sustained and there was relatively little progress in internally stabilizing these economies. Public enterprises were not brought under control and there have been relatively few successes with privatization. Trade regimes remain highly distorted and protection continues to be high in many countries. While fiscal deficits were reduced, they remain large in a number of cases and there has been backsliding in some others. The net effect has been disappointing. The question arises as to why the commitment of these countries to adjustment has not been stronger. To answer this question, one must examine the criteria for success and look at some of the major issues of macroeconomic adjustment.

A macroeconomic adjustment programme must meet three criteria to succeed. First, it must reduce sources of instability and not merely shift disequilibrium from one part of the economy to another part where it will produce another crisis. Second, the programme must be economically sustainable in the sense of leading, with high probability, to restoration of growth in per capita income. Third, it must be politically sustainable in that it does not generate too much opposition while generating enough support to keep the implementers of these policies in office. Let us look at these criteria in more detail. Reducing inflation and cutting the external deficit are key objectives of most adjustment programmes. They establish the basic parameters for re-establishing growth and help to determine the political sustainability of adjustment. In order to generate political support and establish credibility, it is important, initially, that programmes yield rapid and visible progress in reducing inflation. The government, typically, has only limited opportunities to sell necessary but unpopular measures like 'budget cuts' aimed at stopping inflation. Restoring economic growth is essential for the long-term survival of adjustment but must be achieved within tighter fiscal targets. Rationalizing public enterprises is often a key step in many countries to achieving adjustment with growth. For the country to meet its medium- and long-term adjustment and growth objectives, as well as reduce its external deficit, it is important for decision-makers to use exchange-rate and export-promotion policies rather than simply to rely on the repression of aggregate demand.

Economic growth takes place in and through specific sectors. The financial sector is a primary conduit of macroeconomic policy to the rest of the economy. Conflict often arises when high real interest rates accompany stabilization since they can result in financial distress of borrowers and in a generalized deterioration of portfolio quality across the financial sector. If such problems become acute, restructuring and recapitalizing the financial sector becomes necessary and, thus, the fiscal restraint necessary to sustain stabilization can be undermined. On the real side, productive sectors respond with lags to changed incentives while stabilization is being achieved and these lags vary between the sectors because of differences in their technology and institutions. A key issue is how to design adjustment programmes so that they link institutional reform to increased sectoral response. Finally, the social impact of adjustment is critical for both political sustainability and economic sustainability. Growth ultimately depends on people – on their education, health and perception of prospects of finding employment.

Analytical framework
What is the macroeconomic framework for adjustment with growth? How has thinking about this process changed in recent years in response

to what has occurred in the developing countries? Countries with a major imbalance in their external accounts of the type experienced by the high-debt, middle-income countries must, at some point, adjust to a situation in which they have command over fewer real resources. Adjustment can occur in several ways. It can take place automatically through direct income and monetary effects since reduced real income leads to declines in consumption, imports and investment. (In practice, investment – especially private investment – is apt to contract more sharply than consumption. Public investment is also likely to fall more sharply than public consumption since it will be easier for the government to cut investment than to compress recurrent expenditures – the largest share of which is wages and interest on public debt – as the tax base and public revenue contract.) As a consequence, the country's resource balance moves towards the surplus required to service external debt.

Indirect monetary effects, too, operate to bring about adjustment when other things, such as monetary policy, remain equal. Reduced command over earnings, related to lower commodity prices, is reflected initially in a loss of foreign-exchange reserves since the country is no longer able to finance the increased current-account deficit through increased external borrowing. This situation leads to a fall in the real money supply and an increase in real interest rates which, in turn, produce a decline in investment and consumption spending. The adjustment experienced during 1981–84 by most Latin American countries contained elements of these two mechanisms. Income, consumption, investment, imports and foreign-exchange reserves declined sharply. Output declines, accompanied by increases in unemployment and reduction of capacity utilization, were severe. Note such automatic adjustment mechanisms do not distinguish between external and internal balances since the former is achieved at the expense of the latter through reduction of the level of economic activity.

In practice, governments can adopt and have adopted policies aimed at accelerating or retarding adjustment. What policies speed up elimination of external imbalance? Do such policies simultaneously have an effect on internal balance or are there policies which would make it simultaneously possible to achieve both external and internal balance (that is, to achieve external balance without sacrificing either employment or expansion of the domestic economy)? Three types of policies can be identified. The first are 'absorption-reduction' policies which alter the level of domestic demand and can be used to achieve external balance by reducing utilization or absorption of resources. These policies are the conventional tools of demand management. By reducing domestic expenditure, demands for both exportables and import substitutes fall – promoting improvement of the trade balance by simultaneously cutting outlays on imports and freeing domestically-produced goods for export. The shortcoming of such policies is that they too do not distinguish between internal and external balance. Again they achieve external balance at the expense of output, employment and capacity utilization in the domestic economy. Thus, while output of tradeable goods may not decline when absorption is reduced (since tradeable goods, freed by the decline in domestic demand, can be exported), output in the non-tradeable-goods sector (construction and services, for example) will decline if prices for such goods are inflexible downward.

The second type of policies involves 'switching'. By increasing the prices of tradeable goods relative to those of the non-tradeable goods, resources are reallocated or 'switched' from the non-tradeable-goods sector, where there is excess supply, to the tradeable-goods sector, where they can be used to produce for export or to substitute for imports. Contemporaneously, there will be a shift in domestic demand away from higher priced tradeables to non-tradeable goods. Absorption reduction and expenditure switching occur in the short run but output switching may only occur over time and it may require a mix of investment and complementary policy measures to bring about the desired reallocation of productive resources. Simultaneously to achieve internal and external balance, both absorption-reduction and switching policies are required. Absorption reduction without switching will result in a decline in output and increased unemployment. Switching without absorption reduction will achieve neither internal nor external balance. If domestic demand is not reduced, excess demand will be created for non-tradeable goods, prices will rise in that sector and the policy-induced change in relative prices will be eliminated.

Absorption-reduction and switching policies alone may not result in growth of output if the economy is operating at or near full employment. To the extent that the economy is *not* operating at full capacity, policies stimulating expansion of tradeables can simultaneously result in restoration of external balance and growth of output. Here growth will be greater to the extent that unemployed resources can be utilized directly without modification in the production of tradeables. In practice, however, substantial investment in human capital, infrastructure, and plant and equipment may be required if idle resources are to be adapted and employed in production of tradeables. Even with full employment, switching policies may be effective in expanding output of tradeables only if substantial investment is undertaken to adapt sector-specific or activity-specific resources to their newer uses. Such investment requirements may be large relative to national savings, especially if a significant proportion of savings is transferred abroad to pay interest on external debt.

Table 12.1   Summary of potential policies

Absorption Reduction:
  Fiscal   – deficit reduction in public sector
  Monetary – interest-rate and reserve policies, reducing domestic expenditure
  Incomes   – delaying rise in income relative to increases in output

Switching:
  Exchange rate
  Tariffs and export taxes or subsidies
  Factor and product pricing
  Factor-mobility enhancement

Supply-oriented Growth Policies:
  Measures to enhance allocative efficiency and X-efficiency
  Shifting composition of private-sector expenditures in favour of investment
  Measures to enhance domestic savings
  Shifting composition of public-sector expenditures away from recurrent expenditures and
      toward investment
  Changes in current governmental expenditures (for example, from subsidies to main-
      tenance)
  Sectoral stimuli

In summary, a country which is attempting to overcome external imbalance might pursue absorption reduction, switching and supply-oriented growth policies so as to achieve higher employment and non-inflationary growth while strengthening its external position. (These three types of policies are summarized in Table 12.1.) It is likely that switching is generally *easier* in larger and more advanced countries but it may also be true that the scope for efficiency *gains* is greater in the smaller and poorer countries.

Recent experience indicates that there is more to the adjustment process than is given in this analytical summary. First, output switching itself requires investment. For the highly indebted countries, resources for investment were reduced because of interest payments on external debt, which reached 10–11 per cent of GDP in some cases. Second, investment-output lags slow the adjustment process and increase the degree of absorption that is necessary. To sustain the adjustment process over time, investment and growth must be restored. (The primary objective is to restore what Corden refers to as the 'underlying rate of growth'.) Since resources for investment have often been reduced, these countries must double their efforts. Chile, for example, successfully increased its domestic savings from 9 per cent of GDP in the early 1980s to 20 per cent at present but half of this increase went to additional investment while the other half serviced its debt. The price paid by Chile was a prolonged period of substantial decline in consumption.

Some practical matters – issues, strategic design and targets
There has been considerable discussion of the relative benefits and costs
of orthodox and heterodox stabilization programmes. Heterodox
approaches used by countries experiencing chronic inflation, such as
Brazil (Plan Cruzado) and Argentina (Plan Austral), initially appeared to
be successful in arresting the inertia of rising prices without sacrificing
growth. They focused on the use of currency reform, incomes policy and
price policies to slow inflation and to control expectations. The conclusion
emerging from our experience with these approaches is that, while such
measures can help to overcome initial inflation and can be especially effective tools in managing inflationary expectations, they are unlikely to be
successful in the medium term – unless they are supported by orthodox
stabilization policies, especially by tight fiscal management. An additional
issue of strategic design is how to reduce investment, output and switching
lags so as to achieve the desired supply response to increase growth. A
related question is the impact of macroeconomic policy on these lags –
there are no easy answers here but it is an area which clearly deserves more
attention.

Turning to the choice of appropriate targets for adjustment programmes, other complex issues arise. Consider the problem of targeting
net international reserves. If this variable is chosen as a target contingent
mechanisms must isolate the effect of temporary external shocks (for
example, interest-rate and terms-of-trade shocks). In the absence of this
safeguard, rolling adjustment-programme targets may be excessively
tightened in response to external shocks and efforts to re-establish growth
will be derailed. Consider too the issue of real versus nominal targets. If
nominal targets are used and the inflation target is missed, than all of the
other nominal targets will not be attained (and in a sense become irrelevant). Since inflation is not controlled by any one policy instrument but
rather occurs as the outcome of many simultaneous forces – including
policy interventions, exogenous shocks and expectations about future
inflation – forecasting of future inflation rates is very imprecise. This is
particularly true in the high and volatile inflationary situations that now
exist in many of the middle-income, high-debt countries.

When real targets are used, we need a nominal anchor. It is widely
recognized that achieving real targets (real output growth) requires use of
proper incomes and price policies to obtain a real wage which is consistent
with the real targets. However, fixing prices and the nominal wage is
extremely difficult in practice because of imperfect knowledge about the
cost structure of the economy. Moreover, if these are incorrectly chosen,
distortions will arise to undermine the sustainability of the stabilization
effort. For these reasons, it may be preferable to allow the real wage to

be determined by market forces and to use monetary and exchange-rate policies as the nominal anchors which guide the response of economic agents.

Overall macroeconomic management is complicated by the existence of a large overhang of external debt. The public sector is ultimately responsible for servicing this debt while savings are usually generated in the private sector. Thus resources must be transferred from the private to the public sector. Since there are limits on the size of transfer which can be achieved, many high-debt countries resort to the use of an 'inflation tax'. At the same time – because bonds compete domestically for a portion of the available resources and because of arbitrage between internal and external markets for government paper – many high-debt countries experience excessively high and sustained real rates of interest, which crowd out private investment and impede resumption of adequate rates of economic growth. The result is destabilization of macroeconomic conditions,which are likely to become worse and will further interfere with recovery if they are not directly dealt with.

There are solutions to these management problems but their implementation is difficult. One solution is to cut government expenditures but, in practice, investment spending is usually the easiest to cut. Also, while it is often possible to identify some public-sector investments not to undertake, further investment cuts (beyond these particular ones) may make difficult attempts to resume sustained growth. Another management issue is how to increase resources for adjustment and the role of concessional debt relief in this context. A third issue is how to design underfunded adjustment programmes so they can be effective. Is this even possible? If not, what is the consequence? Finally, how should high-debt countries manage their capital account? Given the need for restructuring external debt, the capital account must be closed. Private foreign investors will be able to get in but they will be unable to get out. The result is less foreign investment than would otherwise be forthcoming. Similarly, capital 'flight' is unlikely to flow back to a high-debt country (in large amounts) while the capital account remains closed. On the other hand, if the capital account is open to attract more foreign investment and capital-flight reflows, a dual exchange rate must be adopted and this, itself, will create further distortions.

Three conclusions emerge from this discussion. First, macroeconomic management for the high-debt countries is complicated by the existence of such debt. Second, the sustainability of adjustment programmes may depend upon proper handling of the debt restructuring process. Finally for some countries, concessional debt relief must be part of the solution if adjustment programmes are to work.

Comment by B. V. Gestrin

My remarks focus on the financial-market access for the LDCs. Such access is important as it relates to the financing of trade-related investment and enlarged trade flows. Participation in international trade provides many benefits to developing countries since the domestic market of even the largest developing countries is relatively small. Generally speaking, the more outward-oriented developing countries have fared better than inward-oriented countries in terms of economic performance. This has been true in calmer periods as well as during the last 15 years of external shocks. Obviously, for an outward-oriented approach to succeed, markets must be available and for this we need economic growth in the major OECD countries. However, supply-side (rather than demand-side) variables have dominated export growth in the developing countries during the postwar period. Export success in the LDCs has been primarily related to favourable internal factors influencing their ability to compete and diversify rather than to the situation in the developed countries.

The interest of both the developing and the industrialized countries is clearly to promote those internal factors in the LDCs which will act to restore growth by rehabilitating investment levels. To this end, new financial flows and debt restructuring can play an important role, with a view to regaining financial-market access at as early a date as possible. Sufficient additional financing must be made available to those countries which show that they can use it productively. In this context, it is useful to highlight four main areas of the developing world; namely, the least developed countries, the heavily indebted LDCs, the newly industrialized countries (NICs), and the 'new' NICs. As far as the countries in the first group are concerned, market access will be virtually impossible without official guarantees. Fortunately aid flows appear to be on the increase to them. For the third group of countries, market access is generally no problem and all of them have an interest in integrating further with the world's financial markets. In the fourth group, we generally find countries, such as Thailand and Malaysia, which are developing on the basis of export-oriented production linked to manufacturing in Japan and the United States. Often we find here a relative shrinkage of the role of the public sector (and, hence, traditional syndicated lending to this sector) in favour of private-sector investment and lending. My comments are primarily directed to the second group of countries where progress in resolving the debt problem is alarmingly slow, requiring some new initiatives.

We have already seen a number of promising developments during the last couple of years with a whole new 'menu' of options being introduced – including debt/equity, debt/debt swaps, exit bonds, buying back of debt, debt discounting and various rescheduling approaches. While this menu approach is helpful and is likely to be further refined, it will (in the final analysis) contribute only to a limited extent towards providing a solution. The banks clearly cannot assume an expanding role for themselves in this process. One can expect private creditors to adopt a market-based solution such as debt discounting to reduce their debt claims, while official creditors ensure that net flows to the debtor countries are adequate to support required investment. The governments of the major countries and the multilateral institutions must step in to provide the required funds for investment and growth in the developing countries and to prevent an economic collapse from taking place. Financial support will also continue to be available from private sources (for example, from direct investment) but more and more only with the support of creditor-country governments and international financial institutions. World Bank guarantees and improved conditions for co-financing are just two possibilities in this connection. Proceeding in this way, market access for a number of LDCs can be achieved over time. A number of helpful suggestions were made in the report *Restoring Market Access*, issued by the Institute of International Finance a year ago.

There is no specific plan which can be uniformly applied to all debtor countries to assist them in preserving or in gaining market access. A common theme of any approach must be to bring debt-service requirements within the reasonable limits of existing resources, while providing scope for growth in the future. To reach this goal, debt forgiveness by the banks may be appropriate in some particular circumstances. Rather than having banks lending 'new money' to pay themselves interest, it may be better to consider forgiveness of interest and/or principal. However, the concept of debt forgiveness is extremely difficult. Providing debt relief this way could be very damaging. Just as some borrowing countries have used the past five years of debt-rescheduling to postpone rather than accept adjustments, so would generalized debt relief, by itself, provide no lasting solution. If not carefully handled, debt forgiveness could compound the vicious circle of low investment and growth, thereby pushing further into the future the day when debtor countries return to international financial markets. Reduction or cancellation of debt could rule out for decades any possibility of reviving creditworthiness – destroying what must be the ultimate objective of international efforts to resolve the debt issue.

In the final analysis, a restoration of confidence, allowing a return of market financing of LDC development, will only result from sound economic policies and reforms. These include programmes to increase the supply of savings through strengthening domestic financial systems and the repatriation of flight capital, programmes to improve the efficiency

of investment, improved tax collection, and the removal of strong inflationary biases. All this may sound rather difficult to achieve but the cases
of Korea and Taiwan show what can be done even in the absence of natural
resources. So does the case of Japan where per capita GNP in 1958 was
less than that in Argentina. Economic programmes that seem to have the
best chances of success are those built on cooperative relations with bank
creditors and voluntary market-oriented mechanisms to provide the LDCs
with effective cash-flow relief and a considerably enhanced role for
governments in the provisions of 'new money'.

For many observers, a major problem in achieving such cooperative
approaches is that the interests of governments are very different from
those of the banks. The solution advocated to banks by governments has
basically been to lend more money to the developing countries – that is,
the same approach that caused the present problem in the first place.
Governments, for a variety of reasons, have a considerable interest in
keeping the present approach going provided this does not lead to financial chaos. Unfortunately, such a system is liable to break down as debt
levels and ratios are taken to clearly unsustainable levels. A serious flaw
of this approach is that it seems to postpone, almost indefinitely, the
chance for many countries to return to the market on commercial terms,
even in situations where this would otherwise be possible within a reasonable time horizon.

The current approach tends to drive the indebted countries and their
creditors further apart rather than leading to cooperative solutions. In
some cases, there is even the temptation among the developing countries
to precipitate a breakdown in relations with the banks. Such a confrontation – involving unilateral debt cancellation – would most certainly not
benefit the LDCs. Instead, these countries would then be likely to become
even more inward-looking than before, dooming them to financial con-
finement and stagnation for years to come. There is an urgent need to find
more beneficial outcomes. I feel that an approach such as that outlined
above, combining an expanded role for governments with an enlarged
menu of options, will move us closer to a solution.

*This paper reflects only the views of the author and should be used and
cited accordingly. The findings, interpretations, and conclusions are the
author's own. They should not be attributed to the World Bank, its Board
of Directors, its management, or any of its member countries.

13 A return visit to the international debt problem of the LDCs

Lorie Tarshis

A conflict between the views of the 'establishment' (including bankers, politicians and officials in power) and those of the 'anti-establishment' (academic economists, intellectuals, journalists and of course the representatives of the LDCs) is not without precedent. In connection with my topic, a typical establishment view is that if only they would try hard enough, the LDCs could work their way out of their debt problem on their own. The counter-view is, of course, that the debt crisis has become so serious that its resolution will require a timely, enormous – but most unlikely – input by creditor and other developed countries, and that if these inputs are not supplied in time and in proper measure, the world economy will either become a 'basket-case' or instead the debtors will – by accident I suppose – bail it out by refusing to follow the rules.

Such a scenario is bound to remind optimists of the French success in paying the indemnity demanded by Prussia after the Franco-Prussian War, and of the success of the United States, Canada, Japan, Taiwan and many others in repaying the debts they had incurred during and in pursuance of the development process. However, the anti-establishment view also has its supporting examples, most notably that of Germany after the Peace Treaty of Versailles. For more than a decade after 1921, Germany managed – by following rules set for her – to dig herself and later most of her creditors through recession and into depression. (Incidentally, the guiding rules were notably less stringent than those imposed by the IMF after 1981 on the LDCs.) Eventually, Germany announced that she would no longer even try to pay the sum that had been scaled down over the years to a mere 2 per cent of its initial level. Meanwhile, the debtors paid only funds borrowed from innocents abroad and the creditors received nothing except part of the funds they had loaned. Both suffered costs that were several times larger than the amount initially claimed as a result of the failure of efforts to pay reparations. There have, of course, been other developing countries that failed to develop as scheduled, though none (until this decade) imposed so heavy a cost as did Germany in the post-Versailles decade.

Examples abound and, if they are carefully selected, they can make a convincing case for each view but they will only persuade those already convinced. My proposal is that we look instead at a few key questions that must come up in any serious analysis of the processes involved. First, we consider whether the LDCs can, acting on their own, work off their international debt. Then, still hoping for a full repayment, we ask what creditor countries can do to help debtors service their debt, and also, what obstacles they could expect to encounter. Afterwards we ask what can be done if the debtor–creditor combination fails to facilitate repayments. In general, there may be sensible reasons for scaling down the debt to help not only debtors but also creditors, as was done for Germany several times between 1922 and 1932. On a practical level, three further questions emerge: Would it help to extend the period in which repayments are made? Would it help to scale down the interest charges that debtors are obliged to pay on outstanding debt? Finally, can rules be formulated to guide efforts to bring the debt down to size?

Can the LDCs work themselves out of debt?

After the reality of the debt crisis gained recognition, most observers seemed to believe that, since many individual countries in the past had managed to pay off a debt that had become excessive, the individual countries that make up the LDCs can also succeed. Of course it would require a severe tightening of the belt but, with proper self-discipline, each of them could manage. The example of Germany in the period of reparations – the one clear example to the contrary – has evidently been forgotten. I call this stress of discipline 'the IMF view' because, in frequent talks, the two managing directors of the IMF during 1982–88 seemed to be completely confident as to its validity.

Looking at a single country, the four-fold solution to the problem was, they argued, obvious. First imports have to be lowered by structural adjustment of the debtor economy (not by using tariffs) so that its industries can compete successfully with foreign industries in the domestic market. Second, exports have to be encouraged not by making use of subsidies but rather again by encouraging structural adjustment to make its industries more competitive, so that it can squeeze into foreign markets. The importance of these two factors to a country which seeks to pay off a part of its debt is obvious and they should not be overlooked. However, how can a country so heavily in debt that it appeals to no lender, undertake structural adjustments, which almost certainly require new machinery? Third, the money supply must be tightened and extravagance in government has to be curbed. Finally, the pricing mechanism should be allowed to operate freely. This is a neat, persuasive package and if a few debtors remain with too much debt, they deserve a full measure of blame. As M. Camdessus recently said, 'These countries need to be more steadfast in their efforts to deal with their imbalances and structural weaknesses.' Not for the first time has a head of the IMF sounded like a Boy Scout leader talking to his troop about what used to be called 'the sin of self-abuse'.

This crude perspective, which blames the debtor for being in debt and assigns to it alone the responsibility for solving its problems, in effect lets the creditor off scot-free. Since creditors are not in debt, their sole responsibility is to refrain from making use of protectionist measures. The IMF view is, of course, more sophisticated than this. It recognizes that a country's international debt will rise when its balance of current transactions is in deficit. Thus all it needs to enable repayment of its debt is to transform the deficit balance account into a surplus.

Shortly after the IMF began operations, it issued rules to ensure that its members' balance of payments accounts would be standardized. In effect, it urged that the transaction that country X records as an export of $100 million to country Y, be recorded by Y as an import of $100 million from X. When procedures are truly uniform as amongst members (and non-members too) the sum of the surpluses of all surplus countries must equal the sum of the deficits of all deficit countries! (When this equality is found to exist, nothing can be inferred about the state of the world economy. The equality implies nothing more than that all countries are following a uniform set of rules and all the data needed in preparing each country's payments statement are consistent.) It follows then that when a group of countries manages to convert their aggregate balance of payments on current account from a deficit of, say, $1000 to a surplus of $2000, the balance of current payments for all the rest must drop from a surplus of $1000 to a deficit of $2000. If the LDCs are to reverse the change in their international debt from a rise of $1000 a year to a repayment of $2000 a year, the aggregate balance on current account for the rest of the world must shift from a surplus of $1000 to a deficit of $2000.

This arithmetic does not demonstrate that the LDCs cannot repay their debt. All it says is that a necessary condition for such a repayment is that the balance on current account of the rest of the world must serve as the counterpart of the LDCs' success, and so it must fall into a deficit. Clearly if one of the LDCs becomes a little Japan and another, a little Taiwan, they will be able to achieve a large surplus in their aggregate balance on current account. There is, however, another side to the condition which one must not forget. France and West Germany will have to bewail their terrifying deficits or the deficits of other LDCs must rise. The LDCs can succeed in repaying some debt only if they can 'shoe horn' their exports into markets formerly served by industrialized countries or into newly-created markets. In addition, the growth in their exports and the decline in their imports must be large enough to create deficits in the current payments balances of the developed economies.

These latter countries would have two reasons to object and perhaps to fight back. First, the decline in the size of the domestic and foreign markets for their product will cause a slump in business profits, output and employment unless their governments are willing to adopt offsetting measures to develop markets at home. Since government is usually reluctant to move in that direction, an LDC acting alone or in concert with others will meet with less resistance from the developed economies if conditions in the latter are generally very prosperous. There is a second problem for success by the LDCs may also jeopardize the financial standing and international reserves of the developed economies – though, if loans are being repaid, their reserves should be well maintained, at least during the process. Some, looking into the future, may still find cause for worry and the alternative, namely holding debt paper which may lose all value, should give them even more reason to worry.

A major doubt remains. South Korea and Taiwan were able to raise themselves from the shambles into which war plunged them and their growth and competitive position are by now remarkable. Why, if they were able to succeed, is such a task apparently beyond the capacity of Mexico, Brazil and the rest? Obviously, the rush to take off by Taiwan and South Korea occurred earlier when the developed countries were enjoying high levels of prosperity; those happy circumstances are no longer in being. I suspect that a second factor – that these two countries received very substantial aid from the US government – was also highly significant. Much of this aid was direct and did not have to be repaid. In addition, both countries were able to import capital, paying equities in return rather than debt instruments; moreover, by the time the price of crude petroleum had soared, both countries had developed a strong export potential. This fact meant that they could finance the expensive petroleum they needed to keep their economies in operation with the proceeds from their exports.

Japan and West Germany could now do as much for another patron. Indeed, such a move would probably help the protector country as well as the patron, except for one factor. If Mexico, Brazil or Argentina were selected as patron, the first beneficiaries would *not* be the debtor-country or even Japan and West Germany, but instead the private bank creditors of the selected LDC. In short, the next Taiwan or South Korea will probably have to be a country like Bolivia or Chile whose international debt is relatively low, since the first beneficiaries of the largesse of, say, Japan, acting as the investor in and sponsor of a selected LDC, would be the banks which hold the loan paper of that country. If its debt were very high, the new Japan would have to export about \$80–120 billion of new funds to the selected LDC before the debtor could start to pay off its major creditors – including the banks of the United States, Canada and Europe. The ideal patron, of course, would then be an LDC with practically no debt and a strong strategic position.

Clearly it is not possible to give a confident answer to the question with which this section began. However, in the circumstances of today, anyone who asserts that the LDCs will succeed in working themselves free of debt faces a daunting task; namely, how to convince us that his optimism is justified. While an individual debtor may well succeed, success is likely to be purchased at the expense of other debtors whose debt will increase.

Collaboration to resolve the debt crisis
A striking feature of recent developments is that, although the debt crisis had obviously been close to the surface as early as 1975, very few observers expressed concern about it until 1982. While LDC debt grew conspicuously in the early 1970s, so too did LDC export earnings. Also, since there seemed to be another readily opened 'tap' of dollars namely from the banks to the LDC debtors, it seemed unlikely that they would run out of dollars. By 1982, this happy dream had been brought to a sudden end by the rapid invasion of a 'tight money' front, with accompanying high interest rates. (Tight money was not the only cause since other deflationary measures were adopted to slow down inflation but it was probably the measure most commonly employed in creditor countries.) The tightening of the money supply raised fears about the financial strength of heavily indebted debtors – as a result, the tap became much harder to open – and it also produced a dramatic decline of aggregate demand in creditor countries, including their demand for imports. There was an especially sharp fall in their imports from the LDCs; the exports of debtor- to creditor-countries declined sharply. Thus the two sources of dollar funds that had opened wide from 1975 to 1980–81 were quickly blocked. Suddenly the debt situation had become one of crisis.

The debt situation was under control so long as the industrialized countries were enjoying prosperity and reasonably rapid growth and while they were unready to turn to protectionism. If there is any value in this observation, can the debt crisis not be salvaged by persuading creditor-countries to try to attain higher levels of prosperity and faster growth? The Baker Plan, which reflected the observation, made sense. The members of the Group of Seven (that is, the United States, Britain, West Germany, Japan, France, Italy and Canada) committed themselves to a programme of reducing unemployment, more rapid growth and relatively stable prices without turning to protectionism. In addition, members of the group joined together in recognizing the urgency of a renewal of capital exports to the LDCs. The LDCs, themselves, were to restrain imports and to check private capital flights.

So far, the subsequent record of achievement has been dismal. Several members of the Group fell more deeply into recession and another has remained dormant – well below the required level of prosperity. Only Japan enjoyed a state of high prosperity while the United States experienced a satisfying recovery. The rate of growth of the Seven has remained below the target level. Thus it is hardly surprising that the current payments accounts of the Group still show a surplus and the corresponding account of the LDCs as a whole remains in deficit. No wonder, then, that the aggregate international debt of the latter has grown instead of declining. This growth in debt, however, does not indicate that the industrialized countries have undertaken a renewed programme of exporting capital to the LDCs. Most of the increase in LDC debt reflects unpaid bills for interest and emergency lending by the international agencies, which had been undertaken to persuade the larger private creditor banks to postpone (again) the dates when interest payments from the LDCs come due. In fact, however, these agencies and especially the IMF have done even worse. The IMF has taken back more funds from its debtors than it has loaned out.

The question as to why most members of the Group of Seven were actually unwilling to seek higher prosperity and more rapid growth demands an answer. The response most commonly put forward – that they believed that inflation lurked dangerously near – cannot be accepted. There is another answer which, it seems to me, is more persuasive. These countries, with the exception of Japan and West Germany, were not being foolish to want to build up their international monetary reserves. They had seen how rapidly any country can lose reserves and hence begin to lose control over a fall in the value of its currency. Note too that firm adherence to the Baker Plan would expose each country to substantial reserve losses given the ultimate goal of actual repayments of LDC debt. Any of them would realize that if it decided to loosen its adherence, it could check its reserve losses without seriously hurting the LDCs – especially if it believed that the other members would assume that responsibility. Therefore, it could readily convince itself to take a free ride but so too could the other group members. In the end, the Plan would fail because it could not be implemented.

By way of summary, the LDCs will be better placed to service their international debt the more prosperous are the developed countries and the lower is the ratio of the required improvement in the LDCs' current payments accounts to the exports of the industrialized countries.

Lighting a fire to fight a fire

In the discussion within the Group of Seven about the Baker Plan, members agreed to urge their larger banks to lend more freely to the LDCs than in recent years. This programme raises two questions. First, how can additional loans to countries already too heavily indebted be justified? Second, if more lending can be expected to help not only the debtors but also the creditors – as many experts have argued it would – how can the failure of many of the larger banks to lend more freely be explained? Clearly if that failure helps to explain the prolongation and – as many would say – even the worsening of the debt crisis, we must assess what can be done to encourage more loans to the LDCs.

Additional loans to the LDCs, as they are drawn down by borrowers, contribute to the debtors' efforts to repay their debt. These loans enable LDCs to buy machinery and equipment in amounts and of a type that cannot be secured otherwise. The most seriously indebted of the developed countries are far more likely to encounter deficiencies in capital stock than in their labour force as they seek to produce larger amounts; as they try to produce them more efficiently – necessary if they are to compete for markets abroad and at home – and as they do what they can to vary the character of their aggregate output – necessary if they are to respond appropriately to changes in the demand of their various markets and to the changing ability of their competitors in supplying these markets. Without access to more and different capital goods which they can only purchase with funds supplied by developed country leaders, the LDCs' lot as exporters would generally be too little, too late and too unresponsive. For most LDCs, access to loan funds is a necessary condition for building up a sufficient stock of capital assets.

Experience in 1972–82 illustrates that such access is not a sufficient condition for this purpose. Too large a share of funds was often frittered away to pay for imports of luxuries and military supplies and to help pay for real estate and bank accounts in such safe havens as Florida, Hawaii, the Riviera and Zurich. Also, a great deal was spent to purchase the petroleum needed at home. At the end, the stock of assets needed to strengthen LDC economies was not much bigger than at the beginning. If the LDCs are to qualify for loans in the future, they should control the use of any inflow of scarce funds. This is the more important when, after the funds have been used for the private advantage of some individuals or groups, the country is left with a debt to be serviced in foreign funds with insufficient new assets to enable a matching increase in export proceeds. The examples, suggested earlier, of countries that made good use of borrowed funds to develop their productive and export capacity, permitting them to service higher debt, show that the procedure can work.

A second possible contribution of access to loan funds involves time. A borrower country postpones the day when payment is due. If the market for the exports of the LDCs is temporarily low, the ability to borrow allows the debtor to service its loan at a date which, it hopes, will be more favourable. However, 'waiting' also increases the costs of servicing because interest due but not fully paid adds to the amount owed by the debtor. This feature may be especially important when the debt in question is international. As we have seen, the debtor needs an export surplus in order to finance debt. To build up adequate exports requires that the markets for them be unusually prosperous but waiting for the United States, West Germany, France and other developed countries to regain high prosperity takes time. If the creditors will not give time, the debtors face default and the creditors lose as much from this as do debtors. There is an asymmetry here that should be recorded. When the LDCs are borrowing, they can readily service their growing debt because they are likely to order much of what they need from the developed countries. If anything happens to interrupt that process, it shows up first in the suddenly noticed inability of debtors to service their debt. They are bound, then, to curtail their imports from the developed economies which because of their drop in exports are likely to join the LDCs in recession. The process may then become cumulative – the more so since the LDCs, after borrowing heavily for some years, now face a far heavier bill for interest than occurred at the start.

This process can be stopped if the creditors undertake both to lend enough to the debtors to keep them buying and to counter the deflationary pressures that will otherwise push them into depression. Such policies call for firmness. The creditor-countries will find their balance of payments on current accounts tilting into larger and larger deficits and the LDC debt can (at most) be reduced by the amount of the aggregate deficit of the developed economies.

Turn now to the reluctance of banks to lend more to the LDCs. Creditors do not want to throw good money after bad. Yet, bearing in mind the interest of all creditors in an uninterrupted flow of loan-funds to the LDCs, each would see that it should lend in the social interest but it does not do so. Once again the 'free rider' virus has been on the attack. The failure of a recent effort – engineered by the Mexican government, the US Treasury and Morgan Guaranty Trust Company – to enable Mexico, in effect, to buy up to 10 per cent of the debt paper held by banks provides a clear instance. In future, if anything like this is to be tried, participation by all the banks should be mandated – perhaps by the threat that non-participating banks would not later qualify for government compensation. Perhaps this rule should also be applied to banks that refuse to lend more to the LDCs or 'to throw good money after bad'.

Principles to apply in debt reduction

There is no reason to review the details of the problems a debtor faces when it attempts to service its debt. They are clearly more serious when the debt is high and when creditors are mired in severe depression. They are also serious when the debtor, because of limits on its productive resources, competes strongly with other economies. Finally, they are serious when most creditors hold a very small share of the world's international reserves and urgently want more. Sometimes debtors will become convinced that their task is practically hopeless at least for the time being. Meanwhile costs, real and not simply financial, accumulate and an outright default by the debtors becomes likely. In a way, that particular solution is the worst possible. The costs imposed on the creditors reflect prior strategic positioning by various debtors as well as chance and there is no reason to believe that the solution will be equitable. Secondly, it may come at a time that does not suit the convenience of the various creditors. The results would be less unsatisfactory if they could be worked out in the course of discussions between debtors and creditors but again it is necessary to urge that decisions should not only reflect private deals involving the major parties at interest.

There is no time to discuss the principles of an ideal solution. It will be enough to note that the solution should be equitable as between debtors and creditors and amongst the various classes of creditors. The private banks seem to believe that, whatever happens, they should be paid in full. If that is indeed their attitude, they should be reminded that all their losses should be covered only when their officials and directors had absolutely no responsibility for their bad or excessive loans. Moreover, if they have written off part of their LDC loan portfolio, compensation should not extend into the written-off section. They have already had compensation in the form of a reduced tax on their profits. The solution should also be rapid although final payments have to be made so quickly.

In closing my discussion, three other points must be made. First, the scaling-down of debt can take several forms. A creditor can agree to stretch out the servicing of debt over a longer period or a creditor may reduce the interest rate charged on outstanding debt. Some of the larger debtors have already pressed for such concessions. The results would be tidier and comparisons amongst creditors and debtors would be simpler if the same body were assigned supervisory powers over all these renegotiations. Second, if anyone believes that all compensatory payments to the banks have to be financed from tax revenues, I urge that they look at other, more sensible ways of handling that problem. Consider, for example, the procedures followed by the Bank of Canada or the US Federal Reserve when they purchase T-bills on the open market or discount paper from member banks. Finally, when an individual creditor (even all the creditors) of a single country decide to ease the terms of the claim, the beneficiaries are likely to be, in the first instance, other creditors. To illustrate, if Canadian chartered banks decide to reduce their claims against Mexico by, say, 30 per cent, her other creditors (such as US commercial banks) would be the gainers. Mexico's gain would be conditional on a scaling down of all claims against her to something below the level that she could meet given existing constraints. It seems to me that this consideration calls for international consultation aiming at a concerted move by the creditors of all countries to reduce their claims equitably. In these negotiations each country will have a very strong incentive to act as a free rider.

Comment by M. H. I. Dore

Tarshis has recently written two papers dealing with international debt and the problem of LDCs, one of which is reproduced above. He states some important macroeconomic facts; namely; (a) the LDC debt, made up of cumulative balance-of-payments deficits, must reflect cumulative surpluses of the developed countries; (b) the repayment of this debt requires the LDCs, as a group, to run up surpluses with the developed countries, which must therefore be in deficit; (c) given the large surpluses of Japan, West Germany and the Asian NICs, the deficits required in the rest of the developed countries would have to be astronomic if the LDCs are to make a dent in their mountain of debt. Given this backdrop, such trade deficits would involve massive unemployment in the developed countries, which they would find unacceptable. The logical conclusion is that it is impossible for the LDC debt to be repaid. As I am in agreement with Tarshis, I hope to corroborate his evidence and to strengthen the argument for his proposal to resolve the debt problem.

As Tarshis indicates, the debt crisis has an historic parallel in the German reparations crisis of the 1920s. By the Treaty of Versailles, Germany was required to pay more than $30 billion to the Allies as war reparations. Germany was unable to pay and, after a number of tortuous 'reforms', the Allies finally cancelled Germany's debt at the Lausanne Conference in June 1932. Twelve years earlier, Keynes warned of the disastrous nature of the reparations policies. In *The Economic Consequences of the Peace* (1920), he wrote:

> It might be an exaggeration to say that it is impossible for the European Allies to pay the capital and interest due from them on these debts, but to make them do so would certainly be to impose a crushing burden. They may be expected, therefore, to make constant attempts to evade, or escape payment, and those attempts will be a constant source of ill will for many years to come. A debtor nation does not love its creditor, and it is fruitless to expect feelings of goodwill . . . if their future development is stifled for many years to come by an annual tribute which they must pay us.

The German debt was between sovereign nations; we are concerned here with the LDC debt that is owed by sovereign nations to commercial banks, which face bankruptcy – and with it a serious worldwide financial crisis – if the debt is not paid. At the time of writing (June 1988), France had just proposed cancelling one-third of its official debt to sub-Saharan African countries. Britain, West Germany and Canada have made similar proposals but such proposals only deal with debt between countries. As far as is known, no major proposals have been made by the governments to deal with the debt held by commercial banks.

Almost all schemes so far proposed for the solution of the debt crisis suffer from one fundamental flaw; namely, a non-cooperating creditor bank stands to gain for, as the other creditors accept partial capital loss, the non-cooperating bank will see its paper debt rise in value and thus it expects to be a 'free rider'. In game-theoretic terms, such solutions are unstable. For a similar reason, sales of debt on the secondary market have not been successful in reducing the debt burden. Tarshis assesses the recent Morgan Trust–Mexican government plan and finds that it is unstable (in the sense stated above) before declaring that it has been a failure.

On the positive side, Tarshis makes his own interesting proposal that involves the Central Bank of the creditor-nation buying a portion of the commercial banks' debt (say, 20 per cent per year) and crediting the commercial banks' reserves. Of course, any fear of excessive increases in the money supply can be sterilized. The following six points must be noted regarding this proposal. First, the proposal is a stable solution. Each bank within a given jurisdiction (say, the US) sells the same portion of its debt to the Central Bank (the Federal Reserve). Thus the relative indebtedness of the banks remains unchanged. As the debtor-countries have the right to repay a part of the loan at face value, the commercial bank is indifferent between the debtor-country redeeming the debt and the Federal Reserve redeeming it. Thus no bank has the possibility of a 'free ride' by not participating. A non-participating bank will simply carry a larger debt, but there is no incentive for not participating.

Second, the Central Bank is assuming a paper asset that has no real market value as the paper will earn no interest. From the social point of view, the capital loss occurred when the LDC failed to service the debt. Nothing can change that fact. The transfer to the Central Bank is a bookkeeping transaction designed to contain the adverse effects of the social (capital) loss on the monetary system; that is, the loss having occurred, the Central Bank is recognizing the social nature of the loss. The underlying assumption is that the Central Bank does not wish to permit the bankruptcy of any major bank due to this debt. Third, the paper asset need not be a complete loss. As the Central Bank is acting as an insurer, the paper assets can be transferred to a special reserve account. It can be recouped over a long period of time by imposing a special levy on future bank profits. Indeed, in the future, the levy can be used to build up a special insurance fund against sovereign risk.

Fourth, the proposal is highly incentive-compatible. Any Central Bank that institutes the scheme will enable banks in its jurisdiction to enhance trade credit so LDC imports from that country will increase. Once one Central Bank of a developed country adopts the proposed scheme, other Central Banks are bound to follow due to pressure from their export industries. Fifth, the proposal is superior to the status quo, in which the commercial banks are left to cope on their own by rescheduling debt and pretending to carry paper assets that have no market value. In the meantime, the log-jam created by the burden of debt has reduced capital inflows into LDCs to a tiny trickle, major development construction projects have come to a halt, and LDC imports from the developed countries have fallen dramatically. Growth in world trade has reduced and income growth retarded in the developed countries. Finally, the proposal is a monetary solution to a monetary problem – too much credit extended by the commercial banks. It can be further honed until free of fiscal side-effects, unlike the Morgan Trust–Mexico plan, which required the US Treasury to absorb the losses. Goodhart argues that the Central Banks would now contribute lower profits to their respective governments as each Central Bank is wholly owned by its government. However, as indicated above, the social loss has already occurred. The alternative is to let the banks absorb the loss, pay lower or no taxes and, in addition, threaten the world financial system. Surely the Central Bank can act as an instrument of policy!

To use Keynes's words, the debt service has become 'an annual tribute', constituting a serious impediment to world trade and income, and threatening the stability of the international monetary system. Perhaps twelve years from now, there will have to be the equivalent of the 1932 Lausanne Conference but we need not wait that long for Tarshis's proposal is a workable and viable alternative.

Comment by Charles Goodhart

The purchase of LDC debt by Central Banks from commercial banks would have monetary implications unless sterilized by offsetting sales of government debt, which latter could be done easily enough. A more serious problem facing the Tarshis proposal is that it would probably also have immediate fiscal effects unless the LDC debt were sold to the Central Bank at its 'true' market value, which would immediately crystallize the loss for commercial banks and make them unwilling to participate. Assuming that the Central Bank purchases the LDC debt at a book value in excess of market value, it would than face an accounting loss. Unless normal accounting procedures were put aside, this would reduce its profits and, since many Central Banks have a small balance-sheet, probably impose a severe accounting loss. In virtually all cases, the residual (seignorage) profits of a Central Bank are transferred to the Treasury and, thus, Central Bank losses would also have to be made good by the tax-payer. Accordingly, the assumption of (part of) the loss made by commercial banks on LDC debt by Central Banks would then flow through directly to the taxpayer.

14 LDC debt: towards a genuinely cooperative solution

Benjamin J. Cohen

Attitudes on LDC debt are changing. In the first years following Mexico's dramatic financial collapse in the summer of 1982, mainstream opinion in the banking community and capital-market countries, as well as at the multilateral credit agencies (the IMF and World Bank), remained adamantly opposed to any form of direct relief for heavily burdened debtor nations. Third World debtors were effectively illiquid, we were told, rather than in some sense insolvent. Their long-term ability to service external obligations was, in most cases, fundamentally unimpaired; their liabilities were inherently sound. The problem was simply to give LDC governments the time and encouragement needed to institute appropriate economic policy reforms at home while continuing to maintain full interest payments abroad. Assistance should be limited, at most, to periodic debt reschedulings plus some new lending in selected instances – all carefully tied to policy conditionality, administered formally or informally through the IMF and World Bank. The view was institutionalized in the multilateral debt strategy that has framed creditor–debtor relations throughout the decade – defended by its proponents as the only viable route back to creditworthiness for LDCs and denounced by its critics as little more than muddling through.

Initially, critics could be dismissed as uninformed or unduly alarmist. However, as the debt problem dragged on year after year, and LDCs continue to stagnate under the burden of their foreign obligations, more of those involved are coming to realize that muddling through may not be enough – that the liabilities of many developing nations may not be inherently sound and that some form of debt relief, in at least some cases, seems called for. Evidence of changing attitudes can be seen everywhere: in the widening discounts quoted in the secondary market for LDC debt; in the sizeable write-offs and large-scale increases of loan-loss reserves announced recently by major US banks; in the persistently depressed stock-market prices for the equity of the most heavily exposed lending institutions; and, most importantly, in growing talk in banking circles

174

tsonabout 'debt fatigue' and 'getting out'. As summarized guardedly by the IMF in the latest edition of its authoritative capital-markets survey (Watson *et al.*, 1988, p. 12), following extensive discussions with bankers in all the major financial centres: 'Virtually no major banks were prepared in the present environment to contemplate generalized forgiveness of principal . . . [On the other hand,] banks indicated that the situation of [some] countries might eventually have to be regularized by a negotiated reduction of claims.'

Increasingly, the issue seems to be not whether the prevailing debt strategy should be fundamentally reformed, but how. For the many troubled debtors of sub-Saharan Africa, whose loans came primarily from official sources, a variety of relief measures have already been implemented or are in the works (Klein, 1987; Stoga, 1987; United Nations, 1988). For the middle-income, commercial borrowers (concentrated mainly in Latin America), new plans and approaches are being proposed at a rapidly rising rate – not just by scholars and academics, as one might expect (Sachs, 1986; Sachs and Huizinga, 1987; Islam, 1988; Broad and Cavanagh, 1988), but also by present and former international officials (Amuzegar, 1987; Sengupta, 1988; Rotberg, 1988), members of the US Congress (Bradley, 1986; LaFalce, 1987; Pease, 1988), and even commercial and investment bankers (Kuczynski, 1987; Robinson, 1988).[1] The commonly agreed objective is durably to ease the cash-flow strains on debtor-countries in a context of both renewed economic development and continued stability in world financial markets. The question is: what is the best way to get from here to there?

One point is clear. Given the complexity of the problem and the variety and number of actors involved – including transnational actors such as commercial banks and the multilateral agencies, as well as state actors in both debtor and capital-market countries – cooperation on a global scale is obviously needed. Unfortunately, most of the reform proposals that have surfaced until now fail to make clear how the necessary cooperation can be encouraged. My focus, therefore, will be directed to this central issue of incentives. I aim to sketch a possible framework for a genuinely cooperative solution to the problem.

For analytical purposes, cooperation may be defined in terms of mutually beneficial adjustments of behaviour. Using the language of game theory, cooperation is a function of a particular class of pay-off structures where joint gain is possible but not automatically achieved. Two key conditions are essential to the attainment of cooperation in a given issue area of international economic relations. First, there must be a consensus among all the principal players in the game that, despite elements of competition, a potential for joint gain exists. Second, there must be some mechanism or incentive structure sufficient to ensure that, despite unenforceability of contracts, players will undertake the requisite mutual adjustments of behaviour. Lacking the first condition, actors will proceed as if the game is zero-sum even if it is not: they will not perceive any interest in cooperation. Lacking the second condition, actors will proceed as if the joint gain is unrealizable even if it is not: they will not be willing to take any risk for cooperation. Both conditions are necessary for co-operation to emerge on an issue such as debt; together, they are sufficient.

Unfortunately, in today's strategic interaction between LDC debtors and their creditors, only the first of the two conditions appears to obtain in practice. Analysis elsewhere (Cohen, 1988, a, b) suggests that, while an opportunity for joint gain does exist in creditor–debtor relations, it has yet to be exploited, in good part because of the still-determined resistance of lenders to the idea of debt relief. The durability of that resistance, in turn, is attributable to a quite singular alignment of political forces – centred, above all, on the preferences of a small number of large banks, in tacit alliance with Finance Ministries and Central Banks in the capital market countries – that has so far successfully surmounted intra-industry differences and coordination problems to shape the collective behaviour of creditors. Despite evidence of increasing fluidity of alignments on the lender side, there seems little reason to anticipate that the dynamics of the debt 'game' itself might suffice to persuade creditors as a group to take any risk for cooperation. The needed incentive structure will not emerge spontaneously. Institutional innovation, therefore, will be required to overcome existing obstacles reform of the prevailing debt strategy; that is, a mechanism to promote a genuinely cooperative solution will have to be actively designed to be effective. The practical purpose of this chapter is to outline how that vital task of institutional innovation might best be accomplished.

My premise is that joint gain in creditor–debtor relations would be realized by an alternative, more cooperative strategy of debt-relief in appropriate cases. (By debt-relief, I mean any measure to reduce the present value of future contractual obligations.) The following sections consider how, in practical terms, such a strategy could be successfully for-mulated and impemented. The first section takes up the question of leadership – the issue of who, if anyone, will take the initiative needed to get a process of reform started. The other two sections then take up the question of design – what revisions of existing structures might work best to induce all concerned to undertake the requisite mutual adjustments of behaviour. I argue that the task of institutional innovation might best be accomplished through the creation of an international mechanism for debt-relief on the model of Chapter 11 of the US Bankruptcy Code. A key here would be a new institution, the 'International Debt Restructuring Agency', established to set the framework for a negotiated resolution of LDC debt-service difficulties on a case-by-case basis, consistent with the interests of all the parties concerned.

Leadership

Who, if anyone, could be counted upon to take the first steps to overcome existing obstacles to cooperation? That someone is needed to take the first steps should be fairly obvious. The strategic interaction between creditors and debtors is an example of market failure caused by the unwillingness of any one actor, or group of actors, to take responsibility for the collective good of a genuinely cooperative solution. Such goods are characterized by non-excludability; that is, no one can be excluded from their use once they are provided. Hence, for most actors individually, there is little or no incentive to contribute to their production. No one wants to pay costs that could conceivably be avoided: everyone wants to be a 'free rider'. Thus there is a tendency for collective goods to be underproduced or, perhaps, not even produced at all – equivalent, in game-theoretic terms, to saying that any potential for joint gain may well be destroyed by the individual player's temptation to defect.

Out of this dilemma comes the theory of hegemonic stability – the familiar argument that order in international relations requires the presence of a single strongly dominant actor (a hegemon) prepared to provide the collective good of stability.[2] Not everyone can afford to be a free rider. Dominant powers, in particular, are constrained by the potential systemic consequences of their own actions, as well as by potential feedbacks from the wider system to themselves that may result from their actions. Since they presumably have the biggest stake in the system, they must be concerned about possibly adverse 'ripple effects' that could flow from their individual behaviour. From this, follows an interest in taking some responsibility for systemic stability and maintenance, even should that mean bearing a disproportionate share of the cost. This interest leads to the two central propositions of the theory of hegemonic stability: first, order in international relations is typically created by a single dominant power; and second, maintenance of order requires the continued presence of hegemony. The core of the argument was succinctly stated by Kindleberger (1973, p. 305): 'For the world economy to be stabilized, there has to be a stabilizer, one stabilizer.'

Since Kindleberger wrote, all kinds of caveats have been introduced to qualify the bluntness of his assertion, leading to a general consensus that neither of the two propositions can be taken entirely at face value. As summarized by Keohane (1984, pp. 31–2): 'There is little reason to believe that hegemony is either a necessary or a sufficient condition for the emergence of cooperative relationships. Furthermore . . . cooperation does not necessarily require the existence of a hegemonic leader. . . . Post-hegemonic cooperation is also possible.' As summarized by Snidal (1985, pp. 612–14): 'The theory of hegemonic stability is a special case. . . . There can be no single neat answer.' This does not mean that leadership is therefore unimportant, particularly in so far as the first proposition is concerned. Quite the contrary, in fact, as both Keohane and Snidal have been quick to admit. Keohane concedes (1984, p. 31, 49): 'There is some validity in a modest version of the first proposition of the theory of hegemonic stability – that hegemony can facilitate a certain type of cooperation. . . . Hegemonic leadership can help to create a pattern of order.' And Snidal (1985, p. 613): 'While dominance by a single actor may not be necessary, models of collective action indicate that *some* asymmetry may be useful in reducing the number of [actors] whose participation is necessary for cooperation to succeed.' Leadership may not be the *sine qua non* for generating the collective good of stability but genuinely cooperative solutions will almost surely be a good deal more difficult to organize without it.

The importance of leadership as a facilitator of cooperation is certainly evident in the context of the debt problem. If successful collective action is unlikely to emerge spontaneously in this complex setting, a genuinely cooperative solution must be organized and that calls for initiative by those most capable of bringing everyone to agreement – that is, those with the greatest capacity to threaten or cajole others into accord. In the words of Krugman (1987, pp. 13–14):

> [T]he costs incurred by a failure to reach agreement represents a real social cost (e.g., through disruption of trade, financial flows, political stability, etc.). It may be worthwhile for the [debtors] and their bankers to accept this cost in order to demonstrate their toughness, but it is preferable from the world's point of view, and possibly from the point of view of the parties themselves, if agreement can be reached more quickly. Thus there is a potential albeit problematic role for [third parties] as facilitators of agreement [who] can use sticks and carrots to induce quicker agreement between the bargainers.

This situation does not mean that the leader (or leaders) must end up bearing a disproportionate burden; the issue of the distribution of costs and benefits at the outcome is quite separate from the issue of what side-payment or sanctions may be needed to get the process started. Nor does it mean that the maintenance of agreement requires the continued presence of a dominant power; in that respect, analysts like Keohane and Snidal may be correct in arguing that international cooperation can, in principle, be preserved even after hegemony. It only means that someone must take responsibility for getting the ball rolling in the first place.

Someone must lead, and who could that someone be today other than the US? Its global hegemony, since World War II, may have declined substantially across a broad range of economic issues but, in so far as the LDC debt problem is concerned, there is still no other obvious candidate. The US (despite its own debtor status at present) is unique in its capacity to exercise effective influence over lenders and borrowers alike, by means of bribes or side-payments or by threats to withhold assistance. Moreover, it remains the universally acknowledged leader. As Strange (1983, p. 179) has written, in presenting an avowedly 'European' view of the debt issue: 'Nothing happens unless the United States leads.' If the necessary initiative is to come from anywhere, it would appear that it must come from Washington. In the words of investment banker Rohatyn (1986, p. 21): 'The real question we are facing is whether our government will take the lead in proposing to negotiate some . . . plan with Latin America, Europe, and Japan in view of all the political benefits we could derive from such an initiative. Or will we wait for a desperate Mexico or another country to unilaterally default on its payments, denounce its debts, and set off a crisis?' In fact, a good deal of initiative already has come from Washington, first in originating and then in managing the debt strategy that has prevailed since 1982.

Within the singular alignment of political forces that until now has successfully shaped the collective behaviour of creditors, no actors have been more influential than those of the US: the major money-centre banks of New York, Chicago and California, together with the Federal Reserve and, most importantly, the Department of the Treasury. Other players on the creditor side generally tend to defer to US leadership in dealing with Third World debt problems (Aggarwal, 1987, ch. 3). This reflects not only the key role of the dollar as the currency of denomination for most LDC paper (making the Federal Reserve, in effect, the *de facto* lender of last resort in the event of a debt-induced banking crisis) but also the dominant market share of US lenders in the most prominent of the troubled debtor-nations (for example, Latin America and the Philippines). Bank advisory committees, which have become the standard vehicle for negotiations with LDC debtors, traditionally tend to comprise (at most) a dozen or so of each country's largest creditors. This has given big US money-centre intermediaries, backed by the Treasury, by far the greatest influence in setting the tone of discussions (Holley, 1987, pp. 25–6). It is no accident that the 'multilateral strategy' was first articulated by a US Treasury Secretary back in 1982 (Regan, 1982). Nor is it an accident that all major adjustments of the strategy since then have also emanated from

Washington – for example, the Baker Plan of 1985 and the 'menu-of-options' approach of 1987 (Cline, 1987).

The trouble with all these initiatives is that they largely focused on purely financial aspects rather than on, say, diplomatic or commercial implications. Consistent with the priorities of any finance ministry, relatively little weight has been attached at the Treasury to possible threats of political disruption or lost export opportunities in the Third World. US policy, in practice, has been conditioned most directly by concerns for the safety and soundness of lending institutions – and since the largest institutions have been most at risk, their interests have tended to receive the most attention (Sachs and Huizinga, 1987, pp. 555–7). As one former Treasury Department official (Broad, 1987) noted: 'Treasury actions have catered to the short-term profit of large American banks.' The interests of other players on the creditor side, such as smaller lenders or exporters, and debtors may not have been wholly ignored but they certainly have been effectively discounted. No wonder a genuinely cooperative solution has so far proved elusive!

The challenge, then, is not to get the US to lead – Washington has already been taking a lead – but rather to get it to lead in a different direction and that obviously requires a new coalition of political forces, sufficient to prevail over the now dominant, albeit tacit, alliance between big US banks and the US Treasury. Only an altered political equation at home will bring about a fresh set of policy priorities abroad. If new steps are to be taken to persuade all players – in particular, creditors – to accent the requisite risks for cooperation, a deliberate effort must begin to change the underlying configuration of power that is the determining factor of US policy in this area. Although an opportunity is offered by indications of increasing fluidity of alignments on the creditor side, little evidence suggests that a new and stronger alliance of forces can be expected to emerge spontaneously (Cohen, 1988b). Rising strains among the interested parties are not enough: resentments and frustrations must be translated into effective collective action if the political equation is in fact to be significantly altered, which means a superior use of power to alter the pay-off structure confronting the largest lenders – new tactics of side-payments or sanctions to overcome the big banks' continued resistance to the idea of debt relief. This can be accomplished only by some degree of political organization among other players inside the financial community and/or outside of it. The status quo will not be abandoned without a struggle.

Regrettably, efforts along these lines have not so far proved very fruitful. An early case in point was provided by the debt-relief scheme proposed by Senator Bradley of New Jersey back in 1986. Under this plan, all outstanding loans to eligible countries would have been written down by 3 per cent a year for three years and interest rates would have been reduced by three percentage points over the same period – with eligibility tied directly to a debtor-government's commitment to a programme of trade liberalization designed to promote imports from the US and other industrialized nations. By linking trade and debt so explicitly, Bradley plainly hoped to attract export interests into the policy-making process as a counterweight to the prevailing influence of the money-centre banks. Despite some initially favourable reactions (see, for example, AFL-CIO, 1986), the plan soon faded into oblivion owing to the persistent, and determined, opposition of the US Treasury. Much the same fate has also awaited similar proposals promoted more recently by other members of Congress, such as Representative LaFalce of New York or Representative Pease of Ohio. Still, there seems little alternative to more efforts of the same kind. The problem, until now, is the lack of either a tradition or an institutional base for effective collective action by exporters and other interested parties on the creditor side, such as smaller US lenders or the large European banks. The more such ideas are floated in the public domain, however, the more likely these diverse actors will come to appreciate just how great are the interests they share in common – hence, the more likely a new and stronger coalition of forces could be forged. Nothing is certain in politics, admittedly. US policy priorities may not change, if at all, in time to avert an outright breakdown in creditor–debtor relations. However, the opportunity is there if it can be seized by political representatives in Congress or a new US administration. One can only hope that it will not be too late.

The design of an appropriate mechanism

Much will depend on the altered pay-off structure offered large lenders to persuade them to abandon the status quo. This brings us to the most fundamental question of all: the design of the mechanism needed to promote a genuinely cooperative solution. What structure of incentives would work best to induce all concerned to undertake the requisite mutual adjustments of behaviour? One possibility, obviously, would be to coerce the largest lenders into accepting the idea of debt relief. According to some legal sources, it is within the authority of the US government to use pre-emptory action to reduce claims of private US citizens on foreign sovereign entities.[3] Precedents exist in the settlements negotiated in the late 1940s with a number of Latin American nations, giving US bond-holders no more than a few cents on the dollar for defaulted debts dating back to the 1920s; as well as in the more recent series of cases arising out of the freeze of revolutionary Iran's assets in the US financial institutions in 1979. In similar fashion, commercial bank claims on LDCs today could conceivably be marked down without the direct consent of the lenders involved, as a result of direct government-to-government negotiations. However, a solution imposed on creditors could hardly be described as cooperative and could, quite possibly, be dynamically unstable in so far as banks might be tempted to 'defect' from any further lending in the Third World. Far more stable (and certainly more practicable in political terms) would be a solution based on positive rather than negative incentives for creditors.

What might such positive incentives look like? What concessions from other parties would be most likely to draw creditors into voluntary concessions of their own? Clues are provided by what creditors themselves have to say about debt relief. Mostly they object, of course. Even with evidence of changing attitudes in the financial community, resistance remains undeniably strong and vocal. An analysis of why creditors object, however, can help us understand what sort of safeguards or side-payments might make the idea less unpalatable to them in the future – in effect, to help us understand what revisions of the 'rules of the game' might be regarded as a fair price for their cooperation. Creditor objections to debt relief traditionally encompass a wide range of arguments of varying degrees of intellectual sophistication and rigour. For analytical purposes, it is convenient to group these arguments under six major headings: contagion, creditworthiness, discipline, moral hazard, legal issues and politics. While none of these arguments is without its self-serving elements – lenders are not disinterested bystanders – all deserve to be taken seriously for what they can tell us about perceptions and motivations on the creditor side.

Contagion
Perhaps the most self-serving arguments stress the possible 'contagion effects' of a widespread mark-down of Third World debt obligations. Heavily exposed lenders express concern not only about what such a step might mean for their own safety and soundness but, more broadly, about what it could do to the banking industry and world financial markets in general. Given the manifold links that exist between creditor institutions, a single major insolvency could produce potentially disastrous ripples and feedbacks. At a minimum, many intermediaries could be significantly weakened while at worst, a full-blown financial crisis might occur. Empirically, we may point to a degree of exaggeration inherent in contentions of this kind. Vulnerable though they may be, banks have been remarkably successful in building up their defences against any threat of losses on their Third World exposure. Not only have they bolstered

general capital ratios quite substantially since the Mexican crisis in 1982; they have also been active more recently in augmenting loan-loss reserves and, in some instances, in writing off or selling into the secondary market selected portions of their LDC portfolios (Cohen, 1988b). Moreover, talk of a possible financial crisis tends to discount the effectiveness of present prudential supervisory practices as well as the powerful role of Central Banks as lenders of last resort. Also note the potentially positive impact that debt relief might have on the equity prices and credit ratings of major banks, which until now have been depressed by market doubts about the true value of the LDC paper on their books (Sachs and Huizinga, 1987; Sachs, 1987). While the risk of contagion effects is undoubtedly real, this is unlikely to be as serious as sometimes suggested.

More constructively, we may point to safeguards that could be developed to minimize whatever risk may remain and thus ease the concerns expressed by creditors. At least two such safeguards could be imagined. One possibility would be to insist on selectivity; that is, to limit reductions of contractual obligations to those countries that, by objective analysis, appear to face something approximating insolvency rather than mere illiquidity. This is what I meant earlier by appropriate cases. A differentiated, case-by-case approach is already employed as part of the prevailing debt strategy. An equivalent approach, applied in the context of debt relief, would substantially diminish potential hits to bank earnings and balance-sheets. A second possible safeguard would involve greater flexibility in accounting for all such hits – regulatory changes or reinterpretations permitting banks to avoid an immediate write-down of existing capital assets when obligations are in fact reduced. Such reforms are well within the scope of supervisors' present authority in most of the capital-market countries. In the US, for instance, ample precedents exist under current accounting rules for flexibly stretching out lenders' capital losses in selected instances – for example, under the system of Allocated Transfer Risk Reserves for LDC loans that have been classified as value impaired (Cohen, 1986, pp. 300–1). Why not authorize banks to spread out the costs of debt relief in the same way? Neither safeguard would remove all the pain on creditors, of course, but they would certainly help significantly to reduce levels of discomfort and so contain any threat of contagion spreading from one financial institution to another.[4]

Creditworthiness

A second line of argument – also somewhat self-serving – points to possible consequences for debtors rather than creditors – specifically, the potential damage that debt relief could do to the long-term credit standing of developing nations. Like any bankrupt enterprise or individual, LDCs could find their access to market financing severely curtailed, perhaps even totally blocked, for an indefinite period should their creditors be obliged to cancel some fraction of outstanding contractual obligations. In the words of one New York banker (De Vries, 1986, p. 10): 'If banks are required to write down their loans, simple prudence . . . would surely inhibit new lending to troubled countries for years to come.' The result could be to delay even longer a recovery of healthy economic growth in LDCs. The logic of this argument might be more persuasive but for a simple fact: troubled countries already appear to have suffered severe damage to their credit standing. In fact, no new money is now going to debtors apart from concerted ('involuntary') lending agreements. Even in those instances, a perverse relationship has developed between debtor performance and credit availability. Any improvement in a debtor's economic health tends to be reflected in a reduction rather than an increase of capital inflows as concerted lending is cut back – meaning, in effect, that success in complying with the prevailing debt strategy is punished rather than rewarded by creditors. In Krugman's words (1987, p. 45): 'This amounts to a tax on the country's efforts to adjust its economy.' Seen in this light, creditor expressions of concern for LDC creditworthiness seem disingenuous.

Indeed, the logic of the argument could be stood on its head in so far as debt relief might actually enhance the capacity of LDCs to service their remaining obligations. Foreign-exchange earnings presently absorbed by interest payments abroad could, instead, be used to promote accelerated investment and economic reforms at home; and creditworthiness might ultimately improve as a result. Much depends, of course, on what debtor governments do with their newfound degrees of freedom. From the creditors' point of view, the pain associated with debt relief would surely seem a good deal more tolerable if they could be assured that developing countries would not waste the additional resources made available to them. This suggests a third safeguard (already well established as part of the prevailing debt strategy) to help minimize the risks of an alternative approach; namely, conditionality, making relief contingent upon pursuit of appropriate policies by debtor governments.

Discipline
The third line of argument stresses the risk that debt relief would critically dilute present incentives to adopt tough measures for domestic adjustment and reforms. The advantage of the prevailing strategy, creditors insist, is that it encourages overall responsibility in economic management. The disadvantages of an alternate approach, as put by Morgan Guaranty Bank (1987, pp. 5–6) is that it 'would only weaken discipline over economic

policy and undermine support for structural reform'. Debtors, it appears, are like little children who must be kept under close watch lest they go astray or misbehave! Here too the logic of the argument could be stood on its head in so far as present incentives are already diluted by the perverse relationship that has developed between debtor performance and credit availability. The effective tax on successful adjustment actually tends to discourage rather than to encourage a continued commitment to the current terms of the game. Moreover, there is also the question of incentives for banks, which have paid little direct price for their own imprudent lending. No formal concessions of any significance have yet been extracted from commercial lenders in most instances, apart from the rescheduling of maturities and some modest reductions of interest margins. With few exceptions, bankers insist on holding debtors to their full contractual obligations, while carrying the loans on their books at 100 per cent of face value. Lacking some explicit loss on existing claims, what discipline is there to ensure that banks will exercise appropriate caution in the future?[5]

Given the intense distributional struggles that underlay economic policy-making in any country, creditors have a point with the discipline argument. Any government is apt to be irresponsible if presented with a free good. However, why should we assume that debt-relief need be granted without strings attached? To the contrary, the case for retaining conditionality as an integral part of such an approach is reinforced. Incentives for responsible management could be strengthened if directly linked to a reduction of outstanding contractual obligations.

Moral hazard
Parallel to the discipline argument is the issue of moral hazard – the risk that some developing nations might take deliberate steps to worsen their economic performance in order to qualify for debt relief. Any compromise of the prevailing strategy, we are told, would appear to reward wasteful or inefficient policies at the expense of those who, until now, have done everything possible to keep up with their contractual obligations. In the words of Angermueller (1987, p. 5) of Citicorp: 'Such proposals ... make a mockery of the good policies and sacrifices of troubled debtor countries that have adopted measures to work their way out of the problem.' The danger is that these countries too might be tempted to relax their domestic discipline. The answer to this argument, plainly, is the same as before: make any approach contingent upon pursuit of appropriate policies. Moral hazard might indeed be a problem if the strings attached to debt-relief appear too loose. With a real price to be paid, governments would be deterred to the extent that the costs of qualifying for relief exceed

any benefits to be accrued. The trick, of course, would be in determining how high that price should be – high enough to be effective as a deterrent to moral hazard yet not too high to drive away those that are truly in need.

Legal issues
A fifth line of argument stresses legal problems involving everything from the definition of obligations and the identity of obligors to the relationship and priorities among various foreign claimants. An even more fundamental objection concerns the sanctity of contracts; namely, the fear that *any* abrogation of contracts (voluntarily entered into in the past) would severely, if not permanently, undermine the basis for any further commercial lending in the future. Why should creditors ever again put money into the Third World if full repayment cannot be assured? These are consequential issues and clearly must be confronted head on. They are, however, within the wit of humans to resolve as most nations amply demonstrate in their domestic arrangements for dealing with the challenge of insolvency. Basic legal theory has long held that occasions arise when contracts should not be enforced but rather should be rewritten – particularly when, as a result of low-probability contingencies not foreseen when the contracts were originally written, they place extreme and unexpected burdens on debtors (see, for example, Posner and Rosenfield, 1977). The concern is whether rigid insistence by creditors on full adherence to contractual obligations could so endanger a debtor's capacity to pay that both sides might be better off with some form of relief. The means for resolution at the national level are already well developed in mechanisms such as Chapter 11 of the US Bankruptcy Code (or analogous regulations elsewhere). There seems little reason, in principle, why similar mechanisms could not be used at the international level. From the creditors' point of view, the key safeguard here would appear to be a need for mutuality: explicit recognition of rights and obligations on both sides.

Politics
The final line of argument is that any scheme for debt relief would surely intrude politics into the creditor–debtor relationship. Is this necessarily so? One could argue just the opposite; namely, that the issue (which obviously is already highly politicized) could be defused by any orderly procedure that manages to ease the cash-flow strains of debtor countries in a context of both renewed development and continued stability in financial markets. Much depends on the degree to which some political authority would be directly interposed between creditors and debtors in setting the terms of relief. Commercial lenders, understandably, would be

happiest with a minimum of political intervention, preserving as much as possible of the voluntary and market-oriented character of today's negotiating framework. A final safeguard, therefore, would be to reaffirm the basic autonomy of actors on both sides. In practical terms, this could prove to be the most important incentive from the creditors' point of view.

Towards a practical model

My analysis of creditor objections has suggested five crucial safeguards that could help reduce resistance to the idea of debt relief. These are:

- selectivity – a differentiated case-by-case approach;
- flexibility – rule changes to stretch out costs to creditors;
- conditionality – a direct link between relief and appropriate policy commitments by debtors;
- mutuality – explicit recognition of rights and obligations on both sides; and
- autonomy – preservation of an essentially voluntary and market-oriented negotiating framework.

These safeguards may be understood as the working principles for a new and truly multilateral strategy on debt. The challenge is to translate them into a practical and effective design to promote cooperation.

As indicated, a useful model is provided by Chapter 11 of the US Bankruptcy Code, or analogous mechanisms elsewhere, which deal with problems of insolvency at the national level. Under Chapter 11, debtors unable to meet their contractual obligations can appeal for protection from creditors while they reorganize their affairs (under the supervision of a bankruptcy court) and work out mutually satisfactory terms for a resolution of their difficulties. Settlement terms, subject to certain conditions, may include just about anything to which debtors and a qualified majority of creditors can agree through direct negotiation – deferral of principal, reduction of interest rates, conversion of debts into alternative claims, and so on. The role of the court, in the first instance, is to facilitate negotiations with creditors (for example, by establishing representative committees for each class of claimant, setting timetables for discussions, and acting as a conduit of communication) while exercising general surveillance over the relevant managerial decisions of the debtor. More broadly, the court's responsibility is to use its adjudicatory powers to ensure that creditors receive equitable treatment at the same time that debtors are given the breathing space needed to put their affairs back in order.[6]

The attractions of a Chapter 11 procedure are obvious for it embodies all of the working principles identified above. Mutuality and actor autonomy are preserved by an (essentially) voluntary and market-oriented negotiating framework, based on explicit recognition of respective rights and obligations. Selectivity is embodied in the right of the debtor to make the initial decision to seek protection while flexibility is inherent in the virtually unlimited scope provided for final terms of settlement. Also conditionality is respected in the assignment of a supervisory role to the court over the debtor's ongoing operations. Debtors may benefit from the opportunity to get back on their feet without being driven to the wall. Creditors too are safeguarded in so far as conditions are attached to the assistance provided obligors. Relief does not come without a price.

Parties interested in the problem of Third World debt have long lamented the absence of something like Chapter 11 at the international level (see, for example, Dell, 1985; Williamson, 1985). As one respected legal authority (Suratgar, 1984, pp. 155, 159) has written, events since 1982 have exposed 'the shortcomings of the framework for international bankruptcy . . . What is needed is some international variation on the Chapter 11 approach.' Until now, institutional innovation along these lines has been effectively blocked by the determined opposition of creditors. However, with attitudes on LDC debt now changing in the financial community, the time may be ripe for serious consideration of an alternative approach. What shape might it take? To begin, an appropriate institution must be established; namely, some entity authorized to play a role comparable to that of the bankruptcy court at the core of the Chapter 11 procedure. Negotiations between creditors and debtors may be direct and voluntary but, if the two sides are to take the requisite risks for cooperation, there must be some neutral intermediary capable of assuring them that their respective rights and needs will be respected. A new set of 'rules of the game' would not suffice to overcome the misgivings over motives and commitments inherent in any such strategic interaction. Players also require a degree of confidence that the rules will be interpreted and implemented in a fair and equitable manner – ensuring creditors that moral hazard will be effectively deterred and ensuring debtors that the price paid for relief will not be punitive. As investment banker (and former Peruvian government minister) Kuczynski (1987, p. 142) argued: 'A plan [for debt relief] would work only if it were monitored by a widely trusted international agency and subject to reasonably objective standards of application.' In short, we need some sort of referee.

Precedents for such an institution are not lacking at the international level. One example is provided by the Iran–US Claims Tribunal established in 1981 as part of the agreement negotiated between Washington and Tehran to unblock Iran's frozen assets in exchange for the release of American hostages held since 1979 (Riesenfeld, 1982; Cohen, 1986, ch. 4). Another is provided by the International Centre for Settlement of Investment Disputes (ICSID), an affiliate of the World Bank created over two decades ago to provide a forum for resolving conflicts between states and foreign investors (Soley, 1985; Shihata, 1986). ICSID functions as an arbitrator for any investment dispute submitted to it. The process is voluntary in the sense that the interested parties decide whether to consent to the ICSID machinery but the process is binding in that once consent is given it cannot be revoked, and all judgements are final. Disputes covered by ICSID concern every possible type of foreign direct investment, from wholly-owned or joint ventures to technical and licensing agreements. Specifically excluded are conflicts relating to purely financial transactions of the sort with which we are concerned here.

  For our purpose, there is a key problem with these precedents; namely, the extent of the powers to be conferred on the referee. In principle, a wide range of alternative models for conflict resolution may be distinguished, depending *inter alia* on the degree of authority accorded a designated third party to fix settlement terms between disputants (Goldman, 1985). At one extreme are procedures based on governmental fiat or its equivalent – models that are clearly incompatible with the principle of actor autonomy. At the other extreme are approaches relying exclusively on direct negotiations between the actors involved, formally independent of explicit intervention by third parties – essentially the method embodied in the prevailing debt strategy. In between these extremities, there are other models that attempt, in effect, to compromise between them – for example adjudication or arbitration, where neutral third parties are empowered in some degree to resolve differences on the basis of settled principles; and mediation or conciliation, where the role of third parties is limited to facilitating negotiations by one means or another. Existing precedents are all placed further towards the government fiat end of the range than is likely to prove acceptable to either sovereign borrowers or commercial lenders. Chapter 11 depends on the broad adjudicatory authority of the bankruptcy court while both the Iran–US Tribunal and ICSID act in an arbitrational capacity. Such precedents are therefore imperfect analogies for my purpose. If political intervention in the creditor–debtor relationship is to be minimized, consistent with the other working principles, the powers of the referee will necessarily have to be more restricted. A new approach must rely on mediation or conciliated negotiation if it is to be workable in practical terms.

  An effective alternative to the prevailing debt strategy might thus be designed along the following lines. An appropriate institution would be established by multilateral convention to set the framework for a negotiated resolution of LDC debt-service difficulties on a case-by-case basis, consistent with the interests of both creditors and debtors. The institution could be called the International Debt Restructuring Agency (IDRA). Ideally, it would be organized as a new and independent entity in order to underscore its neutrality and objectivity. In practice, its creation might be more feasible and quicker if IDRA started as a joint subsidiary of the IMF and World Bank, relying on the expertise and experience of existing staff who would be seconded for this specific project. LDC debtors would have the right to apply to IDRA if they believe that their circumstances warrant some degree of debt relief. In doing so, they would irrevocably commit themselves to a process of conciliated negotiation with their creditors as well as to some degree of surveillance of their policies by IDRA. Relief would be provided only where all the concerned parties concur that it is justified. The terms of relief would be anything to which the debtor and a qualified majority of creditors can agree. Following agreement, terms would be supervised by IDRA until such time as the country is back on its feet and, hopefully, its external creditworthiness restored.

The general role of IDRA would be to facilitate negotiations between creditors and debtors on a fair and equitable basis. Following application by a debtor, IDRA would establish or (where such negotiating groups already exist as in the standard advisory committees for medium-term bank debts) certify representative committees for each class of claimant. Once such creditor committees exist, IDRA would set timetables for submission of initial negotiating positions, responses, counter-proposals, and so on. IDRA would investigate the policies and financial conditions of the debtor, in order to provide a common factual basis for negotiators on both sides. More controversially, IDRA might be authorized to go beyond mere fact-finding to undertake formal evaluation of the policies and financial conditions of the debtor, with the aim of providing an objective analysis of its overall economic circumstances and prospects. In effect, the purpose would be to determine, in as neutral a manner as possible, whether the country faces something approximating insolvency rather than mere illiquidity; and if so, to what extent.

Even more controversially, IDRA could be authorized to *propose* its own possible formulae and terms for settlement to help bridge gaps between positions and identify areas of potential agreement. It could even be authorized to *compel* agreement in the event of deadlock. For example, dissenting creditors might be obliged to accept terms agreed by a qualified majority if IDRA declares the proposed settlement to be 'fair and equitable', in the best interests of all concerned – this authority would parallel the 'cramdown' rule that is part of the Chapter 11 procedure (Weintraub, 1980, ch. 12). Alternatively, both sides might be obliged to accept a settlement that is proposed by IDRA itself if agreement cannot be attained within the limits of the specified timetable. Obviously, this function would distinctly shade IDRA's conciliator role into the area of arbitration and thus could prove too much for either lenders or borrowers to accept but if included as only a last-resort element in an otherwise flexible and unencumbered negotiating process, it might have some appeal to all concerned. Finally, as part of any settlement, IDRA (or another agency designated by IDRA, such as the IMF or World Bank) would be responsible for monitoring the debtor's economic performance in order to ensure adherence. Creditors would be permitted to withdraw concessions if IDRA determines a debtor is out of compliance with its policy commitments.

Would such a design be politically feasible? Commercial banks as well as developing countries ought to find it attractive since, like the Chapter 11 procedure, it embodies the five working principles that seem necessary. The banks' home governments should also find it appealing since a minimal demand is put on public revenues. Unlike most other debt-relief proposals that would require some level of funding by the capital-market countries, IDRA would entail no new financial burden beyond operating expenses. Implicitly, to be sure, there would be a cost to taxpayers in so far as they would compensate for any tax deductions or credits legitimately taken by banks when LDC obligations are marked down. This could give rise to charges that public money was being used to 'bail out' private lenders but that would be true only to the extent that the loss of taxable bank earnings implied by any settlement negotiated under IDRA could otherwise be averted – a dubious proposition at best. In any event, the pain for taxpayers would be eased no less than that for banks by any regulatory changes to stretch out the costs of debt relief. Any discomfort remaining should not be politically intolerable – a small price to be paid for a genuinely cooperative solution to the debt problem.

On the other hand, one could argue that the proposed IDRA mechanism does not add much. After all, creditors and debtors already negotiate directly, case by case, on a formally voluntary and market-oriented basis; and as the latest IMF survey of the markets has testified, bankers seem ready to acknowledge the need for selective concessions in appropriate circumstances to ease the plight of troubled debtors. Why interpose some new player in a game where the old players already know all the rules? The answer should be evident: it is because of the dynamic instability that is inherent in the game as currently played – the 'market failure' of an unexploited opportunity for joint gain. Today's approach is costly because it inevitably generates frustration, confrontation and conflict. The great advantage of the IDRA approach, by contrast, is that it would structure incentives in a far more positive way for all concerned.

In the end, an IDRA mechanism would only be as effective as creditors and debtors want it to be. However, in a situation where both sides could potentially benefit as compared with the prevailing strategy, goodwill ought not to be in short supply. So why not try?

Notes

1. A long line of reform proposals stretch back to the very beginning of the debt problem in 1982. For useful discussions of various proposals, see Bergsten, Cline and Williamson (1985); Guerguil (1986); Fischer (1987).
2. For examples, see Kindleberger (1973); Gilpin (1981). For evaluations, see Keohane (1984); Snidal (1985).
3. Opinion in legal circles on this issue is hardly unanimous, however. For a balanced discussion, see Riesenfeld (1982). His main conclusion is that there is much juridicial uncertainty on this issue owing to changing interpretations of underlying principles – in particular, the principle of foreign sovereign immunity.
4. According to one estimate, based on recent years' financial results, a five-year write-down cumulating to 25 per cent of Third-World exposure (beyond the write-down that would already be permitted by previous loan-loss provisions) would require large US money-centre banks, on average, to allocate no more than half their annual pre-tax earnings – painful, clearly, but hardly devastating (Pease, 1988, p. 101).
5. Banks have indeed paid a price through the depression of their equity prices and credit ratings. This, it may be argued, was finally acknowledged with the large-scale increases of loan-loss reserves that were begun by Citicorp and other US lenders in the spring of 1987. However, even with these additional provisions (mostly created via transfers out of existing bank equity), there has been no general write-off or outright forgiveness of existing debts. As David Rockefeller wrote in the summer of 1987, 'this transfer of funds – and that is all it is – has not cost the banks a penny. It does not reduce the obligations of the debtor nations, nor will it diminish the efforts by the banks to recover all the interest and principal represented by their current loans.'
6. For a useful guide to the intricacies of Chapter 11, see Weintraub (1980).

References

AFL-CIO (1986), 'The international debt problem', Statement by the AFL-CIO Executive Council, 5 August.

Aggarwal, V. K. (1987), *International Debt Threat: Bargaining Among Creditors and Debtors in the 1980s*, Institute of International Studies.

Amuzegar, J. (1987), 'Dealing with Debt', *Foreign Policy*, **68**, Fall, 140–58.

Angermueller, H. H. (1987), 'LDC debt: a fork in the road', in *A Current Perspective on LDC Debt, Views* by H. H. Angermueller and J. D. Guenther, Citicorp, 1–6.

Bergsten, C.F., W.R. Cline and J. Williamson (1985), *Bank Lending to Developing Countries: The Policy Alternatives*, Institute for International Economics.

Bradley, B. (1986), 'A proposal for Third World debt management', Speech presented in Zurich, 29 June.

Broad, R. (1987), 'How about a real solution to Third World debt?', *The New York Times*, 28 September, A25.

Broad, R. and J. Cavanagh (1988), 'How to approach Third World debt', *The New York Times*, 3 March, A31.

Cline, W. R. (1987), *Mobilizing Bank Lending to Debtor Countries*, Institute for International Economics.

Cohen, B. J. (1986), *In Whose Interest? International Banking and American Foreign Policy*, Yale University Press for the Council on Foreign Relations.

Cohen, B. J. (1988a), *LDC Debt: Is There an Unexploited Opportunity for Joint Gain?*, forthcoming.

Cohen, B. J. (1988b), *LDC Debt: Is Activism Required?*, forthcoming.

Dell, S. (1985), 'Crisis management and the international debt problem', *International Journal*, **40**, 655–88.

De Vries, R. (1986), 'LDC debt: debt relief or market solutions?', *World Financial Markets*, September 1–11.

Fischer, S. (1987), *Resolving the International Debt Crisis*, forthcoming.

Gilpin, R. (1981), *War and Change in World Politics*, Cambridge: Cambridge University Press.

Goldman, A. (1985), 'Settlement of disputes over interests', in R. Blanpain (ed.), *Comparative Labour Law and Industrial Relations*, 2nd rev. ed, Kluwer, 359–80.

Guerguil, M. (1986), 'The international financial crisis: diagnosis and prescriptions', in Economic Commission for Latin America and the Caribbean, *Debt, Adjustment, and Renegotiation in Latin America: Orthodox and Alternative Approaches*, Lynne Rienner Pub., 29–62.

Holley, H.A. (1987), *Developing Country Debt: The Role of the Commercial Banks*, Chatham House Papers No. 35, London: Routledge and Kegan Paul.

Islam, S. (1988), *Breaking the International Debt Deadlock*, Critical Issues Series No. 2, Council on Foreign Relations.

Keohane, R.O. (1984), *After Hegemony: Cooperation and Discord in the World Political Economy*, Princeton, N.J: Princeton University Press.

Kindleberger, C.P. (1973), *The World in Depression, 1929–1939*, University of California Press.

Klein, T.M. (1987), 'Debt relief for African countries', *Finance and Development*, **24**, December, 10–13.

Krugman, P. (1987), *Private Capital Flows to Problem Debtors*, forthcoming.

Kuczynski, P.-P. (1987), 'The outlook for Latin American debt', *Foreign Affairs*, **66**, Fall, 129–49.

LaFalce, J. (1987), 'Third World debt crisis: the urgent need to confront reality', Statement presented in Washington, 5 March.

Morgan Guaranty Bank (1987), 'LDC debt realities', *World Financial Markets*, June/July, 1–14.

Pease, D. (1988), 'A congressional plan to solve the debt crisis', *The International Economy*, **2**, March/April, 98–105.

Posner, R.A. and A.M. Rosenfield (1977), 'Impossibility and related doctrines in contract law: an economic analysis', *Journal of Legal Studies*, **6**, 83–118.

Regan, D.T. (1982), 'Statement', *International Financial Markets and Related Matters*, Hearings before the House Committee on Banking, Finance and Urban Affairs, 21 December, 34–39.

Riesenfeld, S.A. (1982), 'The powers of the executive to govern the rights of creditors in the event of defaults of foreign governments', *University of Illinois Law Review*, **1**, 319–331.

Robinson, J.D. (1988), *A Comprehensive Agenda for LDC Debt and World Trade Growth*, The Amex Bank Review Special Papers No. 13, American Express Bank.

Rockefeller, D. (1987), 'Let's not write off Latin America', *The New York Times*, 5 July, Sect. 4, E15.

Rohatyn, F. (1986), 'The new chance for the economy', *The New York Review of Books*, 24 April, 18–23.

Sachs, J. (1986), 'Managing the LDC debt crisis', *Brookings Papers on Economic Activity*, **2**, 397–431.

Sachs, J. (1987), 'A debt writedown would send bank stocks up', *The International Economy*, **1**, October/November, 96–7.

Sachs, J. and H. Huizinga (1987), 'U.S. commercial banks and the developing-country debt crisis', *Brookings Papers on Economic Activity*, **2**, 555–601.

Sengupta, A.K. (1988), 'A proposal for a debt adjustment facility', Prepared for IMF Executive Board Seminar 88/3, 9 February.

Shihata, I.F.I. (1986), 'Towards a greater depoliticization of investment disputes: The roles of ICSID and MIGA', *ICSID Review*, **1**, 1–25.

Snidal, D. (1985), 'The limits of hegemonic stability theory', *International Organization*, **39**, 579–614.

Soley, D.A. (1985), 'ICSID implementation: an effective alternative to international conflict', *International Lawyer*, **19**, 521–44.

Stoga, A. (1987), 'Can Africa be saved?', *The International Economy*, **1**, 66–71.

Strange, S. (1983), 'The credit crisis: a European view', *SAIS Review*, **3**, 171–81.

Suratgar, D. (1984), 'The international financial system and the management of the international debt crisis', in D. Suratgar (ed.), *Default and Rescheduling; Corporative and Sovereign Borrowers in Difficulty*, Euromoney Publications, 151–60.

United Nations (1988), *Financing Africa's Development*, Report and Recommendations of the Advisory Group on Financial Flows for Africa.

Watson, M. et al. (1988), *International Capital Markets: Developments and Prospects*, International Monetary Fund.

Weintraub, B. (1980), *What Every Credit Executive Should Know About Chapter 11 of the Bankruptcy Code*, National Association of Credit Management.

Williamson, J. (1985), 'On the question of debt relief', Appendix to the Statement of the Roundtable on Money and Finance, New York, 13–14 December, North–South Roundtable.

External debt: The moral dimension
Comment by Rita Tullberg

Tarshis and Cohen illustrate two approaches which can be taken by academic economists when asked to provide solutions to real-world problems: do we look at the economic consequences of a situation or proposal and then make policy suggestions, or do we make an analysis of the morality of the situation before offering our advice? Generally speaking, economists would shy away from any involvement in ethical problems. However, the debt issue seems to be different, for it is so frequently discussed in terms of 'blame' – greedy bankers versus profligate governments; 'living within one's means' versus responsible lending practices; debt which needs to be 'forgiven' as if it were a sin! This, to my mind, is most unfortunate since it distracts attention from the central issue of the current debt crisis; that is, what to do about it before we are all its victims.

Tarshis leaves ethics alone, sticks firmly to his task as an economist and hammers home a few simple economic truths: what is one country's balance-of-trade surplus is another country's deficit; if LDCs are to repay their existing debts, the rest of the world must adjust their economies so that they can import large quantities of goods and services from the LDCs whilst selling them very little. He directs our attention to a study of an earlier 'debt' problem – one, significantly, with very heavy moral overtones – and that is the question of German reparations after World War I. He might have added that we would do well to approach the current debt problem by first reading *The Economic Consequences of the Peace*. As Harcourt has pointed out, Keynes wrote this book in a white-hot fury. However, the fury was not over the alleged guilt of Germany for four years of destruction and carnage but rather over the stupidity of those who thought reparations could be paid without ruining the economies of all concerned. Those economists who allowed themselves to be swayed by the morality of the reparations issue did a great disservice to the world economy in the post-war years. Further, whatever the motives that lay behind it, was not the Marshall Plan an economically sounder approach to the reconstruction of the war-torn economies on both sides after World War II?

Cohen offers us a very valuable analysis of why debtor-countries accept the current situation of slow (or no) growth, conditionality, negative transfers and constant renegotiation crises, and why they are likely to become less and less inclined to acquiesce to creditor bullying. He also analyses why banks in general fear debt relief, classifying their arguments under such stern headings as 'contagion', 'discipline' and 'morals' – all of which sound so much like warnings from a British nineteenth century blue book on reform of the Poor Law! In so far as these terms are descriptive of the principles which guide bank and client behaviour, no objection can be made but the writer enters the ethical battle by explaining how morally suspect are bankers who lent 'too much' in the first place, how relief would be limited to 'appropriate cases' amongst debtor nations ('the deserving poor'?) and that conditions should be coupled to relief programmes so that LDCs do not waste any additional resources made available to them. This step is a pity since his proposal for a new institution to deal specifically with the problem of LDC debt (along the lines of the modern bankruptcy legislation) offers an impartial and pragmatic solution which does not apportion blame – though this would be more obviously the case if it were not confined simply to LDCs. Perhaps, too, there is something to be learned from the history of bankruptcy legislation when a failure to repay debt was no longer something to be punished as a crime but a civil matter to be regulated by arbitration and negotiation. Indeed, Cohen's scheme provides what Tarshis admits his own scheme lacks. This is the international cooperation and control which would help solve the 'free-rider' problem. Unfortunately, Cohen did not expand the details of his scheme here, particularly in respect to the hegemonistic role he assigns the United States as the prime mover to break the debt deadlock.

Missing from both papers are some guidelines for the future, for life after the current debt problem is over – when net transfers are again positive and the LDCs are getting the money they need for development. Should we rely on market forces and commercial banks to supply the capital? Should large loan consortia be outlawed? Will money come from governments, commercial banks or existing international financial institutions? Alternatively, do we need a new international loans organization?

15 A neglected monetary standard alternative: gold/commodity bimetallism

Albert Gailord Hart

Most economists will probably agree with McKinnon (*Journal of Economic Literature*, 1988):

> Without a common monetary standard, the remarkable integration of Western European, North American, and the industrialized Asian economies in both commodity trade and financial flows is less efficient, and becoming untenable. Dissatisfaction with wildly fluctuating relative currency values, euphemistically called 'floating' or 'flexible' exchange rates, is a prime cause of the resurgence in protectionism.

If we agree that the lack of a monetary standard must be made good, we are still far from agreeing about what the standard should be – or even what it is likely to do for the world economy. What the world needs from a new monetary standard is above all a foundation for expectations of stability. On the foreign-exchange markets as on the stock markets, the horizon of forward-thinking has become shorter and shorter. As McKinnon points out, we have got into a position where purchasing-power-parity considerations seem irrelevant to the processes that move the relative prices of currencies, although the relative values of currencies become more and more relevant to decisions on trade and on investment in new productive facilities! To recreate a context in which expectations are focused by belief in a norm, we must recognize the pivotal importance of the link between the monetary standard and the 'real' goods and service economy. In the 1950s and 1960s, this link was nominally gold but, in reality, it was the convertibility of the US dollar into US commodities and services and the expectation of product management of fiscal and monetary policy by the United States.

In the heyday of the gold standard, the gold link had more reality but a dispassionate analysis would probably show that the link of the monetary standard – through the pound sterling as key currency – to the powerful and stable goods and services economy of Britain was the main factor in relating people's expectations to a norm. The touchstone of adequacy for a proposed new standard is, therefore, the nature of its link to the goods and services economy. Proposed or implied links should be judged by their strength, comprehensibility to the public, and prospects of support from public opinion in a pinch. Their results will hinge largely on the effect upon the public's expectations about the execution of the transactions to which the standard commits the world's monetary authorities.

It is too easily taken for granted in discussions among economists that adoption of a new international standard requires all countries to adopt immutable fixed parities. The shapers of the Bretton Woods agreement showed wisdom in calling upon participants to set quasi-permanent parities. Revaluation was not barred but was supposed to take place rather rarely, as an adjustment to fundamentals, and only after consultation with the IMF. Such quasi-stability of parities will be appropriate also under any reformed standard. An important deficiency of Bretton Woods was failure to internationalize the standard. In principle, the IMF dollar was the focal point of the system but it was decided not to set up the IMF as a world Central Bank. In the post-World War II context, to 1971, the IMF and US dollars were indistinguishable, and the effective standard was the US dollar. It was the US dollar, not any international reserve currency unit, which was (nominally) linked to gold before 1971. I urge the economic profession to push for an explicitly international unit – to be administered by the IMF, perhaps with collaboration of the BIS. Kaldor's suggestion to name such a unit the 'bancor' would fit admirably.

The creation of stabilizing expectations hinges on public confidence in the commitment of the authorities to buy or sell the monetary commodity, on terms defined in advance, for all-comers. Hence, it is crucial whether transactions between the monetary authority and the private sector will or will not have stabilizing effects in the goods and services economy. Since the days of Cantillon, economists have been interested in the stabilizing characteristics of transactions in gold between the monetary authorities (originally simply the mint) and private parties. The idealized gold standard provided a mechanism through which rising price levels checked the growth of the monetary gold stock (and thus the rise of price levels) by raising the cost of production of gold. Correspondingly in a depression, the combination of falling costs and an assured market at the mint accelerated the growth of the gold stock, checking and reversing the downward swing of price levels. Qualitatively speaking, this effect of the currency/gold link looks like just the kind of stabilizing mechanism which economists seek to get policy-makers to install but quantitatively, the effect was derisory. The gold production cost effect was, at best, strong enough to carry out over a couple of decades what stabilization policy needs to carry out in a couple of years. Besides, the gold standard made room for inflationary surges from bursts of gold discoveries and for long dragging deflations between such inflationary bursts.

A different type of link between a monetary standard and the goods and services economy is offered by the Graham Plan for introducing a commodity-reserve currency. This proposal would link the monetary system to the goods and services economy by establishing convertibility of the underlying money into a basket of standardized commodities with world markets. It would be over-hasty to try to shape generally acceptable guidelines for a new monetary standard without careful examination of the commodity-reserve option. This may show that the commodity-reserve proposal has fatal defects but its potential public and private benefits – if it proves feasible – are enormous. Official interest at the US Treasury in commodity baskets has been signalled recently by Secretary Baker but virtually nothing has been done to prepare public opinion for possible use of such baskets in re-establishing a monetary standard. Close analysis of the commodity-reserve proposal, dealing with its potential benefits, feasibilty, possible adverse side-effects, and the best form for it if adopted, is a task to which economists – both inside and outside the government – should be devoting substantial resources.

The Graham Plan
I offer here a brief sketch of the Graham Plan – in a form which fits the circumstances of the late 1980s and early 1990s. As abbreviations, I use CRC for 'commodity reserve currency' (to indicate the plan or to refer in general to the organizational structure and operating machinery it would entail) and CA for 'commodities administration' (to refer to the multinational central organization which would be necessary to carry on the operation). Graham published (in 1940) a scheme for single-nation operation of CRC in the US and (in 1944) a scheme for multinational operation. In preparation for Bretton Woods, Keynes also provided an ingenious scheme for linking commodities with the IMS, which he called the International Commodity Control. In face of opposition from the British Ministry of Agriculture and the Bank of England, however, the ICC proposal was never presented at Bretton Woods and was not brought to general notice until the publication of the Keynes *Collected Papers*. The Keynes proposal differed from that of Graham by calling for operations in single commodities rather than in baskets. This is a major difference even though it was smoothed over in the Hart/Kaldor/Tinbergen presentation of 1964.

For many reasons, the single-nation variant of the Graham Plan must be ruled out. CRC has to be multinational and the sensible way to run it is to set up the CA as a branch of the IMF. To put the plan in force and to frame directives for the CA calls for a conference of IMF signatories to revise the Articles of Agreement. Gold arrangements must be renegotiated as part of the same process. The key feature of Graham's design is the concept of a 'basket' with fixed physical composition. For operating purposes, the unit basket must be a bundle of wholesale lots of the various commodities. The number of commodities included in the basket will probably fall in a range between 20 and 40. With one wholesale lot as the minimum inclusion and with several lots for the more heavily weighted commodities, a unit basket may well include over 100 wholesale lots, with a combined value of $1 million.

Any effective programme to bring the commodity basket into the system in the role of a new 'monetary metal' would have to provide for *gold/commodity bimetallism*. This is a proposition in political economy rather than in pure economics. It rests on the fact that any workable proposal for a revived monetary standard must conserve the monetary reserves which already exist. A CRC system (like any basic international monetary reform) must be put in place through renegotiation and ratification by member countries of major amendments in the Articles of Agreement of the IMF. Try to imagine the framers of a new monetary set-up telling the member countries:

> We are now entering upon a commodity-based system. Your official gold holdings will no longer constitute part of the monetary base, but will simply become non-monetary commodity assets like petroleum or soybeans. Use the gold to gild the Capitol dome, or dump it in the private market for what it will fetch, as you may wish. The world's central monetary authority will disregard gold in future.

The reaction would surely be explosive. Thus a move towards commodity reserves could not be made – any more than could a move towards a 'gold standard without gold' – without providing a role for existing official gold holdings.

A commodity reserve can be brought into actual operation only by retaining gold as a companion monetary metal. To obviate the well-known stresses of bimetallism, convertibility between official and unofficial gold should be ruled out, so that the proposal calls for what in the nineteenth century was called a limping standard, with the CRC 'metal' providing the only link to the goods and services economy. It should be observed that gold/commodity bimetallism is probably the only system which could mobilize gold-standard sentiment toward international stability. The McKinnon proposal for a 'gold standard without gold' would lack any appealing symbol. A 'real' gold standard under which the only link to the goods and services economy was a posted gold price available to all private traders in gold would not work. To include gold simply as a commodity in the basket, on the same footing as other commodities, would not realize the value of gold as a symbol, nor provide continuity of national reserve arrangements. For gold-standard advocates as well as for commodity reserve advocates, therefore, gold/commodity bimetallism is the only game in town.

Criteria for inclusion

Graham proposed 28 commodities for inclusion in the CRC basket, including several kinds of grain, fibres and primary metals. His initial list from the 1940s no longer fits market conditions but his criteria, with some updating, remain relevant. A current set of appropriate criteria would include:

- *Standardization.* To enter the basket, a commodity must have physical characteristics so definite that a price quotation has a clear-cut meaning to people in the trade. While CRC advocates commonly speak of primary products, it is often the products of first-stage processing (ingots of copper and aluminium rather than copper ore or bauxite) which are best standardized.
- *Persistence in use.* An eligible commodity must have prospects for use over a long future period. Items subject to fashion obsolescence or to rapid displacement as user-industries change technology (or as competing materials evolve) must be ruled out. No important types of finished goods pass this test, though some intermediate products may.
- *Storability.* An eligible commodity must be capable of storage for at least a year without unacceptably high storage costs or deterioration of quality. A factor in cost for some commodities may be the need to provide storage facilities which would not otherwise exist.
- *Availability for purchase* by CA during the accumulation period. Holders of existing inventories, or primary-product producers, must be in a position to sell substantial amounts to CA during the initial period when the reserve stock is being built up. If, for example, governments holding surplus cotton refuse to sell to CA at non-extortionate prices, or if widespread miners' strikes block the mining of copper for a couple of years on end, it may be impossible to acquire these commodities before the composition of the basket must be frozen at the end of the accumulation period.

Accumulation rules

The CA must have considerable (but not unbounded) discretion during the accumulation period. To arrange purchases will require negotiation where existing stocks are controlled by governments or where (as with copper) the bulk of production capacity is in the hands of a few large companies. Also some safeguards must be established against political pressure for excessive purchase volume as well as for excessive prices. A possible trap for CRC would be wildly unbalanced acquisitions during the accumulation period. Graham and other advocates of CRC have suggested that weights in the basket should reflect shares of the component commodities in world trade or (perhaps better) in world primary production but there can be no assurance that availabilities during the accumulation period will fit such a pattern. If the targeted level is, say, 20 per cent of a year's production and CA buys cotton on this scale, it may turn out that few other commodities have such large availabilities, so that, at the end of the accumulation period, cotton could constitute a greatly excessive share of the basket.

An appropriate rule might be that, as of the close of any calendar quarter during the accumulation period, not more than 10 per cent of the cumulative cost of CA acquisitions should be in any one (broadly defined) commodity. This rule would constrain CA to be negotiating (and/or making open-market purchases) on a number of markets simultaneously. If Brazil offers a large quantity of coffee, the US of cotton or Mexico of petroleum, CA may have to state that it can only take part of the offer until it can make a large aggregate acquisition of other commodities. If several sellers for one commodity want to participate at any stage, CA must either start with low bidders or set a uniform price at which it will take part of each seller's offer. A rule of this sort, moreover, will make it unnecessary to add to the list of criteria any safeguard against the impact of cartels and the like. A bugbear of the CRC advocates has been that if petroleum (to give the most crucial example) were weighted at its share in world primary production, a move such as OPEC made in 1973 or 1979 might force the CA to sell baskets on a scale that would sharply depress the prices of all commodities other than petroleum. The suggested acquisition rule will hold the weight of each CRC commodity to a maximum. Supplementary lower maxima might apply to commodities for which carrying costs were high, and the like.

Eligible commodities

As I mentioned above, the commodities commonly mentioned as appropriate for inclusion in a CRC basket have been grouped into foods, fibres and primary metals. There is room also for a group of energy products, and perhaps for some basic chemicals.

The first subgroup that comes to mind under foods is grain. A good fraction of the 'surplus' commodities held by the US and other governments consist of wheat, maize and soybeans. Here the question of excessive carrying costs may exclude or limit the use of some commodities. According to Theodore W. Schultz, the unavoidable losses from turning stocks over to avoid loss of quality rise with the oil content of the grains. For wheat, such costs run to some 5 per cent per annum under good storage conditions, for maize substantially more; for soybeans (today by far the most important 'grain') over 10 per cent. For rice, the storage situation seems to be decidedly more favourable. The decentralized pattern of storage, however, might interfere with the availability of rice for purchase during the accumulation period of CRC. It is possible also that rice could not be included without threatening the nutrition of millions of people in case a bulge in net supply for other CRC commodities obliges the CA to buy rice along with the rest of the basket in a season when the rice crop is bad.

It seems likely, in view of storage and turnover costs, that grains must be represented in the CRC basket well below the share of grains in primary production. Except for rice, it is hard to believe that heavy carrying costs could be avoided. A conference negotiating gold/commodity bimetallism, if it decided to include wheat or maize (let alone soybeans), might feel it essential to limit costs by prescribing a maximum proportion for the inclusion of items of high storage costs. An alternative might be to persuade governments which today carry stocks of 'surplus' grains to meet a large part of the storage costs of CRC grain holdings. Without CRC, governments find themselves facing heavy costs of this type (which over a cycle are therefore 'sunk costs'). To the degree that CRC is a replacement for government holdings of surplus grain, therefore, such cost assumption may be negotiable.

Coffee and cacao (both in the bean) figure in most CRC eligible lists. Despite the presence of a number of distinguishable varieties, these commodities are standardized enough to be actively traded on commodity exchanges and their storage costs will probably not prove excessive. Tea is often spoken of in the same breath but is under suspicion of being much less standardized. Another subgroup of foods where at least some elements are likely to offer a workable combination of standardization and storability is that of fats and oils. 'Corn oil' (from maize), peanut oil and coconut oil all figure as inputs for margarine, cooking oil combinations and salad oil combinations. Several inedible fats are ingredients for soaps. Some of these fats will fail to meet criteria of standardization and low storage costs, but some should pass. Butter and lard might come in question if their market arrangements were suitable but lard is under suspicion of being an obsolescent commodity, whose range of uses shrinks through time. Butter, though a less acute case, seems also to be falling out of favour. Besides, important parts of the butter market seem to be fenced in: the European 'mountain' reflects pricing far above the world market.

A refreshing novelty in recent years is the development of an active world market (with futures contracts) in frozen concentrated orange juice. This has the look of a commodity eligible for inclusion in CRC. A careful search may reveal other foods with good standardization and capable of low-cost storage under refrigeration. Dry powdered milk would seem to be another candidate for CRC, while flour seems much too unstandardized.

Among fibres, cotton has been claimed as an eligible commodity by all CRC advocates and would seem to be acceptable by all criteria. Wool is plainly not very uniform in quality across its many varieties but it has perhaps the longest history of trading on organized markets in the whole commodity domain and the experience of its traders may offer adequate means of relating different varieties to quoted 'standard' grades. Several other fibres would seem to be candidates, though the list is apt to shorten under close scrutiny. Hemp, jute and sisal are generally listed as candidates. I am not clear whether any synthetic fibres have appropriate characteristics, though nylon and a few others might prove to be CRC-eligible. Rubber might conceivably enter but natural rubber is suspect as an obsolescent material and it is likely that synthetic rubber is too heterogeneous and/or too costly to store to be eligible. A few first-stage-processed industrial products derived from fibres might come in question. Burlap and 'cotton grey goods' seem likely to pass CRC criteria but these items may be entering on a phase of obsolescence.

Turning to metals, copper, aluminium and tin always appear on the lists of CRC advocates. All three seem to pass very easily all criteria except perhaps that of quick availability for CA purchase during the accumulation period. Silver (which has almost vanished from monetary use but has become an important industrial input) should also be eligible. These metals, in their standardized ingot form, are produced almost entirely by a small number of multinational companies, each of which has a good deal of market power. These companies are well placed to reach interim agreement with each other and with concerned governments to curtail output when demand is slack – abating both the price cuts and the stock accumulation which typify agriculture in depression. The amount of these commodities actually in storage at times of slack demand is likely to be much too small to permit instant acquisition of as much as might be appropriate for CRC by the yardstick of shares in total world primary production. On the other hand, these products have substantial inactive productive capacity. Besides, they have strong organized markets with futures contracts. If the CA applies the rule of holding physical commodities or futures according as one or the other is cheaper, large amounts can probably be purchased without disrupting markets during an accumulation period of three years or so. Added storage facilities might well be needed but, since the products in question are neither fragile nor easily damaged by temperature or moisture, costs for such facilities need not be enormous.

Considering energy commodities, grounds for concern about the inclusion of petroleum in CRC, as mentioned above, can be dealt with by weighting the commodity so low that it ceases to be capable of distorting seriously the price of the CRC basket. It may be necessary to take care of standardization problems by separate inclusion of two or three varieties of crude oil. If so, the maximum weight would have to be allocated in advance among these varieties. Liquified natural gas is another commodity not on the older lists which seems to meet CRC criteria. Coal is fairly well standardized but presents difficulties because it does not maintain quality well in the loose heaps which are generally used for short-term storage. There have been claims that coal keeps well under water. This or some other technique may permit cheap enough longer-term storage to make coal eligible for CRC.

It is unlikely that the above listing exhausts the possibilities. There may well be standardized and storable commodities eligible for CRC among the basic chemicals. Recent misadventures with chemicals in storage or in transit call for caution, however, and provision for safe longer-term storage might be expensive. Nevertheless, this group of products seems to call for closer scrutiny. Forest products too offer CRC candidates. The existence of futures contracts for lumber may be an indication that standardization difficulties are soluble for cut planks and joists. Plywood may prove eligible. Paper board for packaging seems to be well standardized though it may be too bulky for storage in excess of working inventories. Any listing of the world's best standardized and most widely used commodities can scarcely omit newsprint. This industry may have little existing capacity for storage beyond working stocks but it would seem that facilities for longer-term storage could readily be provided. If so, inclusion in CRC would seem highly appropriate.

Gainers and losers
Prospects of securing the establishment of a new standard based on gold/commodity bimetallism will, of course, depend heavily on the extent to which those who stand to gain become active supporters of the proposal, and those who stand to lose become active opponents. As matters now stand, few of the potential gainers are aware of the CRC option. Here

it is essential to keep distinct the gains and losses of the initial acquisition period from those of the later period of full operation. In quantitative terms, the acquisition period is likely to account for the bulk of the more direct effects. Indirect effects (notably the effects on expectations) will take longer to realize and will be more qualitative.

A crucial moment comes when the accumulation period is over and CRC goes into full operation with posted buying and selling offers. At this point the size, composition and base price of the commodity basket must be fixed. These will grow out of the accumulation process itself. As shown earlier, the CA must work during the accumulation period under rules which lead to a more or less balanced accumulation, with no commodity exceeding, say, 10 per cent of the stock at any stage. The outcome of the accumulation period, however, cannot be specified at the outset because the availability of commodities for purchase will be affected by negotiations with governmental and private holders and by unpredictable events like crop fluctuations and prolonged labour disputes. At the end of the prescribed accumulation period, the stock will simply be what CA has actually acquired. It will be a major policy decision to decide at this crucial moment upon the number of baskets into which the stock is to be divided, and upon the base price for the unit basket. Since such a decision cannot actually be instantaneous, the initial directive to the CA should be framed to provide a pause between the end of the accumulation and the start of full CRC operations, stretching out the 'crucial moment' to perhaps six months.

It will be observed that any procedure must set limits to the risk that CRC degenerates into an international explosion of 'pork-barrel' politics. In the initial negotiations, governments which want their favourite commodities heavily weighted can, of course, campaign for high target levels but during the accumulation period, they will be limited by a maximum-acquisition rule and will have to make good their claim to whatever weight is assigned by assuring availability for purchase. The likelihood that pork-barrel politics will affect the initial negotiations is abated by the balance of the interests governments will feel they represent. With almost all eligible commodities, there will be some governments with a stake in producer interests. However, in respect of any specific commodity, most governments will have consumer interests which outweigh their producer interests. Furthermore, some major countries enter primary-product trade almost exclusively as importers. Hence the initial directives to CA must be expected to focus on safeguards rather than on producer-interest price-boosting. Since CA discretionary powers during accumulation (and during the extended crucial moment) will have to include some scope for the negotiation of purchase prices, however, we must expect political pressure toward higher prices of specific commodities in the accumulation stage. It may be appropriate for the initial negotiation to set up a watchdog body to protect the integrity of CA price decisions during accumulation.

The first group of gainers hold 'stabilization' stocks. In such a case as the overhanging stock of US cotton, the effective owner is the US government if a sale is made below the support price and a grower if the sale is made above the release price. A fair deal would probably be to transfer cotton to the CA at market price – or at some very substantial fraction (perhaps 90 per cent, say) of the support price – whichever is lower. The holding authority will actually benefit by such a deal even if it books an accounting loss. The overhanging 'surplus' is shifted to a position where it can come back onto the market only after the accumulation period and, then, only when the price of the basket rises to the posted selling level. Where the immediate seller is a government body, the CRC plan should call upon this government to apply the bancor realized to debt reduction. Thus governments which have both large external debts and large stocks of surplus commodities can simultaneously place their commodities in safe hands and abate their external-debt service costs. The US government will then use the proceeds of sales of cotton to CA to pay off the holders of dollar reserves, reducing the interest item in the US fiscal budget and in the US balance of payments. The Brazilian government will use coffee proceeds and the Mexican government will use petroleum proceeds to pay off overseas bank loans – at a discount if this can be arranged. The bancor which, in consequence, will flow into the reserves of the US and other countries whose banks hold the loans overseas, again, will be applied to paying off dollar reserves and similar liabilities. Thus the world's debt pyramid can be appreciably whittled down and current-account receipts of debtor countries released to buy needed machinery and intermediate products. Even with procedures to retire newly emitted bancor, the accumulation of the CRC reserve is likely to generate some net expansion of the aggregate of national monetary reserves. To limit such expansion, the revision of IMF statutes should perhaps include authority for the IMF to issue and to repurchase securities of its own within the various national financial markets and/or on the Eurocurrency market – giving the IMF power to carry on 'open-market operations' as can a national Central Bank.

A second group of immediate gainers will be the producers of CRC commodities. The CA acquisitions during the build-up period will unavoidably boost the prices of the commodities to be bought – perhaps in the course of the build-up period itself, or perhaps earlier by revisions of expectations during the preliminary negotiations. The extent to which the gains for producers of a broadly defined 'commodity' will be confined to the producers of the specific highly standardized varieties purchased by

CA is hard to say. The elasticity of substitution both in production and in use between these varieties and less standardized varieties must be substantial when two or three years are allowed for adjustment. Yet, if there are cases where the standardized varieties dominate other varieties for important uses, withdrawal of standardized varieties into CRC stocks may generate relative price shifts that will not wear off quickly.

Consumers of commodities and services (for which CRC commodities are inputs) will be losers by the acquisitions of the initial period. The corresponding rise of living costs will tend to restart inflationary spirals in various countries so national monetary authorities may have to run more restrictive policies, with some danger of increased unemployment. The outcome for traders seems doubtful, except as holders of eligible (or closely related) commodities at the outset. Whether the opportunity to take the initiative in organizing transactions between the CA and the private sector is of value to traders seems debatable. Fluctuations in price for individual CRC-related commodities are likely to be of smaller amplitude and more predictable – with extreme movements in the short term substantially less likely. It seems likely that the total of private plus CRC stocks will be greater for many eligible commodities than the recent total of private and government-owned stocks. If so, the service of storage will have an enlarged market.

Inflationary consequences during the accumulation period will be mitigated because part of the expansive effect of creation of bancor to buy CRC commodities can be taken up by absorbing unemployed workers. The world's industrial sector, as a whole, is seriously depressed. Except for the US and Japan, all important industrial countries have high and refractory unemployment. The part of the industrial economy which is located in Latin America, the Philippines and Africa is prostrate. The perceptible redistribution of world income in favour of the primary sector tends to stimulate the market for products of Third World industry on its home ground. Besides, the fuller availability of new equipment and intermediate products will enhance the ability of Third World industry to fill the demand which already exists. Taking one thing with another and considering that, worldwide, the primary sector generates only 10 per cent or so of the total costs of final products, the inflationary consequences of CRC accumulation should not raise price levels by more than 2 or 3 per cent. Worldwide, the resultant of price changes and changes in employment is likely to yield net gains rather than net losses for most consumer households.

A major channel for indirect effects of CRC is financial. Here there is a prospect of widespread gains. The financial systems of the industrial countries – especially of the US – are rendered fragile by the asset weaknesses generated by rash lending to Third World debtors and to the primary-product sector in the industrial countries themselves. Furthermore, the tissue of fictions cultivated to maintain the pretence that bad loans are still 'performing' compounds the difficulty by giving banks and other financial institutions an incentive to make more bad loans. Settlement of a substantial fraction of Third World loans can do a great deal to clear up the debt mess and ensure solvency of financial institutions. The industrial and primary sectors will both be better off if the risk of a financial crash can be abated in this way. Governments will be better placed to introduce measures to curb excess liquidity and to reduce the churning of financial portfolios without concern for the efficiency of enterprises whose stocks are held or traded.

As stated at the outset, the underlying case for a reformed monetary standard is that it is necessary to rescue the world economy from a situation where no norms for expectations exist and all asset valuations 'hang from sky hooks'. The world economy shows strong signs of racking itself to pieces, and setting up destructive political movements that seek autarky. Unfortunately, monetary reform is necessary but not sufficient for the cure of capricious expectations. In the pivotal US economy, enormous financial resources are wielded by outside players who are only beginning to understand the working of our goods and services economy. US players, on their side, are only beginning to understand how to compare US and overseas assets. The pension funds, insurance companies and the like who hold the lion's share of US equities and of debt securities that command leverage over management of companies are obsessed with quick gains from treating companies as 'assets' and neglect their responsibility to get companies managed with operating efficiency. Thus the major instrument in the private sector which might create and put meaningful values upon wothwhile 'fundamentals' is out of action. In the US tax system, the deductability of interest payments is a major distortion. The brand of efficiency which maximizes the exploitation of this enormous loophole is the dominant element of efficiency as valued by the stock market, the 'takeover artists' and managements defending their turf. Further, US society is burdened with a gambling addiction. Risk-taking is essential to our economy but we must slant the structure of rewards in favour of those who take risks on behalf of authentic productive activity rather than in favour of mere financial manipulation.

Comment by John N. Smithin

Proposals for the establishment of a commodity reserve currency are not new, of course. They go back at least to Irving Fisher, and Hart himself has been a distinguished contributor on previous occasions. A new wrinkle in the current proposal is the reference to commodity gold 'bimetallism' but this turns out not to be a really central issue and is simply a concession to the practical politics of getting the scheme accepted in a world in which several nations continue to hold stocks of gold as part of their international reserves. Hart does not dwell on the theoretical or conceptual case for moving to a commodity-reserve standard. This is taken more or less for granted. Instead, the focus is on implication. The argument is essentially that, at the present time, there is a unique 'window of opportunity' for bringing a commodity-reserve system into being. This is so for two reasons; first, the current dissatisfaction with the floating exchange-rate regime may make the international community more receptive to alternative ideas and, secondly, during the 1980s there has been an 'overhang' or surplus of many primary commodities on world markets. The latter would make the accumulation process easier and have beneficial side-effects for the commodity-producing nations.

There is obviously room for debate as to whether the exchange-rate difficulties of the 1980s really require a new system (either of the CRC or some other type) or simply a commitment by the major players to pursue more appropriate fiscal and monetary policies. This issue is the subject of many papers at this conference and does not require belabouring here. One does wonder, however, if in spring 1988 the window of opportunity provided by depressed commodity markets is not already disappearing. The financial press has recently carried a number of reports of more rapidly rising commodity prices, which seem to indicate a greater degree of tightness in certain areas. For those of us who are not experts in commodity-market developments, it would be interesting to hear Hart's interpretation of the recent reports and their implications for the CRC scheme.

Hart gives meticulous attention to the details of the implementation of the system. Potential candidates for inclusion in the basket of commodities are identified, the mechanics of the accumulation process are set out, logistical and storage issues are dealt with, and the short-term gains and losses from the implementation process are estimated. He offers a clear account of the political-economy aspects of the proposal and this represents a considerable advance over many of the more abstract schemes which have appeared in the literature. A sceptic, however, would still have plenty of scope to argue about the 'why' of the CRC system rather than the 'how'. Obviously, the purpose of the proposal is to stabilize the purchasing power of actual media of exchange (at both the international and national levels) but the extremely large physical lots of commodities suggested by Hart cannot themselves become the international exchange medium. The latter will actually be the liabilities of the central institution, Hart's 'Commodities Administration'. This institution must, therefore, be sufficiently powerful and pursue policies which are sufficiently responsible to maintain the unit-of-account value of its liabilities. In other words, our commodity-reserve system must still be 'managed' by what is effectively a world Central Bank – just as, arguably, the old-fashioned gold standard was effectively a sterling standard managed by the Bank of England. If we must assume the existence of such a powerful and prudent institution, the question immediately arises as to what additional payoff there might be from tying up potentially useful physical resources as the reserve? Why could not such an institution (if it existed) be relied upon to pursue a similarly responsible policy even in a purely fiduciary environment? This is a rather venerable question, but it does require an answer.

Comment by Robert W. Dimand

Hart usefully directs attention to a commodity reserve currency as a means of restoring stability in the international monetary system. As he stresses, a new monetary standard must provide a foundation for expectations of stability. It is curious to recall that the case for flexible exchange rates made by Friedman (1953) and Johnson (1969) was that flexible rates would allow a country to pursue a stable monetary-growth rule, insulated from imported inflation or deflation as well as contributing to efficiency by having one more price determined by the free market. Since the breakdown of the Bretton Woods system, however, large fluctuations in exchange rates, often fuelled by speculative bubbles, have led to disenchantment. In the place of earlier claims that flexible rates would provide stabilizing insulation against external shocks, McKinnon advocates a shift from flexible rates to a 'gold standard without gold' while Mundell proposes a return to the gold standard. Rather than worrying about insulating a stable domestic monetary policy from external shocks, the more recent proposals for monetary reform attempt to place external constraints on potentially erratic and unstable domestic monetary authorities.

Hart rightly objects to a monetary standard based on gold or other precious metals because these are individual commodities with prices subject to speculative or other fluctuations – as the price of silver rose and then fell dramatically at the time of the Hunt brothers' speculation. CRC is an extension of Fisher's tabular standard. Fisher proposed that, in place of a fixed gold value of the currency or a fixed money supply, the Central Bank should vary the quantity of money to keep constant a price index which is based on a bundle of widely-traded commodities. Graham's 1944 proposal and Keynes's plan for postwar international commodity control envisaged an international agency that would maintain the fixed monetary value of a basket of commodities – by trading directly in the commodities, not just by altering the quantity of the monetary standard. Hart prefers the Graham proposal, where transactions would be in the complete bundle of commodities, to the Keynes–Kaldor suggestion of discretionary trading in individual commodities, which would leave the commodity authority more open to restrictionist pressure from producers.

Fisher's tabular standard could be maintained, if the monetary authorities had the necessary will, without any trading by the monetary authorities in the basket of commodities whose composite price is being held fixed. Graham and Keynes came to CRC, however, from previous concerns with commodity buffer stocks as a means of reducing fluctuations in the prices of individual commodities, that is in relative prices. This was the concern of Graham in *Storage and Stability: A Modern Ever-Normal Granary* (1932), and of Keynes's *Economic Journal* paper in 1938 entitled 'The Policy of Government Storage of Foodstuffs and Raw Materials'. It was natural for them to combine the problem of a stable international monetary standard with the problem of financing an international buffer-stock scheme to stabilize the prices of individual commodities. It is not so evident why, when the question of a new monetary standard is considered on its own, the CRC scheme of accumulating buffer stocks and intervening in commodity markets is to be preferred to Fisher's proposal for pegging the monetary value of a bundle of commodities by varying the money supply appropriately. A possible answer is implied by Hart's response to the McKinnon proposal. He prefers gold/commodity bimetallism to McKinnon's 'gold standard without gold' because the latter lacks any appealing symbol. The monetary authorities could manage their currencies so as to maintain a fixed nominal value of a bundle of real goods and services, without accumulating any stocks of commodities or creating an international mechanism for trading in commodity markets. The tangible stocks of gold and other commodities (and the announced offer to buy or sell any number of commodity baskets at a fixed price in terms of bancor) serve an important symbolic function. They contribute to the appeal of entering the system and, as symbols of commitment, to the formation of expectations for stability.

I must express a reservation about Hart's view that the creation of bancor through the initial accumulation of CRC commodities will not have as great an inflationary impact in the transition period as might be expected – because there are large numbers of unemployed workers in Latin America, the Philippines and Africa who would be absorbed into employment by the demand stimulus. Recent experience indicates that unemployment in Brazil and Argentina has not prevented demand stimulus from causing inflation so that the accumulation of stocks of Brazilian coffee and Argentine grain might reasonably be expected to generate additional inflation. Industrial expansion in developing countries might also be hampered by the rise in the relative price of raw materials. These points are, however, peripheral to the main thrust of Hart's efforts, which provide valuable insight into the question of a new international monetary standard.

16 The international monetary system: a look ahead

Bernard M. Wolf

Held just over two weeks prior to the Toronto Economic Summit of the Group of Seven industrialized countries, our Conference on the Future of the International Monetary System identified the key problems facing the world economy as it approaches the 1990s and considered a variety of solutions. No consensus was reached but relevant options were aired. The same major problems discussed by the Conference participants were recognized in the communiqué issued by the leaders of the G-7 countries following the Toronto Summit. These include large imbalances in the major industrialized countries, the substantial volatility of exchange rates and the debt-servicing difficulties of many developing countries. However, the modest international initiatives taken at the Summit fall far short of resolving the world's economic problems. More attention will have to be paid to comprehensive solutions as suggested by the papers in this volume.

In seeking solutions we must recognize that the present world economy is vastly different from that of two decades ago. Economies are much more interdependent than earlier. Not only is production viewed on a global basis by multinational corporations but capital markets have become increasingly integrated as a result of deregulation and improvements in communications technology. Indeed, inter-country capital movements are often far larger than the flows across exchange markets arising out of current-account transactions. Furthermore, the US is no longer the overwhelmingly predominant player on the international monetary scene. The international economic system has expanded to include a buoyant Pacific Rim which, coupled with the emergence of a stronger Europe, has resulted in a non-hegemonic system, loosely led by a triad of the US, Japan and the Federal Republic of Germany. The present IMS, unlike that of the gold standard, the Bretton Woods system or the EMS, cannot rely on strong leadership by a single major power.

This concluding chapter provides an overview of the chief unresolved issues which confront the IMS as we approach the 1990s: exchange rates and policy coordination, the LDC debt problem and the role of multinational institutions.

Exchange rates and policy coordination

With the demise of the Bretton Woods system, major currencies floated against the dollar. By February 1985, as a result of an unfortunate monetary–fiscal mix, combined with an overall low savings rate in the US, the dollar had become extremely overvalued against the Japanese yen and the European currencies, especially the German mark. Subsequently, it began a steep decline, possibly accelerated by the 1985 Plaza Agreement. What happens now? The Summit endorsed the April 1988 conclusion of the G-7 finance ministers and central bankers leaders that 'a further decline of the dollar, or a rise in the dollar to an extent that becomes destabilizing to the adjustment process, could be counterproductive by damaging growth prospects in the world economy'. Clearly, the leaders have called for stability at the moment but how is that to be achieved?

Left to its own devices, with merely a signal from the Summit, the market may decide that current exchange rates are appropriate. If not, concerted intervention by Central Banks in foreign-exchange markets may be able to assure these rates. However, such intervention, even if effective, only works in the short run. From a longer perspective, decisions will have to be made about how much flexibility there should be in exchange rates. Proposals range from freely-floating rates at one end of the spectrum to a common single currency for all the major industrialized countries at the other extreme. Obviously, if it can be maintained, a single currency by its very nature avoids fluctuations entirely. However, the costs in terms of unemployment and regional disparities may be too high unless there is an adequate combination of labour mobility, wage flexibility and fiscal transfers.

Stable exchange rates eliminate uncertainty in international trade and finance but exchange-rate changes can be a useful weapon in the arsenal of a country's policy instruments when it comes to adjusting for structural change or for differing rates of inflation among countries. They can be the least painful way of adjusting especially when a real shock must be absorbed; for example, the four-fold increase in petroleum prices for an oil importer in the 1970s. The question is how much flexible rates can be relied upon when 'over-shooting' of equilibrium rates is a clear possibility and when, as recent experience with the US trade deficit so clearly demonstrates, the lags associated with the impact of exchange-rate changes can be long, variable, unpredictable and asymmetric in the sense that they may differ substantially when a currency is rising as compared to when it is falling.

Many of the proposals for the reform of the IMS advocate that, in the absence of a totally dominant economic power, the leading industrialized countries coordinate their domestic policies to some degree, especially monetary policy. Some propose relatively fixed rates such as target zones, which in order to be maintained will require policy coordination. Others argue that the coordination of policies in itself will lead to exchange-rate stability as a by-product. In any event, coordination is problematic to achieve since it requires relinquishing a substantial degree of economic sovereignty. Countries are reluctant to concede sovereignty particularly when they have very different trade-offs between unemployment and inflation. For example, at the time of the Summit, the US resisted additional fiscal restraints to remove the imbalance between government and investment spending on the one hand and tax revenue and saving on the other, while Europe was reluctant to adopt more fiscal and/or monetary stimulus.

Moreover, even if sovereignty were not an issue, one is left with the problem of deciding what formal indicators should be chosen in determining policy coordination. As an illustration, to determine whether central bankers should raise or lower the average level of short-term interest rates, they could focus on income or price level targets or some combination of both. With respect to income, they might consider the aggregate growth of nominal income in relation to some target growth level for the participating countries. Alternatively, they might be guided by changes in an index of commodity prices.

A system of exchange rates fixed within relatively small bands but subject to periodic changes has been adopted by the major EEC countries with the notable exception of the UK. The EMS is based on the idea that fixing the rates would encourage coordination of domestic policies but, where there was insufficient coordination, the rates could be changed from time to time. As Bernstein reports in Chapter 5 above, the success of the EMS has been in maintaining orderly exchange markets and in facilitating 'the necessary adjustment of central rates in small steps to offset changes in the price-competitive position of its members'. In effect, nominal exchange rates acted like a crawling peg to achieve approximate real exchange-rate stability. Of course, the concept of real exchange-rate stability itself poses the problem of validity for the notion of relative purchasing power parity in the long run. Moreover, high rates of unemployment in Europe have accompanied real exchange-rate stability as the EMS adopted the strong anti-inflationary posture of its anchor, the Deutsche Bundesbank.

The 12-member European Community has announced that it will strive to achieve a fully integrated internal market and an end to the remaining capital controls among member countries within a few years. In the process, the EEC is looking at changes in the EMS, including the possibility of establishing a European Central Bank and a redefinition of the ECU as a European reserve currency. Certainly, the EMS experience deserves further scrutiny for the lessons it might offer for the IMS as a whole.

Linked to the type of exchange-rate scheme is the question of international reserves. Currently, reserves are created when countries intervene in the foreign-exchange market to buy up other key currencies, when gold is bought by Central Banks, and when, from time to time, Special Drawing Rights are issued by the IMF. This *ad hoc* process certainly does not provide for orderly reserve creation. If the world does not opt for a common currency, should a new reserve asset be created or should the characteristics of SDRs be altered so that they no longer take a back seat to gold and national currencies? What role should the IMF play in the system?

LDC debt
The only concrete measure taken at the Summit with respect to the LDC debt problem was the proposal to ease the debt-service burden of the poorest debtor countries, mainly in sub-Saharan Africa. The external debt of these countries accounts for only about 8 per cent of the more than $1 ¼ trillion LDC debt. Creditor-governments in the Paris Club will reschedule official debt by choosing among either concessional interest rates (usually on shorter maturities), longer repayment periods at commercial rates, partial write-offs of debt-service obligations during the consolidation period, or a combination of these options. However, the implementation of even this small step has still to be worked out. One difficulty is the need to compare the contributions of the different Western countries when they choose different options. Clearly this debt relief is an important first step but it does not go far enough; the sub-Saharan African countries need a very substantial write-off of their debts given their extremely low per capita income and poor growth prospects.

For the highly indebted middle-income countries, which are chiefly in Latin America and account for the vast majority of LDC debt, the Summit communiqué brought no new initiatives. The leaders merely applauded measures such as an increase in World Bank capital and the increasing recourse to innovative financing techniques whose important characteristics are that 'they are voluntary, market-oriented, and applied on a case-by-case basis'. No one can deny that the Mexican debt-swap schemes of

1987–88 and the Brazilian refinancing arrangements of June 1988 are helpful. However, are they sufficient steps on the road to solving the debt problem or do they merely postpone the day of reckoning?

There is a substantial voice that suggests the LDCs should no longer be asked to severely curtail their domestic demand in order to service debt since this provides neither for rising standards of living nor markets for the exports of the industrialized countries. Measures ought to be found which will assure a net positive flow of funds to the LDCs in the form of private and multilateral lending, aid, new investment and the return of flight capital. These measures must address the following questions:

- How is the burden of eliminating the excessive debt overhang to be apportioned among the LDCs, industrialized countries, and the commercial banks? This is more difficult in the case of the middle-income countries than for the sub-Saharan countries since their debt is owed to private banks rather than to governments.
- What role should institutions such as the IMF, the World Bank or newly created entities play?
- How can 'the free-rider' problem be avoided so countries or banks which do not participate actively in debt relief do not benefit by the action of others? For example, banks not participating in the Mexican debt-swap increased the likelihood of having their loans repaid at a lower discount rate or even in full.

Any solution to be viable must maintain confidence in the IMS and make some progress in generating economic reforms in the LDCs. There is no shortage of plans, some of which are discussed by our contributors. However, for their adoption, such plans must acquire the endorsement of the key industrialized countries, especially the US, and the acquiescence of the commercial banks.

Multinational institutions

A well-functioning IMS is a prerequisite for an open, multilateral international trading system. Without it, the world would quickly move down the slippery slope of protectionism. In the post-World War II period, successive rounds of trade negotiations under the auspices of the General Agreement on Tariffs and Trade greatly liberalized trade, yet protectionism in the form of non-tariff barriers seems now to be on the rise. The Summit leaders call for a strengthening of the GATT, particularly with the regard to the surveillance of trade policies and dispute-settlement procedures. However, words must be channelled into concrete initiatives at the mid-term review of the Uruguay Round in Montreal, December 1988.

Particularly in need of attention, in addition to the above, are agricultural subsidies, trade in services, national treatment of investment, and intellectual property rights. The issue of agricultural subsidies is a particularly explosive one and if not solved could lead to a trade war.

Finally, when protectionism, the debt of the LDCs, reserves, exchange-rate volatility and misalignment, external imbalances and the coordination of domestic economic policies are viewed as interdependent world economic problems, the question arises whether institutions such as the GATT, the IMF and the World Bank should forge greater links and/or whether new institutions should be created.

The leaders at the 1988 Toronto Summit congratulated themselves on having weathered the October 1987 financial crisis and having kept up the momentum of growth while generally restraining inflation. However, the euphoria will be short-lived unless measures are taken to solve the world economy's pressing problems. A strong, yet flexible IMS will certainly be a prerequisite in the 1990s in order to achieve high rates of economic growth since the system will be severely tested by the need for the US to transform its huge trade deficit into a large trade surplus; the surplus being required to service the surging US foreign debt as it adjusts to being the world's largest debtor country. In addition, if the debt problems of the LDCs are not solved, the resulting financial crisis could shake any international financial system; only a robust one could remain operational.

Name index

Adams, C. 70, 79, 80, 83
Adenauer, K. 39
AFL/CIQ 192
Aggarwal, V. K. 179, 192
Agglietta, M. 41
Akyuz, Y. 94, 115
Al-Nowaihi, A. 83
Amuzegar, J. 175
Angermueller, J. 175
Aoki, M. 71, 73, 83
Avramovic, D. 141, 148

Baker (Plan) 90, 102, 103, 107, 111,
    139, 164–6, 180
Balassa, B. A. 48, 64
Bernstein, E. 20, 216
BIS 198
Bradley, B. 175, 180–1, 192
Bretton Woods 29–32, 38, 45, 54, 62,
    89, 90, 99, 100, 102, 110–11,
    134, 136, 147, 198, 199, 212,
    214–15
Broad, R. 175, 180, 192
Buiter, W. 70, 71, 73, 78

Carey, R. H. 137, 148
Cassel, G. 42–5, 52, 64
Cavanagh, J. 175, 192
CFF 100
Chirac, J. 40
Citicorp 185
Cline, W. R. 180, 193
Cohen, B. J. 176, 180, 183, 189, 193,
    195, 196
Committee of Twenty 35–6, 100,
    113–15
Cooper, R. N. 95–6, 112, 115
Corden 119–22, 125, 127, 154
Cornia, A. C. 109, 115
Crocket, A. D. 115
Culpepper, R. 139, 148
Currie, D. 71, 84

De Gaulle, C. 39
Dell, S. 94, 96, 115, 117, 188, 193
De Vries, M. G. 95, 113, 115
De Vries, R. 184, 192
Dornbusch, R. 15, 21, 26, 64, 69, 70,
    77, 83, 102, 119, 122

Edison, H. J. 70, 83
EEC 36, 38, 39, 119, 216–17
Eichengreen, B. 116

Federal Reserve 12, 13
Fischer, S. 192, 193
Fisher, I. 210, 212, 213
Fontenelle, A. 183
Frankel, J. A. 82, 84
Frantz, O. 40
Frenkel, J. 42, 51, 64
Friedman, M. 68, 69, 84, 121, 212
Fukuda, S. I. 71, 84–6, 88

General Agreement on Tariffs and
    Trade (GATT) 110, 218
Geurguil, M. 192, 193
Giavazzi, F. 70, 84
Gilpin, R. 192, 193
Giovanni, A. 70, 84
Giscard D'Estaing, V. 39
Godley, W. 124
Gold, J. 101, 115
Goldman, A. 189, 193
Goldstein, M. 115
Graham (Plan) 199–202, 212
Gros, D. 70, 79, 80, 83
Group of Five (G-5) 106
Group of Seven (G-7) 106, 114, 140,
    147, 164–6, 214–15
Group of Ten (G-10) 90–1, 95–9,
    103–6, 114–15, 129, 147
Group of Twenty Four (G-24) 90, 91,
    99, 103–7, 114–15
Guitian, M. 101, 115

Haberler, G. 147
Hamada, K. 71, 84–6, 88
Harcourt, G. 195
Harrod, J. 99
Hart, A. G. 23, 26, 102, 199, 210,
    212–13
Healey, D. 101
Herman, F. 40
Hirschmann, A. O. 146
Holley, H. A. 179, 193
Huizinga, H. 175, 180, 183, 193

Institute of International Finance 158
Interim Committee 26, 105, 115
International Centre for Settlement
    of Investment Disputes (ICSID)
    189
International Debt Restructuring
    Agency (IDRA) 177, 190–2
International Monetary Fund (IMF)
    6, 7, 10, 11, 30, 34–6, 46–7, 50,
    90–1, 95–6, 100–1, 103, 105,
    107–12, 114–15, 132, 134, 141–2,
    160–2, 174, 190–1, 198, 200, 207,
    218–19
Isard, P. 42, 64
Islam, S. 175, 193

Jazwinsky, A. H. 71, 84
Jolly, R. 115
Jones, M. 88

Kaldor, N. 91, 102–3, 115, 198–9,
    212
Kalecki, M. 100
Kant, E. 36
Kenen, P. 106, 115
Keohane, R. O. 177–8, 192–3
Keynes, J. M. 2, 93, 100, 114–15,
    119, 123–4, 143, 146, 170, 195,
    199, 212
Khan, M. S. 142, 148
Kindleberger, C. P. 36, 177, 192–3
Klein, T. M. 175, 193
Knight, M. D. 142, 148
Kohl, H. 39
Komiya, R. 48, 64
Krugman, P. 14, 178, 184, 193
Kucynski, P. P. 175, 188, 193

Lafalce, J. 175, 180, 193
Lamfalussy, A. 93, 116
Levich, R. 42, 64
Lindbeck, A. 48, 64
Lucas, R. 71

Marston, R. 48, 64, 85, 88
McCloskey, D. N. 45, 64
McKinnon, R. I. 15, 21, 23, 26,
    43, 54–5, 64–6, 68–70, 73,
    78–81, 84, 88, 91, 93, 124,
    197, 200, 212–13
Meade, J. E. 15, 124
Meese, R. 42, 64
Merrill Lynch 138
Miller, M. H. 70, 73, 83–5, 87–8
Mitterrand, F. 39
Moggridge, D. 114–15
Morgan Guaranty Bank 184, 193
Morse, J. 35
Mundell, R. 119–22, 212
Mussa, M. 42, 51, 64, 119

New Cambridge Group 124

OECD 46–7, 50, 56–7, 59–60
Ohno, K. 21, 26, 51–2, 64–5
OPEC 101, 144, 202
Oppenheimer, P. 127, 129

Pease, D. 175, 192–3
Pohl, O. 40
Poole, W. 85–6, 88
Portes, R. 115, 116
Posner, R. A. 186, 193
Poterba, J. M. 70, 72, 78
Prebisch, R. 147
PRISM Package 71, 83

Reagan, R. 36, 119, 122, 134
Regan, D. T. 179, 193
Riesenfield, S. A. 189, 192, 193

Robinson, J. D. 175, 193
Rockerfeller, D. 192–3
Rogoff, K. 42, 64, 88
Rohatyn, F. 179, 193
Rosenfield A. M. 186, 193

Sachs, J. 71, 84, 85, 88, 175, 180,
     183, 193
Schmidt, H. 39
Sengupta, A. K. 175, 194
Shaunessy, T. 138
Shihata, I. F. 189, 194
Shultz, G. P. 101, 116
Smith, A. 27
Smyslov, D. V. 39
Snidal, D. 178, 192, 194
Soley, D. A. 189, 194
Stein, J. 85, 88
Stewart, F. 115
Strange, S. 179, 194
Summers, L. H. 70, 72, 84
Swoboda, A. K. 116

Tarshis, L. 110, 116, 170–3, 195, 196
Taylor, L. 71
Thatcher, M. 122
Tinbergen, J. 102, 199
Tobin, J. 15, 93, 116
Triffin, R. 38, 45, 64, 144, 148

UNCTAD 102
UNICEF 109
United Nations 175, 194

Volcker, P. A. 118

Watson, M. 175, 194
Weintraub, B. 191, 192, 194
Werner Plan 41
Williamson, J. 68, 70, 73–4, 79, 80,
     81, 83–5, 87–8, 188, 192–4
World Bank 6, 7, 98, 107–8, 111,
     112, 131–2, 136–7, 139, 143, 148,
     174, 190–1, 218–9
World Development Report 131, 136

Zecher, J. R. 45